camino del sol

Camino del Sol

A Latina and Latino Literary Series

camino del sol

Fifteen Years of Latina and Latino Writing

Edited by Rigoberto González

The University of Arizona Press   Tucson

The University of Arizona Press
© 2010 Rigoberto González

www.uapress.arizona.edu

Library of Congress Cataloging-in-Publication Data
Camino del sol : fifteen years of Latina and Latino writing / edited by Rigoberto González.
    p. cm.—(Camino del sol)
    Includes bibliographical references.
    ISBN 978-0-8165-2813-4 (pbk. : alk. paper)
    1. American literature—Hispanic American authors. 2. Hispanic Americans—
Literary collections. I. González, Rigoberto.
    PS508.H57C36 2010
    810.8'0868073—dc22

                                                              2009034569

Publication of this book is made possible in part by the proceeds of a permanent
endowment created with the assistance of a Challenge Grant from the National
Endowment for the Humanities, a federal agency.

♻

Manufactured in the United States of America on acid-free, archival-quality paper
containing a minimum of 30% post-consumer waste and processed chlorine free.

15   14   13   12   11   10   6   5   4   3   2   1

In respectful memory of our three
Chicano poets who passed away in 2008:
raulrsalinas, Alfred Arteaga, Luis Omar Salinas
¡PRESENTE!

Contents

Fiction

Nonfiction

camino del sol

Camino del Sol

Lighting a Path for Chicano/Latino Literature in the New Millennium

In alphabetizing these selections, and in opening this reader with poetry, I have ushered in a happy coincidence: Francisco X. Alarcón's *From the Other Side of Night/Del otro lado de la noche* is once again the title at the beginning of a journey.

In 2002, the year the University of Arizona Press released Alarcón's volume of new and selected poems, I had just been given an extraordinary opportunity by one of a few Chicano writers I knew in New York City. Sergio Troncoso (author of *The Last Tortilla and Other Stories*, another Camino del Sol title) had been reviewing occasionally for *The El Paso Times* of Texas, and while we were having lunch in Manhattan, he received a call from Ramón Rentería, the features editor of that newspaper. A few moments into his conversation, he suddenly looked up at me and asked, "Would *you* like to review books?" Little did I know that when I said yes (though with reservations), I would embark on a path that has yet to conclude. Since the summer of 2002, I have been submitting reviews to *The El Paso Times* about twice a month—close to seven years at the writing of this introduction.

I had never written book reviews and had only infrequently read them, especially when it came to Chicano/Latino literature. Books by Chicano/Latino authors were rarely represented in the pages of newspapers, national magazines, or journals I had leafed through at bookstores over the years. Discussions about writings by Chicanos/Latinos were the territory of academics—theses, dissertations, and the scholarly essays that appeared in obscure regional publications. Studies on Chicano/Latino literature were the assigned required texts of college curricula, heavy with jargon and confined to a "theoretical framework."

It dawned on me that a newspaper would be the ideal medium for connecting and communicating—using clear and accessible language—with the average reader. By writing book reviews specifically focused on books authored by Chicano/Latino writers, I would be mediating a conversation between the written word and the everyday bookworm who was also a doctor, a high school teacher, a factory worker, or a retiree. In short, the newspaper reviews would be the book talk stripped of the elitist and alienating vocabulary of scholarly criticism, like the language found in the poems, stories, novels, and essay collections I would be reviewing.

What better example of simplicity of language expressing sophistication of thought and ideas than the verse of Francisco X. Alarcón? *From the Other Side of Night/Del otro lado de la noche* was the first title I reviewed for *The El Paso Times*, printed in the Sunday edition, June 9, 2002. Three months later I reviewed another Camino del Sol title, *Home Movies of Narcissus* by Rane Arroyo. Then another, Juan Felipe Herrera's *Notebooks of a Chile Verde Smuggler*, in January 2003. And yet another, *Work Done Right* by David Domínguez, two months after that. While I kept an eye out for books written by Chicano/Latino writers that were published both by the New York houses and by university and independent publishers, the frequency of my selections from the Camino del Sol Latino literary series spoke to the quality of the titles published by the University of Arizona Press. You see, I had made a conscious decision by then, since newspaper space was rare and becoming more precious each year, to review only those books that moved me to a critical response.

Seven years later, I realize that ours is a parallel journey: the University of Arizona Press prints and distributes the literary works of Chicano/ Latino writers and I review a number of them—both efforts tracking an important thread of Chicano/Latino cultural production during the first decade of the new millennium. This wasn't an agreement, exactly, though after years of interaction with acquisitions editor Patti Hartmann, what began as a professional relationship feels more like an alliance of sorts. At the very least it's a mutual recognition of the importance of our tasks, which were always in service to the reading community at large. That alliance became official once I accepted the invitation to compile this reader.

Camino del Sol: A Latina and Latino Literary Series was the brainchild of well-known editor and writer Ray Gonzalez, a name not unfamiliar to those of us with a vested interest in Chicano/Latino literature. Gonzalez was already building a solid reputation as an editor with vision, compiling early anthologies like *Tracks in the Snow: Essays by Colorado Poets* (1989), *Without Discovery: A Native Response to Columbus* (1992), and *After Aztlán: Latino Poets of the Nineties* (1993), which introduced readers to a critical mass of Chicano/Latino writers—a rich literary community whose many members have gone on to have illustrious writing careers. He was also a well-respected critic, bringing valuable attention to books authored by Chicanos/Latinos through *The Nation* and *The Bloomsbury Review* at a time when there were only a few venues that were taking a serious look at this burgeoning body of work. Subsequently, Gonzalez proposed the literary series to the University of Arizona Press. After much negotiation and discussion, it launched officially in 1994 with Gonzalez at the helm as series editor.

Historically, "Camino del Sol" as a series name gestures toward the now-defunct Tonatiuh Publications/Premio Quinto Sol established by the late Octavio I. Romano, which published the literary series that launched the careers of such Chicano luminaries as Tomás Rivera (with the publication of *. . . y no se lo tragó la tierra* in 1971), Rudolfo Anaya (with the publication of *Bless Me, Ultima* in 1972), Rolando Hinojosa-Smith (with the publication of *Estampas del valle* in 1973), and Estela Portillo Trambley (with the publication of *Rain of Scorpions* in 1975).

And so it was fitting that the first title released in the series was Juan Felipe Herrera's *Night Train to Tuxtla*. Herrera, one of Chicano literature's most prolific and celebrated writers, set a high standard, especially for poetry. But most importantly, the combination of renowned editor and renowned author in the Camino del Sol debut ensured that the series would step onto the publishing landscape as a reputable and recognizable newcomer with promise.

I remember clearly, as a graduate student enrolled in the writing program at Arizona State University, that there was an air of excitement about this launch; it announced a new publication venue for up-and-coming Chicano/Latino writers with dreams of seeing their works in print. The only other presses with a strong Chicano/Latino–specific publishing history were Arte Público Press, directed by Nicolás Kanellos in Houston, and Bilingual Press, directed by Gary Keller in Tempe, Arizona. But a third possibility broke that "two-party system," in place since the 1970s, that had initiated the careers of some of the nation's more recognizable Chicana/o writers such as Sandra Cisneros, Lorna Dee Cervantes, Ana Castillo, Gary Soto, Pat Mora, Alicia Gaspar de Alba, Demetria Martínez, Victor Villaseñor, Helena María Viramontes, and Denise Chávez.

Ray Gonzalez's knowledge and expertise of the literary field set a strong foundation at the University of Arizona Press for marketing and publicizing future titles with Camino del Sol. Though he stepped down as series editor in 1996, he has continued as an essential presence and ally of the project, reviewing and evaluating manuscripts, offering generous endorsements on book jackets, as well as participating in the series itself with seven books of prose and poetry published as Camino del Sol titles.

At the conclusion of Gonzalez's brief tenure as series editor, Patti Hartmann stepped forward as acquisitions editor, guiding Camino del Sol into the new millennium as *the* Latino literary series with unmatched distribution power and visibility, an unparalleled top-caliber stream of Chicano/Latino authors and literary works, and a reliable rhythm of new releases each season—currently six titles a year.

A series that preceded Camino del Sol and is worth noting is the Chicano/Latino Literary Prize, established in 1974, which is still administered by the Department of Spanish and Portuguese at the University of California at Irvine. Under the direction of such legendary figures of Chicano/Latino letters as Alejandro Morales, Juan Bruce-Novoa, and María Herrera-Sobek, the award series gave early recognition in the 1970s to such writers as Gary Soto, Alma Luz Villanueva, Helena María Viramontes, and Juan Felipe Herrera.

Other Chicano/Latino literary series currently providing publishing opportunities on a notably visible scale are the Chicana and Chicano Vision of the Américas, launched by the University of Oklahoma Press in 2002 with the publication of Chicano writer Leroy V. Quintana's story collection *La Promesa*; the Miguel Mármol Prize for a debut book of prose by a Latino writer, launched in 2002 with the publication of Chicana writer Lorraine López's *Soy La Avon Lady and Other Stories*; Writing in Latinidad, with an emphasis on Latino autobiography, launched by the University of Wisconsin Press in 2005 with the publication of Argentinian-Jewish-American Susana Chávez-Silverman's memoir *Killer Crónicas: Bilingual Memories/Memorias Bilingües*; Latino Voices, championed by Ilan Stavans and launched by Northwestern University Press in 2003 with the publication of Sergio Troncoso's novel *The Nature of Truth* and Chicano writer Manuel Muñoz's story collection *Zigzagger*; the Andrés Montoya Poetry Prize, administered every two years and launched in 2004 by Letras Latinas, the literary program of the Institute for Latino Studies at the University of Notre Dame, with the publication of Chicana poet Sheryl Luna's *Pity the Drowned Horses*; and the newly launched Canto Cosas Poetry Series at Bilingual Press with its first title, *The Date Fruit Elegies* by Chicano poet John Olivares Espinoza, in print at the end of 2008. These last two promising series are off and running thanks to the direction of Francisco Aragón, the editor of another recent University of Arizona Press anthology *The Wind Shifts*. And most recently, Texas Tech University Press launched The Americas in 2009, a book series that promises to publish eight titles by U.S. Latino and Latin American authors each year. Among the first releases is *Breathing, In Dust*, a novel-in-stories by the Chicano writer Tim Z. Hernández.

There have been short-lived attempts to foment an interest in Chicano/Latino literature within the larger New York houses, namely RAYO at HarperCollins, which was spearheaded by René Alegría and launched in 2000. This imprint made a brief but noticeable splash, publishing such Chicano writers as Luis J. Rodríguez, Yxta Maya Murray, Michael Jaime-Becerra, and Stella Pope Duarte, before it became, by 2007, exclusively a Spanish-language imprint kept afloat by the sales of Isabel Allende titles. Given the current climate of cutbacks, lay-offs, and downsizing, which has affected the publishing industry severely, it is doubtful that any mainstream press will be attempting a Latino-only imprint anytime soon. It's worth acknowledging, however, that Grove Press (an imprint of Grove/Atlantic Inc.) has been loyal to a handful of its Latino authors over the years, namely the Chicano writers John Rechy, Jimmy Santiago Baca, and Dagoberto Gilb, and the Cuban American writer Pablo Medina. Young writers of note who have started their writing careers in the large New York publishing houses are few. Among them, the Chicano writers Alex Espinoza (HarperCollins), Oscar Casares (Little, Brown), and Reyna Grande (Atria); the Cuban American writers H. G. Carrillo (Pantheon) and Ana Menéndez (Grove/Atlantic); the Peruvian American writer Daniel Alarcón (HarperCollins); the Panamanian American writer Cristina Henríquez (Riverhead); and the Dominican writers Angie Cruz (Simon & Schuster), Loida Maritza Pérez (Viking), Nelly Rosario (Pantheon), and Junot Díaz (Riverhead).

Small, independent, and university presses, however, will continue to soldier on. Besides the aforementioned presses, it's worth recognizing the contributions of the University of New Mexico Press (and its continued support of Chicano writers Rudolfo Anaya and Levi Romero), the legendary Byrd family and Cinco Puntos Press (and their long publishing relationships with Chicano writers Benjamin Alire Sáenz and Luis Alberto Urrea), Bryce Milligan and Wings Press (and their long publishing relationship with Chicana writer Carmen Tafolla), the late Alexander "Sandy" Taylor and Curbstone Press (besides publishing works by seasoned Chicano writers like Luis J. Rodríguez and Ana Castillo, the press has championed early-career writers like the Dominican American writer Annecy Báez and the Afro-Latina poet Aracelis Girmay), and more recently, Johnny Temple and Akashic Books (which has published multiple titles by Cuban American writers Achy Obejas and Robert Arellano, and notable titles by Puerto Rican writer Abraham Rodríguez, Chicana writer Felicia Luna Lemus, and Mexican poet Gabriela Jauregui). It is also worth mentioning the extraordinary work done by the editors at Aunt Lute, which has given the literary world such titles as Gloria Anzaldúa's bestselling masterpiece *Borderlands/La Frontera*. These presses have all made a commendable effort at publishing books by Chicano/Latino writers and poets whose work reflects a varied Chicano/Latino experience.

Though Camino del Sol does not stand alone in identifying exceptional manuscripts and supporting talented writers at different stages of their careers, what sets it apart from all the others is that in such a short span of time it has cultivated an admirable and sizeable list of distinguished contemporary authors, which in turn has attracted a flurry of literary activity—both critical attention and interest from other contemporary authors who want to be part of this on-going series. Other presses can boast such a response, but none can match the volume of active writers and recognizable names in the Camino del Sol series.

Awards and other literary accolades bestowed upon Camino del Sol titles include the PEN/Beyond Margins Book Award to Richard Blanco's *Directions to the Beach of the Dead*; two Before Columbus Foundation American Book Awards, one to Diana García's *When Living Was a Labor Camp* and one to Luis Alberto Urrea's *Nobody's Son: Notes from an American Life*; an International Latino Book Award in poetry to Pat Mora's *Adobe Odes* and a second one in autobiography to Kathleen Alcalá's *The Desert Remembers My Name: On Family and Writing*; the Premio Aztlán to Sergio Troncoso's *The Last Tortilla and Other Stories*; the PEN/Oakland–Josephine Miles National Literary Award to Kathleen de Azevedo's *Samba Dreamers*; and, more recently, Juan Felipe Herrera's *Half of the World in Light: New and Selected Poems* was awarded the prestigious National Book Critics Circle Award in Poetry. He is the first Chicano to win that national literary prize.

Perhaps that's the secret behind the unique success of Camino del Sol: it has generated a "literary buzz" that has intensified the competition and raised the expectations of the quality of manuscript submissions, particularly in poetry. As a frequent reviewer of these poetry manuscripts myself, I tend to evaluate projects by comparing them to the two most outstanding poetry books in the series written by first-time authors: *How Long She'll Last in This World* by María Meléndez and *Work Done Right* by David Domínguez. In my opinion, only a manuscript that matches the quality of these two triumphant titles is worth joining their distinguished company.

In the many years that I have spoken on Chicano/Latino literature at public events, as a writer and as a critic, I have spent unnecessary energy responding to the same inquiries: *Where can I find books written by Latinos?* and *What's the difference between Chicano, Mexican American, and Latino?*; and my personal favorite, *Is Latino literature written in English or is it translated from the Spanish?*

I realize that despite a rich publishing history extending decades, there is still much ignorance about who this population of writers is and how their diverse culture is represented in the written word. But before one faults the general reader, let me announce that those questions, uninformed as they sound, have been asked by editors, agents, publicists, publishers, and accomplished writers outside of the Chicano/Latino community. Unfortunately, I have encountered such lack of knowledge *within* the Chicano/Latino community as well. So despite any strides forward (like Chicano/Latino writers receiving national recognitions, more publishing venues available for Chicano/Latino writers, and the continued publication of Chicano/Latino anthologies and readers, such as the one you now hold in your hands), it is important to recognize that 100 percent of these efforts to enlighten and educate comes from proactive advocates of Chicano/Latino literature.

It is my hope then that this reader will be useful as an introduction to Chicano/Latino letters or, for those more familiar with the field, as an affirmation of how much this landscape has grown, changed, and matured since the Chicano movement of the late 1960s and early 1970s (which I will use as a historical marker). Certainly, American society and politics have been transformed because of decades of interaction with generations of immigrant communities and their respective cultures. And Chicano/Latino literature has been reflecting these social-political shifts through every relevant stage.

But before I discuss what has changed, I'd like to point out a few key elements that have remained the same. The sensibility of this reader still reflects a strong working-class consciousness, since most Chicano writers (the majority represented in this reader) come from working-class roots, and along with that background comes an awareness of social and political struggles, everything from migration to education, and the practice of activism through ink. Writing continues to be a critical component of cultural activism. No matter how apolitical the subject matter may appear to be, it is to be considered a political act by the mere fact that voice, identity, and experience are claiming space and visibility in a venue—in this case, literature—that is still dominated by white artists.

Working-class consciousness is expressed through the stories and poems that take place in the barrios (nearly every prose piece in this collection is set in working-class neighborhoods) or in the work place, such as the sausage factory in the poetry of David Domínguez, the salt mines in the poem by Rita María Magdaleno, and the chicken farm in one of Sergio Troncoso's stories. Descriptions of communal spaces and living conditions that suffer from economic depression do not stereotype the Chicano/Latino community as poverty stricken, nor does this romanticize disenfranchisement. Rather, this is a manifestation of a shared history and experience, since, in spite of a quickly growing middle and professional class, the majority of the Chicano/Latino population continues to subsist in low-wage-earning households.

The dominant region giving geographical context to the works in this reader is, not surprisingly, the American Southwest. More specifically, the two dominant urban centers (reflecting a historical trend, particularly with Chicano literature) are Fresno, California, and El Paso, Texas (and their immediate surroundings). This phenomenon has no proper explanation and continues to surprise, since there are now larger urban centers with higher concentrations of Chicanos/Latinos (like Los Angeles and Chicago), but Fresno and El Paso continue to lead an extraordinary literary legacy that reaches back to Chicano writers like John Rechy, Gary Soto, and the deceased writers Arturo Islas, José Antonio Burciaga, Andrés Montoya, Ricardo Sánchez, and Estela Portillo Trambley. It then spirals forward into a newer generation of Chicano writers like Daniel Chacón, Blas Manuel de Luna, Richard Yáñez, Carolina Monsiváis, Sheryl Luna, Javier Huerta, and Emmy Pérez. In this reader, representing the Fresno contingency are Juan Felipe Herrera, Luis Omar Salinas, David Domínguez, and Dixie Salazar; representing the El Paso area are Ray Gonzalez, Pat Mora, Sergio Troncoso, and Christine Granados. The rest of the contributors have roots in Florida, New Mexico, the Midwest, and in other parts of California and Texas. The third dominant region is Arizona. Writers who engage with Arizona's unique cultural landscape include Stella Pope Duarte, Patricia Preciado Martin, Margo Tamez, and Gina Franco.

Migration continues to be a viable metaphor for Chicano/Latino writers. From the early seminal texts, such as Tomás Rivera's *. . . y no se lo tragó la tierra*, which detailed the migrant farmworker experience, to José Antonio Villarreal's *Pocho*, which is a classic American dream/immigrant story, to Ron Arias's *The Road to Tomazunchale*, which outlined the cultural journey of the imagination, movement forms the backbone of the majority of Chicano/Latino prose narratives. But, as demonstrated by the four novels in the Camino del Sol series, the more contemporary narrative is reaching beyond the familiar immigrant struggles or, at the very least, reintroducing them in innovative ways.

Brazilian American writer Kathleen de Azevedo's *Samba Dreamers* and Braulio Muñoz's *The Peruvian Notebooks* might be classified as conventional immigrant narratives dealing with the pressures of assimilation and the internal conflict of navigating a dual identity—being a citizen with loyalties toward the homeland and the adopted home—except that these novels are also clever illustrations of how American cinema and pop culture have bridged distant geographies (South America and North America), providing new models and metaphors through which a Latin American citizen can reinvent and integrate himself or herself into the media-centered American culture. (That energy is echoed in Rane Arroyo's poem "Amateur Filmmaker.")

Puerto Rican writer Fred Arroyo's novel *The Region of Lost Names* (like the essays of Chicano writers Kathleen Alcalá and Luis Alberto Urrea) speaks to the complexities of second- and third-generation Americans: searching for ancestral roots and a better understanding of the family history; weathering the tensions of a generation gap compounded by a cultural one; closely examining the dysfunctional and contradictory values of family and religion; unmasking society's idealized version of the "Latino family"; exploring both self-discovery and leisure; and mining for relevant tropes in an expansive arena that encompasses everything from folklore to pop culture. In brief, the lens of observation, experience, and imagination is shaped by a formal education and access to other resources that are not as readily available to immigrants.

Additionally, de Azevedo, Muñoz, and Arroyo invoke the metaphor of immigrant as exile—a state of being that is presented in more literal terms in the poems by the Cuban American poets Richard Blanco and Virgil Suárez, and in the memoir of Chilean activist Marjorie Agosín.

The novel *If I Die in Juárez* by the Chicana writer Stella Pope Duarte and the essays of Chicano writer Ray Gonzalez examine life along the

U.S.–Mexico border. Perhaps more than any other space, la frontera is the war zone that serves as the foundation—spatial and emotional—for the Chicano writer. The Río Grande, the wall, the fence, the border patrol (now Homeland Security), are but superficial divisions and dividers for the long-contested birthright and ownership of the Southwest. Gonzalez's essays give insight to the historical context, particularly of Tejas/Texas, and how this bi-national, bi-cultural legacy directs and fuels the Chicano writer's imagination. Duarte takes a critical look at the ills of contemporary border culture, from the unsolved femicides to the poverty, pollution, and unemployment of an overcrowded, underserved community. These two visions, one introspective and exploratory, the other humanistic and activist-oriented, provide a full, unflinching view of a dynamic, ever-changing place that refuses to collapse despite the heavy weight of its past and present social and political conditions.

I'd like to affirm that every poem in this project has some political slant, context, or sensibility. Despite American poetry's disdain for the infusion of politics into this particular genre—a position that is in itself political—Chicano/Latino poets insist on engaging, reshaping, or recognizing the discourse of ethnicity, identity, religion, history, language, community, and culture. Indeed, these interconnected discourses are important muses to the poet, but the center of gravity continues to be memory. Memory is preserved and honored through the literary elegy inspired by significant events (as in the poems "Operation Wetback, 1953" by Diana García, "Where the Bodies, Half-Dressed, in Pieces" by Gina Franco, and "The Deer" by Marcos McPeek Villatoro), or it is expressed through the imagery of Catholicism in commemoration of the deceased—what I call the "descanso poem," a word version of an altar to the dead. Examples of the descanso poem in this collection include "Shrine" by Juan Delgado, "World to World" by Valerie Martínez, "Prayer" by Blas Falconer, "Letanía para José Antonio Burciaga" by Juan Felipe Herrera, and "Prayer for My Brother" by Carl Marcum.

Thankfully, women are well represented by Camino del Sol—seventeen out of the thirty-seven contributors. And six of the authors (Francisco X. Alarcón, Rane Arroyo, Lisa D. Chávez, Demetria Martínez, Blas Falconer, and Richard Blanco) openly identify as gay, lesbian, or bisexual, though their works (or my selections) may not necessarily reflect that sexual identity.

In terms of gender, this speaks highly to the University of Arizona Press's efforts to be cognizant of a balance. It is not news that in the early stages of the Chicano/Latino literary movements, men dominated the pages and stages of cultural expression, a trend that shifted in the 1980s with the meteoric rise of authors like the Chicana writer Sandra Cisneros, the Puerto Rican writer Esmeralda Santiago, the Cuban American writer Cristina García, and the Dominican American writer Julia Alvarez. It is important to recognize that the same shift was happening within the Asian American, African American, and Native American literary communities—female writers were now at the forefront of cutting-edge literature. More recently, however, there is an odd gender disparity in terms of literary genres: males continue to dominate poetry (though that's not the case with Camino del Sol). In fact, the Chicano/Latino poets with the more prominent international profiles are all men: the Puerto Rican writers Martín Espada and Miguel Algarín, the Cuban American writer Virgil Suárez, and the Chicano writers Alberto Ríos, Gary Soto, Juan Felipe Herrera, Luis J. Rodríguez, and Jimmy Santiago Baca. The only female poet who matches or surpasses those reputations is Chicana writer Lorna Dee Cervantes.

In this reader, the writings by women offer an interesting multi-generational scope of literary feminism, since at least three generations of women writers are included. As a dramatic point of contrast, I invite readers to compare the prose of Patricia Preciado Martin and the poetry of Pat Mora, which are slightly mannered and domestic compared to the edgier, daring subject matter in the works by younger women like the story writer Christine Granados and the poet María Meléndez.

In terms of sexuality, just as the Chicano/Latino community at large had to deal with its inherent sexism, it has yet, unfortunately, to negotiate properly with its homophobia. This, given the struggles with such charged issues as gay marriage and the adoption of children by gay/lesbian couples, is a challenge on a national scale. Since the 1990s, Chicana/Latina lesbian writers have made many literary contributions that have helped shape a "lesbian of color" discourse. These include Chicana writers like the late Gloria Anzaldúa, Emma Pérez, Carla Trujillo, and Alicia Gaspar de Alba, the Cuban American Achy Obejas, the Chilean American Mariana Romo Carmona, and more recently, the popular young Chicana novelist Felicia Luna Lemus.

Gay Chicano/Latino writers, unfortunately, have made only minor strides toward establishing such a community. The out-of-the-closet role models with prominence and staying power have been few and spread out over the decades. These include Chicano writers John Rechy (since the

1960s) and Arturo Islas (until his death in 1991), Chicano poet Francisco X. Alarcón, mystery-genre novelist Michael Nava, Colombian writer Jaime Manrique, and Puerto Rican writers Rane Arroyo and Miguel Algarín (these last five active since the 1990s). Not until this millennium have the successes of younger gay authors, such as Chicano writers Alex Espinoza, Manuel Muñoz, and Miguel Murphy; Colombian American writer James Cañón; Cuban American writers H. G. Carrillo, Richard Blanco, and Ernesto Mestre-Reed; and the popular spoken-word artist based in New York City, Emmanuel Xavier, offered a critical mass approaching a gay Chicano/Latino community, perhaps even a movement, though it has yet to become formally organized.

Another key observation that deserves mention is the presence of first-book authors under the age of forty (at the time of this publication). The strong writing coming from this fresh generation of writers speaks to the strong academic education that most of them have received through creative writing programs (a young writer without an MFA degree is a rarity these days). An academically trained writer has the advantage of the professionalization that works its way into this education, from the exposure to and interaction with visiting writers on college campuses to the community building that is unavoidable through conferences such as the annual reunion of the Association of Writers and Writing Programs (AWP). Unlike their predecessors, younger writers have the benefit of a lengthy Chicano/Latino literary history and lineage, plus resources such as list-servs and literary cyber-chat made possible on a sizeable scale through the Internet. No matter how esoteric the work or how removed the writer is from an urban center, no artist—unless it's by choice—works in isolation. Indeed the advancements in technology have facilitated not only the quality and quantity of publications but also knowledge of the workings of marketing and publicity. With Facebook, MySpace, and writers' blogs at a young author's immediate disposal, a response to a publication, accolade, or other literary accomplishment can be easily amplified. "Word of mouth"—always the reliable disseminator of information—has now become "word of mouth via hyperlink" and an essential resource for the small press community.

Readers might be surprised by one characteristic of this reader: except for the poetic works of Franciso X. Alarcón, Juan Felipe Herrera, and Albino Carrillo, there is an absence of writers who engage with intralingual wordplay and/or an indigenous national identity (there is, however, a Native American sensibility found in the poetry of Margo Tamez and

Lisa D. Chávez, and a gesture toward Mexican indigenous identity in the chapter excerpted from Stella Pope Duarte's novel). Linguistically, Camino del Sol has exercised a rather conservative selection in publishing authors who generally do not employ Spanglish or an avant-garde poetics (which moves away from the language and traditional forms found in lyrical and narrative poetry). Subversion of language and convention is a feature that has a long history with Chicano writers, dating back to the legendary word acrobat Alurista, who continues to challenge, parody, and provoke with his irreverent and outspoken political verse to this day. Younger voices practice this presentation at poetry slams, open mics, and on the spoken word stage. In terms of finding a home to publish these writings, young performance artists or practitioners of the intralingual poem turn to independent presses even smaller and more financially strapped than the university presses, such as Calaca Press and Chusma House Publications, which published such veteran Chicano writers as the late raulrsalinas and José Montoya.

I would like to note, however, that with the spring 2009 publication season release of *what i'm on* by the Chicano writer Luis Humberto Valadez, the University of Arizona Press took a dramatic first step toward embracing the more linguistically and structurally innovative verse of the new generation of Chicano/Latino writers. That gesture was underscored with the simultaneous publication of *POEMA*, the fourth book written by postmodernist Colombian American poet Maurice Kilwein Guevara, and *Of Earth and Sea: A Chilean Memoir*, the "poetic autobiography" of Chilean writer Marjorie Agosín, beautifully translated by Roberta Gordenstein.

And so this extraordinary journey through fifteen years of Camino del Sol. My expectation is that the social and political scope of this reader provides evidence that "Latino" is not a monolithic designation, that despite sharing common ground, the territory of Chicano/Latino writers is expansive and non-limiting. General categories such as class, gender, sexuality, and ethnicity are unpacked and examined through the varying perspectives of each complex narrator or unique speaker.

In the early stages of this project, the University of Arizona Press representatives and I kept using the term "best of the series." And I'd like to clarify that, according to the selections finalized for the reader, these are choices influenced by the social and political context of that fall 2008 season. A different time period would have produced a slightly different table of contents, but that could be said of any response to a change of temperature in a room. In *my* room was the national election and subsequent triumph of Barack Obama, our first non-white U.S. president; the scapegoating of Mexicans (*still!*) by a political climate that insists on blaming "illegal aliens" for the ills of American society; the collapse of the economy and the temporary suspension of Wall Street parties; the continued toasting of Dominican American writer Junot Díaz, only the second Latino fiction writer (after the Cuban American Oscar Hijuelos) to receive the Pulitzer Prize; the devastating loss of three Chicano writers over the course of a few months—raulrsalinas, Alfred Arteaga, and Luis Omar Salinas (the three poets to whose memory this reader is dedicated)—and my own personal demands as the newly elected treasurer of the National Book Critics Circle, where I also serve as executive board member and am obligated to read the full color spectrum of contemporary American literature.

In rereading the entirety of the Camino del Sol titles, what appeals to me are pieces that provide education and engagement—poetry and prose that teaches readers something about the Chicano/Latino experience at the same time that it invites readers to enjoy a story or to reflect on an image—works that tap into universal truths through a distinct Chicano/Latino cultural lens, and which accomplish description, exposition, dialogue, and lyricism with a strong adherence to narrative and poetic craft. In brief, prose and poetry that are aware of form, content, and context. For the serious Chicano/Latino author of relevant writing, there is no "art for art's sake," no luxury of separating identity from imagination or experience. Such posturing is the indulgence of the privileged—the hobbyist writing of dilettantes and children of leisure disguised as "artistes"—or, more tragically, the insecure scribblings of delusional writers of color who believe they will transcend their ethnic identities and be hailed simply as "writers." In this race-conscious society we all inhabit, such wishful thinking remains a fantasy.

I opted to divide this reader into the three conventional sections—poetry, fiction prose, and nonfiction prose—since I am painfully aware that the general literary readership has three distinct preferences and that educational curricula tend to be designed around convenient categories and labels. The ideal audience, however, is the hungry reader of all three genres.

And finally, the tone of this project is also an acknowledgment of my never-ending nationalistic squabble with any press, series, heading, or label that insists the word "Latino" take such prominence, as is the case with Camino del Sol and with this reader. The fact is that out of the thirty-seven authors here featured, twenty-five of them self-identify as Chicana/o, the other twelve claim cultural heritages rooted in the rest of Latin America and the Caribbean (excluding Mexico, of course). Instead of perceiving this as a shortcoming by the University of Arizona Press to uphold a safe, nationless designation, I'd like to celebrate the continued presence and perseverance of Chicana/o writers whose politicized identity prevails despite the erasure imposed by the label "Latino."

A further note on the selection process: followers of the series will notice the absence of a few Camino del Sol titles from this reader. The parameters of my selections were to include only projects that were originally published in the series, which meant excluding any books reprinted by the University of Arizona Press such as Pat Mora's poetry volume *Agua Santa/Holy Water*, Luis Alberto Urrea's novel *In Search of Snow*, and Ray Gonzalez's essay collection *Memory Fever*. Four authors (Juan Felipe Herrera, Braulio Muñoz, Patricia Preciado Martin, and Ray Gonzalez) have had multiple titles published within the series, and I opted for a representative sample of their best work. I also excluded work from the poetry anthology *The Wind Shifts*, edited by Francisco Aragón, primarily because I wanted to be consistent and select *only* from single-author volumes originally published by the University of Arizona Press. I made a conscious effort to avoid repeating Aragón's selections in terms of the work by poets that appears in both projects, since I consider this project to be a companion reader to *The Wind Shifts*. Finally, the most recent titles to make it into this reader were published in the spring 2009 publication season. These parameters were made to accommodate a deadline and a page-count constraint.

I'd like to acknowledge a few people who were essential in making this book happen. First, thanks to Patti Hartmann, who first tempted me with the possibility of undertaking this massive chore with the coy remark, "But you've read most of the books already!" Thanks also to Kristen Buckles for her guidance and invaluable insights on reshaping the selection criteria. Much gratitude to my "keystroker" Betsy Narváez, to my graduate assistant diego báez, who read over a summer what I had read over a period of a decade, and to my academic home, Rutgers–Newark, the State University of New Jersey, for the generous research budget.

And finally, none of this would have been possible without the trail-blazing vision of the Camino del Sol series founder, Ray Gonzalez, a generous mentor and Renaissance man, the greatest champion of Chicano/Latino literature, our most prolific and hardest-working man of letters, who continues to kick open doors after all these years. Gracias, Ray.

Rigoberto González
New York City, March 2009

Poetry

I pin these poems
on you like stars,
tattoo tears

Where you go, these words
go, forever
my suitcase ready at the door

—*Demetria Martínez*

From the Other Side of Night/
Del otro lado de la noche

Francisco X. Alarcón

Del otro lado de la noche	From the Other Side of Night
qué decir	what to say
ante	about
el silencio	silence
las páginas	the pages
que se quedan	left
sin escribir	unwritten
los libros	the books
en donde	in which
todavía	we are yet
ni somos	to be
ni estamos	appear
ni existimos	exist
esta vida	this life
condenada	condemned
al olvido	to oblivion
aquí	here
nadie sabe	nobody knows
ni sabrá	nor will know

del mar
que llevamos
adentro

of the sea
we carry
within us

del fuego
que encendemos
con el cuerpo

of the fire
we ignite
with our bodies

del
otro lado
de la noche

from
the other side
of night

Plegaria de amor

Love Plea

acógeme
en tus brazos
amor mío

love—
take me
into your arms

que soy
el duelo
de tu mediodía

I am
the mourning
of your noon

este río
sin lecho
sin dirección

this river
with no course
or direction

dame
tu mano
hermano mío

brother—
give me
your hand

que soy
el carmesí
de tu clavel

I am
the crimson of
your carnation

el viento
en busca
de su raíz

the wind
in search
of its roots

ábreme	open
las puertas	your doors
no tardes más	hurry—
no ves	don't
que carnada	you see—
soy	I'm bait
para	for
los perros	the dogs
de la oscuridad	of darkness

¡Tlazoltéotl!

Diosa del Amor
Diosa de la Muerte
Comedora de la Suciedad
Madre de Todas las Estaciones

Madre de los Ríos
baña a tu hijo
con las aguas que brotan
de la Fuente de la Juventud

Madre de los Colibríes
sécale sus últimas lágrimas
bésale todos sus dolidos huesos
engalánalo con flores matinales

Madre de las Montañas
acarícialo con murmullos
llévatelo a tu lecho
el sueño de tu más hondo cañón

Madre de la Noche
llora con nosotros
ilumina su paso con las estrellas
de la Vía Láctea

Madre del Mar
abraza sus cenizas
hazlo coral rojo que brille
entre los grupos de peces risueñores

Madre de Todas las Estaciones
Comedora de la Suciedad
Diosa de la Muerte
Diosa del Amor

¡Tlazoltéotl!

Tlazolteotl!

Goddess of Love
Goddess of Death
Eater of Filth
Mother of All Seasons

Mother of the Rivers
cleanse your son
with waters flowing
from the Fountain of Youth

Mother of the Hummingbirds
dry off his last tears
kiss each aching bone
dress him in morning flowers

Mother of the Mountains
caress him with murmurs
take him into your bosom
the dream of your deepest canyon

Mother of the Night
weep with us
light his path with the stars
of the Milky Way

Mother of the Sea
embrace his ashes
turn him into bright red coral
amidst schools of laughing fish

Mother of All Seasons
Eater of Filth
Goddess of Death
Goddess of Love

Tlazolteotl!

Oración del desierto

montañas:
  abuelas
    olvidadas
      y recordadas

concédanos
  su aliento
    su fuerza
      su salud

para curarnos
  uno a otro
    —como la noche—
      las heridas

Desert Prayer

mountains—
  grandmothers
    forgotten
      and recalled

grant us
  your breath
    your strength
      your health

to soothe
  —like the night—
    each other's
      wounds

Home Movies of Narcissus

Rane Arroyo

Amateur Filmmaker

Close-up. I'm unshaven. It's OK, for I'm invisible in Chicago
tonight. My shadow wears a long coat borrowed from the black
moon.

I get seasick just riding Earth.
Today's happy hour is outside
of bars. Trees with thousands
of fingers tickle my silly shadow.
Downhill on Broadway. Gravity,
kiss me. Clouds weigh my eyelids.

*

From a locker room, I journey into the dark streets and pass
two generations of jazz players, and both are asking for the
same coin in my pocket. I ponder a liquor store's promise: "like
dying & going to Heaven."

Even the priests were naked in
that Catholic pool that was
surrounded by walls with peepholes.
I go down Argyle Street alone.
A human-size dragon drags New Year's
into an ancient New Chinatown.

*

I sit on my porch, my underwear glowing like a verb. My heart refuses to sleep like the rest of Chicago. Lake Michigan looks like a black eye.

Did gods make the stars from
the bones of dead sparrows?
Séance with Charles Darwin:
there's a monkey on the cross
and a smiling ape in my jock.
The moon cannot mirror my skull.

*

A ride on a subway train, heading towards Argyle Street. The Chicago skyline is a white wall, trembling at the thought of graffiti.

A magician on the glowing train
can't stop touching himself everywhere:
a brief letter from you, love?
Sometimes I smell the olives from
the far garden of the Christ of my
hard childhood. Stop, this is my stop.

*

Along the black lake's edge I stumble and spy on fishermen and drug traders, whose presence is revealed only by lit cigarettes, tiny lighthouses.

It's always about loneliness, isn't it?
I'm teaching other people's children
while I have a cat misnamed as Destiny.
Today's horoscope was so mysterious.
I'm mistaking dreams for memories.
Is Judgment Day a big film festival?

People of the Piñata

I'm drunk while my parents
pray at midnight mass with
other people just as surprised

as they are to be old. I'm drunk
after a job interview that took
5 minutes; it took me one hour

to walk home in new begging shoes.
I'm drunk and toast a lost cousin
in jail whose sex life is "now so

very ambitious" while I stay home
to make *Art International* a meal.
I'm tasting rain on my lips from

a beer garden in a storm in which
a cousin came back from the dead;
gossip became manifestos.

I'm drunk, feeling political
like those transvestites in San Juan
who threw lit cigarettes at tourists

who mocked them in their own land.
I'm drunk and circle the piñata
shaped like a mule. I murder it.

That Flag

The Motel 6 clerk thinks I'm
Italian and complains to me
about Puerto Ricans, and I
nod because she has the key
to the last cheap room in town.
I unpack and go for a ride
down Joe Peréz Road and watch
two white, shirtless men do drug deals.
One looks at me, laughs. What does
he see? This sexy thug has
a Confederate flag in his truck
window. He rubs himself again
and again and I watch the way
one is possessed by a wreck.
The deal done, the two men then
slap each other on the ass,
and ride dust storms back to town.
I sit there thinking the fuckers
are right, that they are big
handsome, that they are our
America's perfect heirs and
that I'm not—aging Puerto Rican
homosexual poet exiled
to a borrowed bed. I walk
past the clerk and sing "Buenas
noches," but it isn't one, for I dream
of that flag, of a terrible army
of soldiers in uniforms of skin
sent to steal from me the head
of Joe Peréz. But I've hidden it
inside my own skull. It is safe.

Directions to the Beach of the Dead

Richard Blanco

When I Was a Little Cuban Boy

O José can you see . . . that's how I sang it, when I was
a *cubanito* in Miami, and *América* was some country
in the glossy pages of my history book, someplace
way north, everyone white, cold, perfect. *This Land
is my Land*, so why didn't I live there, in a brick house
with a fireplace, a chimney with curlicues of smoke.
I wanted to wear breeches and stockings to my *chins*,
those black pilgrim shoes with shiny gold buckles.
I wanted to eat yams with the Indians, shake hands
with *los negros*, and dash through snow I'd never seen
in a one-horse hope-n-say? I wanted to speak in British,
say really smart stuff like *fours core and seven years ago*
or *one country under God, in the visible.* I wanted to see
that land with no palm trees, only the strange sounds
of flowers like petunias, peonies, impatience, waiting
to walk through a door someday, somewhere in God
Bless America and say, *Lucy, I'm home, honey. I'm home.*

Translation for Mamá

What I've written for you, I have always written
in English, my language of silent vowel endings
never translated into your language of silent h's.

> *Lo que he escrito para ti, siempre lo he escrito*
> *en inglés, en mi lengua llena de vocales mudas*
> *nunca traducidas a tu idioma de haches mudas.*

I've transcribed all your old letters into poems
that reconcile your exile from Cuba, but always
in English. I've given you back the *guajiro* roads
you left behind, stretched them into sentences
punctuated with palms, but only in English.

> *He transcrito todas tus cartas viejas en poemas*
> *que reconcilian tu exilio de Cuba, pero siempre*
> *en inglés. Te he devuelto los caminos guajiros*
> *que dejastes atrás, tranformados en oraciones*
> *puntuadas por palmas, pero solamente en inglés.*

I have recreated the *pueblecito* you had to forget,
forced your green mountains up again, grown
valleys of sugarcane, stars for you in English.

> *He reconstruido el pueblecito que tuvistes que olvidar,*
> *he levantado de nuevo tus montañas verdes, cultivado*
> *la caña, las estrellas de tus valles, para ti, en inglés.*

In English I have told you how I love you cutting
gladiolas, crushing *ajo*, setting cups of *dulce de leche*
on the counter to cool, or hanging up the laundry
at night under our suburban moon. In English,

> *En inglés te he dicho cómo te amo cuando cortas*
> *gladiolas, machacas ajo, enfrías tacitas de dulce de leche*
> *encima del mostrador, o cuando tiendes la ropa*
> *de noche bajo nuestra luna en suburbia. En inglés*

I have imagined you surviving by transforming
yards of taffeta into dresses you never wear,
keeping *Papá's* photo hinged in your mirror,
and leaving the porch light on, all night long.

> *He imaginado como sobrevives transformando*
> *yardas de tafetán en vestidos que nunca estrenas,*
> *la foto de papá que guardas en el espejo de tu cómoda,*
> *la luz del portal que dejas encendida, toda la noche.*
> *Te he captado en inglés en la mesa de la cocina*
> *esperando que cuele el café, que hierva la leche*
> *y que tu vida se acostumbre a tu vida. En inglés*
> *has aprendido a adorar tus pérdidas igual que yo.*

I have captured you in English at the kitchen table
waiting for the *café* to brew, the milk to froth,
and your life to adjust to your life. In English
you've learned to adore your losses the way I do.

In the City of Smoking Mirrors

Albino Carrillo

H. Writes to His Brother to Assure Him of Continuous Comfort in the Afterlife

Now comes upon us North Star, O smoking
mirror I invoke your charge, brother from
the laudanum sustaining us all. From my visions pray
for us now the war's begun. Healed not,
our hot blood nation rises dear, secret
weapons never used before against children—
the cleft mountain, that green plain you dream of
shattered so no Buddha would come to sit,

no decent man would take his children near.
Brother twin, the advice I give is like
a deep icy breath taken in a snowstorm:
I can't tell you what it's like to love, or
how to court the young natives so they
open gladly arms leading to the inevitable kiss.

Now comes the truth of winter we think. Our
enemies who hold the bomb mean to burn
us all: you & me, the gardens we've planted
in this life, so far. And now, with the One
European God watching from another
galaxy, a far-out thought I have is that
the music will end, we'll find ourselves
in Mixtlán among the dogs, swimming for

sandy shores somehow reminding us of home:
the girls were easy. Blue turquoise eyes,
favorite birthstones, scientist's daughters all.
Just help me as the next life begins in
some suburb or another, coasting clear
of fathers who don't want to know our names.

Animal Time

I cut loose the last rope, my way back home
when we were all lambs and we were all born.
Between the animal meat and my brain
I let go in sunlight: there was a father
in all of this, speaking a dull language
with his dry tongue until the sun goes out
blue smoke filling the animals again.
I'll admit I don't know him, his back,

or his fine neck curving toward heaven—
in the evening when the thick trees turn black
and I am left to my body, slowly
the night rushes my mind to flame
and I cannot count the shuffling stars,
the holy holies who guard wicked doors.

El Espejo Fumeroso

She knew a mirrored twin, began to write
small letters, notes really, in patient script.
He'd then reply with a story about his body,
the hidden left-side liver,
how he died when doctors couldn't find
his sick appendix. But naturally
he came back, urged by the black spot
growing on his heart, that fine muscle
tuned against his nature.
After a while, though, it's all up to the heart, she'd say.
Who's to know the smoke tasted delicious,
that children roamed his hallways? It was when he was alive
with the black desert sky that he forgot
her letters, useless now but understood
in the back-draft as he counted his way
past the minor planets lining heaven.
Words were everywhere those days,
sullen reminders lifting the faithful to new
intersections. It was with these holy
engines he found her, a flashlight shining
with her pulse, a compass point directed
into his body where he felt her skin,
the fine throb of her wet temples humming
and the taste of her mouth.
His mirror surrounded by her mirrors.
The truth: his arrows flew right,
her fractured kin welcomed him back home.

In an Angry Season

Lisa D. Chávez

The Conjuror of the New Century

1893

Step right in, ladies and gents, step
right in and see the conjuror of the new
century, sample the wonders
he unveils. Years will wink past
with a snap of his fingers; his magic
lantern will reveal the glories
of the century ahead, splendor
spread before you like a vast
unsettled plain.

Enter into the darkened tent and there
he is, prophet of the new, the master
magician who makes years disappear. Terribly
tall, impossibly thin, his bony fingers scythe
across the table shrouded in midnight
cloth. What wonders he displays!
Years skitter past like hunted mice
and he flaunts miracles: cities ablaze
with infinite electric lights, ice boxes
that chill without ice, carriages without
horses, life without toil. His lantern
illuminates astounding scenes: a ship shooting
to the moon like an arrow, machines
that move through smoky skies, magic

boxes that store knowledge and spew
it out again. A miraculous machine age!
Opportunity for all, money to be minted, dreams
crafted in credit and cash. Coins appear
between his fingers like winking eyes,
multiplying for new kings of industry
whose riches assault the mind.

Now here's his lovely assistant, blindfolded,
scales in hand. Sprightly she steps
into his oblong box. Swords slide in; muffled
shrieks and her thin blood seeps out,
unnoticed. But don't look away! There's
always more! A mustard-colored jar
produces magic gases, and an entire
generation chokes and falls. This new
centurion is skilled in sleight
of hand, making people disappear:
six million vanish into air, ash. Entire cities
vaporized in twin exploding clouds.
He pulls trinkets out of an empty
hat: famine, war, and plague. A pyramid
of oranges transforms into a pile
of human skulls, all that remain
from the charnel of Bosnia and Biafra,
Cambodia and Kosovo, countries
whose names don't yet appear on the maps
unfurled in boardrooms and war rooms.
And there's still more. He hawks elixirs
to the citizens of this new world: pretty
potions consumed through needles
and pipes in Bangkok and Boston, from
Amsterdam to L.A. The takers fall down
like passenger pigeons blasted
from the sky, and the razor wire
of justice encircles those who remain.

What a century! Money and gunpowder
perfume the age! Riches unimaginable
for some, while others beg, cowering
on their corner of cardboard or concrete
in the wealthiest cities of this world.
Wonder and opportunities unfolding
like a paper fan. Then crushed. The conjuror
introduces his entourage: generals and CEOs,
presidents and peasants armed
with their tools of war—planes, money,
power, pistols. All followed
by vultures and flesh-eating flies.

From the audience, a frightened voice
pipes up: Terrible illusion, take it
away! Too late, he cries, too late.
The entry fee is already paid;
this future is yours. Welcome
to your new world, a century
of dishonor, suffering, and pain.

The Tattoo Artist

I go to get a tattoo. A butterfly, coy flutter on an ankle. I take a
little something to relax. I fear the needle, that gleaming serpent's
fang. But then I think of the tattoo artist's arms, the way an amethyst
panther prowls up one forearm, the way along the curve of his bicep
a dolphin dips into a fantastic sea of starfish and seaweed, the way
bright phantasms brood beneath his shirt. I call to say I'm coming.
His apartment hums with heat. He smiles seriously as he lets me
in; he's naked except for a pair of shorts. And the tattoos. His body
blooms with color: a tropical garden teeming with orchids and
brilliant birds of paradise. A vine—riotous with scarlet flowers—
snakes up one leg, glides beneath his shorts, slinks up the beach of
his belly. His back fecund with fantastic beasts, a bridge between

dreams and waking. A mermaid weeps indigo tears that transform
into fans of diminutive fish. A Chinese dragon exhales a shower of
stars. A herd of plum-colored horses, hooves sparking saffron light.
Hallucinatory color, the electric glow of pigment injected beneath his
skin. A palimpsest of symbols, illustrations from a trance. I would
read those images like braille, my fingers, tongue traveling along the
labyrinths of ink, discovering entire continents between his shoulder
blades, along a thigh. I tell him what I want. He frowns, his face
the only part of him unmarked, a blank banner floating above the
tumultuous images parading across his chest. Then he shrugs. "A
butterfly, if you like. But it is so ordinary, so unlike you. Maybe
something more . . . original?" I nod. He smiles and his teeth catch
the light like pearls. A tangerine tiger shivers, tensed to leap from
beneath bamboo shadows. A leaf green snake undulates on his chest.
"Where?" My ankle seems an unworthy offering, too tame, too far
away from those undiscovered continents of desire. I pull my T-shirt
over my head, proffer one breast. And he busies himself with paper
and pencil, and he rubs the pattern onto my skin. And he slips his
hand under my breast, holds it reverently, as if weighing gold. My
nipple hardens at his touch. Then the needle whines to life, begins
its burn on my skin and I can barely hold still—it's like an itch you
can't scratch—and the needle moves in and in and in and my bright
blood eases out around it and I sink into the sea swirling and swelling
on his arm. "Do you like it?" he asks, hand still cupping my breast,
dabbing at the beads of blood and sweat with a cloth moist as a
mouth. And I rise through his waves to see. I open my eyes and
images surface like leaping fish. On my left breast, a violet flower
blooms. Into its trembling depths a hummingbird—all emerald
green and garnet—inserts its narrow beak, sucking the nectar from
the flower's long throat. The wings vibrate with the rise and fall of
my gasped breath. The flower stems from a bottle green vine that
fades into my skin. If I could only pluck that vine, follow it like a
thread into the maze of patterns yet to be traced. I can almost see
them, the ghostly phosphorous of tattoos waiting to be needled in,
waiting for the hand of the dream master, the vision giver, the tattoo
artist. "Oh, yes," I say. "Oh, yes." My flesh demands design.

The Bad Wife

The bad wife doesn't cook gourmet meals.
The bad wife doesn't flatter your boss.
The bad wife isn't a good housekeeper,
      doesn't wear frilly aprons
      or take pies to the neighbors.
The bad wife doesn't ask about your day.
She doesn't balance the checkbook,
      do the laundry, or fill up
      the car with gas.
She doesn't drive safely.
The bad wife doesn't say she loves you.

The bad wife wears a black leather
      miniskirt, red spike-heeled boots
      and a blonde wig.
She doesn't wear panties.
The bad wife flirts with strangers in bars
      you didn't know existed. She drinks
      bourbon straight, smokes home-rolled
      cigarettes and lets the smoke shoot
      out her nose.
The bad wife carries a .38 in her purse
      and knows how to use it.
The bad wife fights back.
      She is not afraid of anyone.
      Not even you.
The bad wife gets her nipples pierced,
      gets a tattoo that says Mike.
      Which is not your name.
The bad wife takes your credit card, charges
      two pairs of silk, paisley-print boxers,
      a bottle of scotch, some Kama Sutra oil.
      A hotel room. You get the bill.
The bad wife doesn't come home at night.

The bad wife is a scream of pleasure
           heard through the wall of a motel room.
She glows in the dark.
She is blue neon at night.
The bad wife is a roller-coaster ride
           you never want to end
           though you're sick and shaking
           with the pleasure.
She's slow poison and you don't want
           the antidote.
She's ruthless.

The bad wife opens up your chest
           with one long-nailed finger.
She takes your heart in her teeth and shakes it
           like a terrier with a rat.
She's already swallowed your soul.
               And spit it out—insignificant
               stone.
The bad wife grins, terrier-toothed, and
           you let her back in—to your house
           to your heart to your bed.
The bad wife will never leave you.

A Rush of Hands

Juan Delgado

Shrine

Another cross by the roadside,
This one, so like the others,
Has a rosary draped over the arms,
A bundle of stems.
A few wilted petals cling,
And five candles circle the cross,
Reminders of the drive-by shooting.
Only the phone number
Written in silver duct tape
On the cardboard box, a plea
For "Info," is unusual.
You have to do more than that,
More than chapter and verse,
Numbers leading some of us
Nowhere, and others to a place
All too familiar to revisit.
We can so easily fill in
The chalk outline of a body
With a narrative we have heard
So often on the evening news.
Even a clown with balloons
Parading with a large sign
Announcing no down payments
Until the first of the year
Only gets us to tap our brakes.
If you want more than a glance,
You need to do something exceptional,
Something extravagant.

Forget it, don't think
Of planting a tree for the victim—
It's too common nowadays.
Enough with the plastic flowers
And pinned photos—we already have
Too many faces on milk cartons.
Listen: spend some money.
Hire a belly dancer if you can,
Then get yourself a noisy band.
High school marching bands are the best.
Hire a group of men, not too young,
Neatly dressed in suits,
And instruct them to tie
A ribbon between two trees,
Then have them ceremoniously cut it.
Stand by a table with rows of cookies
And provide us with punch.
Then, when you sense we are ready,
In a weak but steady voice
Begin to tell us about him.
What was his name again?
And how old was he?

Backyard

For Scott Francis

I

Her son watches from his window
The leaves of the walnut tree turn into bats,
Their eyes blind as the marbles under his bed.
When he turns toward his room, they appear again
On his wall, dark wings, outlined by the moon.
His finger traces where their faces would be
If they were not tucked under their wings.
Some tremble, opening their wings,
    A cry for flight.

II

Quietly, as she prayed at his funeral,
She pinches off the leaf of a geranium,
Holding it, a kerchief to grieve her son.
She walks through a garden of relatives,
Asking them to please stand and leave
Because she has to water the lawn.

III

The walnut tree's leaves were once a gift,
         Lavish, loosely worn,
           Now fallen.
     A crisp step,
A squirrel flips a leaf and finds
A walnut, then scurries into the shade.

The sky beyond the tree,
         A cage of branches,
Is hungry for the captive birds to fly.

IV

A breeze fills her curtains, the nets of night.
        She unbuttons her blouse
While the bougainvillea's eyes follow her
To the end of the stepping stones.
The leaf creeping, a tilting shadow points
        Her to a spider's arc.
The green that feeds on the underside of moist stones
        Thickens the air.

Nido

With someone on either side of him holding his hands,
The boy runs, faster than he can go by himself,
His feet skipping above the ground,
And over him flies a window that frames
    His grandpa's face.

    Now that the boy's father is dead,
His grandpa shows up more often, mentioning how much
He had to pay so his son could have a decent burial.
Outside the boy counts the stepping-stones
Taking him to his father's grave marker.

    The grandpa throws off his cap;
He's hungry and sits himself down.
The boy spots on the screen door a beetle
Showing off its hairy legs, its yellow-spotted belly.

His shadow spreads across the lawn to the boy.
    He forgot to rake the leaves.
With the quickness of a grasshopper's leap,
The grandpa strikes the boy.

    ✳

    His face stings as he walks
To a porch that is leaf cluttered, reeling.
The window fades when the kitchen light goes off,
And the lawn widens until there is no hiding place.

Work Done Right

David Domínguez

Chilalengua

I dreamed they gave the JFK Peace Prize to an empty chair
for exposing the horrific oppression of
the Chilalenguan government upon its workers.
The chair was lovely: fine mahogany, a green cushion,
and a silk banner draped like
a humanitarian bridge across the armrests.
How useful the morning paper was.
Earwigs, with only a few bits of meat for food,
took weapons and maneuvered
across the production room toward freedom.
A thick club of newsprint stopped them dead.
Their crisp insect corpses became
immobile pinches that dotted the concrete floor
close to that safe spot behind the wall.
Obituaries marked where the dogs slept.
They dreamed of other things,
the warm corner of a couch and a master's
kind odor that lulled them to sleep.
These thoughts alone were a risk, so the dogs
remained obedient and silent to avoid the winter night.
In Chilalengua the weather was fine.
Long rows of skulls baked under the sun.
Their large black orbitals dotted the fields of sorghum.
One skull with a cracked cranium wouldn't keep its mouth shut.

Club Las Palmas

Open vats of red vinegar fermented outside:
108° of Del Sol heat and black asphalt.
Guillermo and I choked on the vinegar's vapor
as we threw cardboard boxes,
still ripe with scraps of guts, into the dumpster.
Pig blood poured from the boxes,
ran under my smock, and down my skin.
"This is no way to live," I told Guillermo.
Guillermo dipped his hand
into a box lined with wax,
used his hand like a wooden ladle,
filled his palm with warm blood,
and he held it very still as if
blood might reveal lost memory
or a life that he had yet to live.
At noon, we ate lunch.
Flies, maddened by raw meat,
stuck to our skin and dizzied the air,
but I still heard, splitting industrial Del Sol,
the freeway where I wanted to be.

I wanted an age too young to remember,
when fog settled across the Valley and my grandfather,
who drove trucks for Ringsby Rocket,
passed by on the 99 and took
the Jensen off-ramp to check in his emptied rig.
At home, he put his soft-bristled wooden brush beside the towel
smelling of shower and shave,
and he sat to eat nopales and chicken
my grandmother sweetened with red chili sauce.
He slipped into the black silk-lined coat
of his best black suit, and opened
the black case of his trumpet,
and after each valve was oiled,
and after the floral-carved bell was polished,
we drove to Club Las Palmas,
and Abraham's Latin Combo began to tune.

At Galdini Sausage, lunch was over.

Guillermo fixed his collar with dignity,
and he undid his belt, and his pants
with dignity, and he pulled out his shirt,
and he pointed at the rope-thick
purple scar sagging hip to hip below his belly
where he once cut himself open
to let out the life he did not want.
"It is better to work," he said, and tucked in his shirt.

Have you seen a man give himself to this place?

Guillermo and I started a pallet of Sweet.
We ground shoulder and cartons of fat.
We added molasses, sugar, and anise,
then sank in beyond knuckle and elbow
and pushed it all through.

Pig

I pulled into Galdini Sausage at noon.
The workers walked out of production
and swatted away the flies desperate for pork.
Pork gripped the men and was everywhere,
in the form of blood, in the form of fat,
and in pink meat stuck to the workers' shoes.
Outside, eighty-pound boxes of pork
melted under the sun, and as the sun worked,
the blood and fat grew soft, and the boxes,
lined with wax, became like thin paper soaked in oil.
Mack trucks came in with unprocessed pork
and took out chorizo, linguica, hot links, and sausage:
German, Sweet, Breakfast, Hot, and Mild.
One man stood straight up into the sky,
closed his eyes, and with his thumb and forefinger,

worked out bits of meat from his eyelashes
glistening like black grease under the sun.
The air conditioner in Mr. Galdini's office
made the papers from his desk float onto the floor.
He gave me a hard hat, a smock, an apron, and a hair net.
"You're in there," he said and lifted the blinds
of a window that partitioned his office from production.
He stood, gut pushed out, and his whole body
swayed with ease as we watched the workers walk out,
humpbacked under the unyielding memory of pig.

The Tovar Bull

Along the downtown sidewalks,
white guayaberas swung in the breeze.
I wanted a white one,
a white guayabera adorned with paisleys,
a white guayabera
that reminded me of my grandfather
who spent the afternoons
under the pecan tree of my backyard.
I'd sit on his lap,
and we'd listen to afternoon boxing on Spanish radio.
I remember the day we heard Joselito Bienvenida,
a boxer I cheered for because
he tattooed his children's names above his heart.
I remember closing my eyes
and the challenger's tassels that danced like fire
as Joselito's eyes swelled shut,
and when Joselito left himself on the ropes,
the beating began.
Joselito, out on his feet,
died in the ring.
My grandfather and I sat unable to speak
until he took from the breast pocket of his guayabera
a handkerchief that he knotted into

a mouse that jumped from his palms and glided
through the air—
white and filled with the sun.
We munched on *chicharrones* from Cielo's Bakery,
and when Grandpa used the handkerchief
to wipe my mouth,
a stream of light passed through the branches,
and I saw the scar in his eye,
a large white scar
like the ghosts floating through my dreams.
"We are Tovars," he told me, "*fuertes como toros.*"
With the tip of my finger,
I traced the *el toro* tattoo on his forearm,
and he told me he saw a Tovar bull
kill the most promising matador in Mexico City.
The bull's neck muscle was so thick,
the matador couldn't push the sword down
and through the barrel of the chest.
The matador gave up
and tried to slice the bull's throat, but the bull,
hidden for a moment behind the cape,
went under the sword,
and pierced the man's groin with both horns.
The bull watched the blood
soak the dirt before other matadors chased it away,
and my grandfather remembered
the bull's black eyes
reflecting the sunlight even at dusk.
The white guayabera I tried on felt like
the skin of a guardian saint,
and I saw Joselito out on the canvas.
I thought about the bull, too,
how he went *under*
the sword and stared at the matador
after the matador was dead.
I looked into a mirror
and admired my white guayabera,
the hide of a bull
all ghosts would fear.

A Question of Gravity and Light

Blas Falconer

To Know You Better

I sleep in the bed you were born in.
Vines of passion fruit strangle the house,
and trees your father planted
still bear their inedible fruit. The taste
is in the leaves, you always said.

The stump in the backyard
must have been the almond tree
where you chained your dog.
And when you left, they say,
the dog walked into the hills,

chain dragging from its neck.
Men gather for the cockfight,
crowd shoulder to shoulder,
but I can still see the birds,
their wings too large for their bodies,

sweeping the ground like small brooms.
At a table, men lower their faces,
dominoes cupped in their dark hands,
each one a secret.
Women burn palms on the beach,

sell fried fish and plantains in bunches.
They tell me nothing.
They recognize your sway in my walk,
Mother, and their heads
are heavy with disappointment.

This

He tries to say, *Stop. Stop talking*, but can't,
and you can't, and he is shaking his head,
sobbing. The trees blur into one green wall,

and you can't recall what it was
you couldn't not say. You think, *When we stop,
he'll get out. We'll never speak again.*

You touch his thigh, and he doesn't move.
Everything sighs a little. *What is this?*
he asks, softly now, and studies your face.

He knows and you know what this is and why,
but you can't say, not yet, and he is still
looking at you, and the road goes on and on.

Letter from the Cumberland

> *You wouldn't
> the years I begged. Would
> the years I wouldn't.*
> —Sandra Cisneros

A crow fell over a field of tall grass,
one wing flapping against its body
uselessly, and I recalled your question:

Even if I would, could you?

                              But first,
I never thanked you for books you sent
wrapped in gold tissue and green ribbon.

They arrived at my door open, but
I saw the bits of tape and paper left
behind.

    The answer is yes. Each night
I fly back home, repeating the word—
If. If.—from your last letter.

            I look
to the cliff where a bronze bird leans
over the edge, tipped wings spread
as if it could.

Epilogue

To the Reader

She stands on the rocks in high heels. She looks
out of place, meaning elegant: a silk scarf
in her hair, a string of pearls, the sea nudging
the shore relentlessly. The photographer winds
and leans into the shot—the story still to come—

in English, of course. Who'd have guessed: a girl
like her from a town like this. . . . The stones
wobble under her weight. A shell cracks. She points
to a hook. Click. The shoes are a lie. The scarf,
a lie. The pearls. Click. Fishermen blush, but

the rest is true—their daily exchange, and more
than half of what she says. Look at her now.
A boy is climbing the tallest tree, a blade tied
to his belt. Below, girls lift their hands into the air.
The bay full of boats. They've come all this way.

The Keepsake Storm

Gina Franco

Darkling

It happened gradually. My hands, always behind me, sore
from picking at ropes, went first.
They began to feel light and hollow, though something prickled
beneath the skin. My fingers closed and fused,
my arms grew narrow and long
until they were twice the length of my body.
Then, my heart. It raced ahead of me
and tried to thrash its way out—
philomel, philomel—
I listened, afraid to speak.
I thought the hush could do me no harm.
But in silence my tongue was severed.
I'd watched it writhe on the ground in front of me, murmuring,
dividing, becoming forked before it slithered off.
When feathers finally appeared in patches, I saw
that you can live, mute and still, with a sharp desire
for your father's country, which is power.
Or you deny your name until it feels like strength,
and give away all but your scarlet hair,
for it might bring recognition
when you feel murderous, waiting, impatient to do nothing,
turning away from a spindly light that burns your eyes.
You sleep all day, wake fitfully in the evening,
dream of a lover as gentle as your father.
Out of any long-chosen habit you will be transformed
if you are living in want.
He will leave again, and he will return, of course he will.
He will leave, brandishing his coiled weapon
that makes you convulse with longing
to sing.

The Walk Like Old Habits

It seems unlikely, how the city repeats itself
without describing your life. Peeling billboards,
chinks in the walls. Girls on the corner make signs
to one another in the dust, balconies turn
from the beggars rearing up like mannequins
and you think truth is there, however unintelligible.
But it does not wake you to street names you imagine
said something adequate in the beginning, if ever
one street was not like the next, if ever this place
was not like Venice, not like Beijing, but itself
the first lone thing under the sun. Like the garden
before it was *their* garden: the sun before ritual,
before gods, sprouting from stones and fountains, mad, mad,
before all things unremarkable, as winter, as excrement.
Nor does the sudden maze of bicycles and storefronts
bring a word to mind, nothing more than concrete,
brick, glass, motion, all useless, really, though you
come across a woman who sorts through a box
of white fruit, her face pocked with scars
you might recognize should the moon appear full
to announce a point of origin or pleasure that is free
of mooning on every waterway you see. If only
love were free of spit and image, and image—interrupted
by the bells, bells, bells calling from towers
in churchyards where lie the beloved in crates—were
free of rivals. Laughter erupts from a place, many,
beyond the canals, the canals below chimneys
and cemeteries and temple steps, the steps
where old men watch boys mock them, now limping,
now drooling, now trying on an old man's palsy
leafing through a book: licks a deliberating finger,
turns to the pages like the living turn to bread.
The corpses. The guillotines reminiscent of lab rats
stand in for revolution in the square, the emperor
moves through the crowd like a crisis coming
to a head. Heads and more heads in the streets,

this street where you open your eyes and find, isn't it
strange, that you do not grieve the bare infant
you gather to yourself from the walk like old habits
reminding you that some things are new, this body
who wakes you, new hands, new eyes. So little
do you know yourself and the light you would make
even here, to the quick, embracing small things
that grasp you—it's me, it's me—that you
look up for the grounds of your blessings.

Where the Bodies, Half-Dressed, in Pieces

For Carmen Rios, flood victim, Del Rio, Texas, August 22, 1998

What blessings are left to them? They heap belongings
on the walk. Stones washed from their walls
lie about like teeth, one ache next to another.
Nature remains. A sodden box of photos, a wet TV.
A pile of Christmas ornaments winks
in the sun, so there is miracle. They find
new mosquitoes in toilets. In the kitchens, mold
creeps over the windows, in the bedrooms, a goat's
carcass, a bag of trash, a used diaper,
a tree. They find they can put their hands
through walls. Of clay. So there is also
belief. Had belief come sooner, had a forecast
arrived—*listen, it's rain—the drought
is over—the flatlands are running over*—but all
is quiet. Not yet a downpour, patient
at doors, not the emergency broadcast system
streaming across every screen. Not sirens,
thunder, screams, houses shuddering,
giving way below those crouching
on their rooftops. Not yet. First came
coincidence, a twist of fate, a man who towed

his motorboat to the nearby lake, trapped mid-storm
outside his neighborhood. Countless he rescued.
A woman hugging a rushing bush, brothers
perched on a truck, the old man who sells
melons all summer: where was he but among
the saved? So there are also numbers.
When the deluge arrived, I felt
eternity. I left my house. I took up
my cane and walked around in the dark, flicking
switches, banging into things, fighting, until I found
the door. I was up to my neck, swirling.
When it was time, water swallowed me too, down
in a cold flash to the streets where the hill
ends, where the bodies, half-dressed, in pieces,
are torn away from dreams. At Devil's Bend, bodies
collected with trees and refrigerators. The water
receded. The crane dug up hundreds rotting
off the bone, nine of whom were identified
as citizens. I am with them and their families
in the paper below the mayor's address. The rest
were mejicanos, so of course there is also home.
In the funeral home where my daughter didn't find me,
there was a body, stripped of all but a ring
that resembled my own, but again, it was not mine,
so for a time there was also hope.

When Living Was a Labor Camp

Diana García

When living was a labor camp called Montgomery

you joined the family each summer to sort dried figs.
From Santa María to Gilroy, Brawley to Stockton, you settled
in rows of red cabins hidden behind the orchards.

You recall how the red cabin stain came off on your fingers,
a stain you pressed to your cheeks so you looked like
Dolores del Río, the famous Mexican actress.

Her high-sculpted glow stunned the boys who dogged you
to the theater, the coolest building in town, where you forgot
the San Joaquín heat and fruit flies.

You wiggled on velvet-backed chairs, split popcorn with
your cousins. When the film's hero, the rancher's son, rode
horseback to the river and spied Dolores washing her hair,

you'd swoon. Just for a moment, a small eternity, the hero's
hacienda, its dark wood beams and low-slung chandelier, were yours.
You were tall and thin and everything looked good on you.

To tell the truth, though, you preferred Lauren Bacall's whistle.
So at the packing shed you eyed your brothers' friends, not
the pickers, the carpenters, those who wanted out

of the fields. You picked one with a full-mouthed smile, not
your mother's choice but a tall man with papers who wanted
to join the army and live in L.A.

And perhaps, in the end, everything didn't look good on you.
Maybe your hair didn't look good dyed auburn; maybe
pillow-breasted women weren't meant to wear sheaths.

You visit the camp each summer reunion. Your sisters snatch
peeks at your husband. His teeth still look good. A cousin
glides you through a cumbia; you dreamt he kissed you once.

You catch the stench of rotting figs, of too-full outhouses.
The nose closes off. You feel how hot it was to sleep, two
to a mattress, the only other room a kitchen.

You thought your arms thickened long ago lugging trays of figs.
You thought you had peasant ankles. You thought you could die
in the camp and no one would know your smell.

Softball and Tomato Fields

They swarm like ants from the edge of the field,
la migra, the brown horde of them. They take
the best away: Manuel, the meanest pitcher

in the league; Frankie, who could have played
for the Brooklyn Dodgers; Monchie, too busy
looking at the clouds to catch a pop-up fly.

They take the best from Texas and Sinaloa,
from Arizona and Nuevo León—
dutiful sons, faithful husbands swept up

in the net. No matter if they're legal,
no matter if they have papers, in this game,
runners caught between bases are all picked off.

Operation Wetback, 1953

The day begins like any other day.
Your daughter soaks a second diaper,
chortles as she shoves her soft-cooked egg
to the floor. Knees pressed to cracked linoleum,

you barely notice as your husband strokes
your belly. *Mijo,* he croons, prophetic plea,
then squeezes your nalgas as if to gauge
for ripeness. As he edges past, you notice

how his blue shirt blurs against the summer sky,
how sky absorbs his patch of blue, then empties.
Moments later, a truck groans, moves on,
carting rumblings of men headed for the fields.

Years later, you tell your son and daughter
of that anguished day, how green card migrants
vanished from the camps. You tell your children
how news gripped the camps of trains headed south

loaded with wetbacks. You never tell your children
what you can't forget: how you failed to squeeze back,
failed to wave good-bye, failed to taunt him
with viejo sinvergüenza. You never tell your children

how you forget this one man's voice—a voice
that brushed your ears, your hair, a path down your back—
a voice that blends with sounds of a truck
that never brought him home.

POEMA

Maurice Kilwein Guevara

Lyric

I snore.

Greedy for the horizon and its multiplication in rain,
I'm digging up the brow of the rust-veined stone,
Howlers in the high trees telling us to move on.
The shadows

Divide your face. Your small hands are wavy in the creek.
I want to paint your fingernails Costa Rican green.
One by one, I want to blow on them.

The white breath of a jet opens the sky.
I want you to open me, Eunice Odio.
I snore.
As I turn on my left shoulder, my bottom leg kicks the cotton sheet.
I want to eat moras out of your palm
And trace the frond shadows focusing
Over the small of your back.

Green line of leaf-cutter ants,
Thread of time-scented molecules,
Poetry is spit and fungus growing underground.

Wake me up, Eunice.
Your lips tumble like the night-red of Arenal.
Your dress on the floor feels aqua-lemon,
The cool skin of orchids.
My mouth is open.

I admit it:
I'm greedy for the entire Pacific Ocean and whales.
I cross the border for roasted iguana and onion.
Tremors at Momotombo. Where are you?

You started, "A woman who was suddenly lost
Because the air wanted her . . ."
What does that mean, Eunice?

I'm snoring,
Little choking sounds.
Please, don't let me sleep past the June hour.

At the Podium

While uniformed corpses fly home from the desert
latest of windy May
the moment of the President's great thrumming
coincides with the Japanese beetle
crawling so far into his tunneled ear
that even a flashlight or a match couldn't sun the dark-
orange and speckled wings
lifting the medieval cape
in warning
in that twisting shell
in his inner ear echoes
of alcazars and shipwrecks
still burning under columns of water
of hooves and exploding sand
of propeller engines earthbound
voices beginning to turn
and descend

What Baby Gertrude Heard

I only saw it from the air so what can I say except that I was
born in Alleghany.
—G.S., 1935

a

Almost daylight crib light barred owl declaiming, "The morning glories are
ravenous. The ravens are mourning. The glories are blaring their trumpets
insidious etcetera soot." I will Pittsburgh my infancy. I will Allegheny all
losses and windy cabbage leaves beyond the trellised window where aftershave
walks away as black hair after he dangles shoelaces from polished black
shoes over me. Periods as soot falling on a crib sheet. Think it. Remember it.
Pittsburgh it as the iron horses carry you into the mountains.

b

Taste of cherry pulp.
Smear of cherry red,
faced.
Tear of bleary salt.
Waste of stems and inky pits.
She is she who is cold a gold bracelet on my cheek.
Don't you try? Wrong wrong wrong.
How do you spell a pair a pare of glasses a pear of shoes a chair of
legs made of cherry wood. You don't even get the same misspelling right.
Smelling is thinking.
Don't cry, remember, let the nap go away, fill your nappy with Carnegie if you
musk.
I will Pittsburgh my infancy.
A bird with mint feathers is lyrical and, therefore, is said entirely to Allegheny.
I will Allegheny all losses down the river in a paper boat made of history.

c

All rivers lead to the Ohio. A book is door to a forest.
One bituminous crow caw-cawed all through filthy mines and mills:
1874 is six months of history because it wears polished shoes or muddy
boots not to mention horseshoes which aftershave tinkles with after
work. Because it changes baby Gertrude who is changed by glamour it
grammars history.

d

I will Pittsburgh my infancy.
I'll Allegheny all losses away.
Night syntax of fireflies lighting the cherry-bruised window.
Temporal and verb confusion, morning glories closing lavender cigars.
Frick it. If I'm wrong, then I'll just have to make it up. Steel it.

border-crosser with a lamborghini dream

Juan Felipe Herrera

blood night café

Burials.
They come, they go.

Young boys with hard shadows on their girl faces
in the chrome box. The face goes with the knife in the coat pocket.
The knife goes with the gubernatorial tie on the screen.

Pick up dirt, make circles over
the fleshy mound of my palm. Stand like Travolta
hands in a flash, my white coat in a hula
wind cuts down over me. Breathe
old woman says to me. Spit.

Walk on
with Black spirituals inside.
Door slams on my tiny heart,
sirens come, go shoot lipstick

on Greyhound station windows.
My father strolls through the aisle,
a licorice cane, a Baptist ghost on fire.

selena in corpus christi lacquer red

In my own Tex-Mex breakdown, suffix
for eternity—I dash to the bottom, refrigerations;
what I could not have, gone white. Come up
with the harmonica for wings. Blow
the G, then strum my ancient brain, in a French hotel.
Blues & Rancheras, tombs, S with an X on her back.
You taste the Goddess, now—Quiet. Me:
in the ashen flower, upright, proud in your rising blood.
Moody & swollen in da cabaret, naked. Grip
me, in the mud, in sudden flame, red
star in Corpus Christi lacquer—going down, maguey milk
into an odd-angled branching needle, a howl Virgin—
the one I wanted to deliver me. Open me, X-Selena
w/your vocal and bruised accordion breast.

Giraffe on Fire

Juan Felipe Herrera

Ofelia in Manhattan, Circa 1943

Girl, you couldn't sport a finer gabardine jacket
with Ofelia Robles going up to the sunrise service
on Easter Sunday at the Radio City Music Hall.
You see, everything was in the shape of a fancy guitar—
even the question mark by her telephone number
in my pocket calendar or the last note scribbled
on a napkin full of your philosophy.
It was all personality, black coffee, and music.
You were there, sister. Drinking post prohibition.
Even the most fancy accountant loved gospels
and occasionally visited the Methodist Broadway Temple.
I can just see it. I never forgot the staging
with that elegance of romance and rosewood;
so many notes curled in there, kind of velvety,
bow ties that you couldn't see, but
they were there, fluttering with a mysterious
sweetness at the center. That's when cousin
Tito played string bass; small, plump, hot-tempered,
polka-dot vest and on Saturdays nothing
but congas with Ralph Gómez, the No. 2 man
because he always stuttered.

In the middle of Central Park,
I was the girl with the baggy corduroys doing a tango.
Me and Ofelia and her Portuguese accent.
She was the only real dancer at 40 degrees
north latitude, baby.

I wanted the war to end. Japan had to lose, right?
The Queen Mary was serving cocktails
and you had ten in small paper cups while
we were waiting in line. Look at the sea, you sang.
It was spitting up pure imagination and ambition.
Flashes as far as the eye could see. Take the Rockefeller Center
beyond ol' Sixth Avenue, for example.
Who lived there anyway?

I just wanted to love Ofelia on the rooftops.
Rum-colored bandannas. Our open shirts.
You could hear all the busboys gripe from up there.
Bad tips, the boss that didn't like you using the phone
in the back room. A few bashful tenor voices by the jukebox.

You were reading the *New York Times* in those days.
Pretty good English.

Going like this:
Oye, que tú, esta cosa está caraja
and Mr. Pickett won't pay me as much because
I don't belong to the golf club; you know, like Wilfredo?
Everyone should live in an oyster bar, right?
That's my philosophy, sister. You used to say
that it was about purpose not just Wall Street.
That's when subways had class. And mink too.
All the women were wearing it. Ofelia looked like a doll
until Jorge, the janitor at the new Woolworth Building
told her the fur was a mutation. She gave me
some binoculars she had gotten at an auction.

Move your fingers and just like that
you could see everything. A thousand miles away, easy.
You could count all the electric peanuts in the sky,
Jesus, that's when I was still trying to get a job
working at the night cleaners. Girl,
you could even eat those sizzling candies
hanging over the park.

What about Sammy Hall,
the guy we used to box when we were kids?
He was pure muscle. Then, a fat badge.
One evening I saw him twirling his nightstick.
The guys used to grunt that he was the only black cop.
You had to be German or Polish, maybe Italian,
if you wanted to be a policeman. And that was it.
Sammy didn't like me teasing him about his floppy cap.
Man, it was just me and Ofelia. "Dizzy legs,"
I called her one night at the Rooster
listening to a little bit of Harlem royalty.
You went there, right? We were "dracula,"
the two of us, in a class by ourselves.
Girl, the clubs were hot. But, I had to move.

It happened so fast. One day I just couldn't
sell anymore of my bullfighter paintings on the street.
Nobody was buying them, anymore.
Maybe something was going to happen.
All of a sudden nobody wanted bulls
and gallant lean men in shimmering bronze suits
on their walls. People started talking about
abstract portraits, squares and upside-down eyes.
How could you eat with that stuff over your head?

Things were changing, I guess. So,
I left. Just like that. It was always about leaving paintings
and some clothes and taking paintings and some clothes.
This time, I didn't know what to take. I am telling you.

I never saw Ofelia again.
Maybe she's still dancing out there.

She had a gift, you know. We said
we wouldn't write letters.
It couldn't work that way with us. It had to be pure chance.
A bird-of-paradise in a vase over a piano top, the way
Ella sang or Uncle Vince roughing you up
with his famous question: how's misery?

You said you could handle it. Just wait—
things were going to get a little better after the war.
You said someday you'd get in touch
and we'd joke about that saxophone
we put five dollars down on at the pawnshop.

I can still see the open case from here,
against the glass, a miniature city of mad sparkles,
so alive, I could step in there, dance to the music,
look sharp forever. It was our island, girl.

Notebooks of a Chile Verde Smuggler

Juan Felipe Herrera

Immigrant Fortune Teller Machine

Lissen,
Bobo Chango—yeah,

you, rope-a-dope blues lover,
writer with a jinx on your ass, time is up
on your side of the block, betta' be adding up
your karma tortillas jus about now, 'cuz,
all the chips you've been collecting be gone
to the wind, man, so
lemme set you straight
in a nice way, got it? So,

whaddaya gotta do,
Chango, is—begin again,
toss out your old coins,
your mamá ashes, your papá whips,
yo' bad boy lover pill-poppin' games
an' mos of all your fast talkin' total whack
communicating genius girl self out the door!

Ahright, Sugar, yeah,
thass what I say,

step on
out now, naked,
everything showing, yo'
true self,

not that slime bug collection you've been
showing at the parlour, no no, noooo
you know whadday mean,
yeah, Chango, now,
iz up to you, you gotta trow out all that razz
matazz affabet', all them piles & stacks
of crosswords, those tiny pronunciation
dictionaries, the ol' memory power
tapes and that self-enlargement machine,
you know whad am sayon, OK?

Out wid it
out with all them hoodlum paintings of yoself,
out out, I said,

this is the lass stop before you
hit Phoenix, you know that next place you say
you are bound for, I see your ol' truck outside,

hissin', gettin' all shook under the sun,
outside, with that fine weasel sitting
on the red leather cushion next
to the wheel,

still rappin' about Desert Storm
comix & the great stash of bodies in the trunk
all the way from Tegucigalpa, yeah, yeah

I know, I heard it true
the grave vine, talking about the Virus in
air, grinning at you, adding up your DNA
like Fritos and bean dip, I can hear it from
here, yo' radio blastin' out,

yeah, about the Chain People,
the Chain Colonies, the hunger artists in search
of chicken sandwiches, the new bands of rape dogs,
it's my language anyway, sucker
so

whadelseiz new,
you going to ask me a new new
question today?

You come up with somethin'
new new? So tell me then, wha?
Did you say new, did you say Shakyamuni?
Did you say Shotinyotoey? In the hall,
the fast destiny velvet ball, is that what I hear

I heard you say
something? Or maybe you were just laughing
in that fast high mariachi voice you got
from whoknowswhere, San Francisco? Yeah,

you jus bopped
in on the sneak,

but I'm tellin' you, don't
you come heah nomo
thinking I'm going to put up wid you &
your razz about yo'self and all those yellow
papers you carry in your fish bag,

yeah thass
what it smell like, fish, good ol' mackerel,
wrapped in newspaper, yeah, yeah, you call it
something else, you always call it something
else, you come out with all those fancy hooks,
those scratchy little phrases, those words, yeah
those hooks,

thass what you call them, wordyhooks,
and you spin around me like an Italian
Puerto Rican boxer with all the moves an'
handsome serious faces you make

saying
you look good in any hat south of Broadway,
but, I'm telling straight up sugar, time is up, see
that door to yo' left,
no that one, muchacho,
the one
to your left I said, yeah

the one cracked
dopen, the one with all those tiny smoky
black bluish candles popping inside, gold
smoke and shadows, red vases blurrin'
wavin' into watery insects on the wall there,
some kind of holiday, like,

come on, now,
I told you all about that door
long time ago, remembrrr, yeah, you remembrrr,
that first almost infinite day
when you came
up to me by yo'self,

yo' mamá and papi
still alive then, I think they were havin'
coffee and apple pie a la mode over there
by the newsstand, and your father was talkin'
big 'bout buyin' some kinda land in Kingman, Arizona
paying thuddy dollars a month from the Welfare check
sayin' he was goin' to leave it you,
but he was jus
a li'l too old for those things, his light was
'bout gone by then, then, well you know the res.
Now sugar, one lass time,

you go now, get on
out now, leave those old cardboard boxes here,
ain't nothin' in them anyway, jus leave them
right heah, & go on out there, time is right,

I can tell by the way people are shuffling
their feet & the shadows 'cross the fences,
time is time, jus smell the wet night rollin' in,
you know how my green blue blouse
always gets a li'l tight jus about now,
rain comin' in, maybe,

my customers drop a coin,
and me 'bout the yellow sparks of sirens, wild crows
flyin' up to the saints carved outside the cathedrals
askin' same ol' questions, perched on the glass
against this glass, jus like you

they shiver and whisper like in an ol'
movie house, 'bout to begin, I tell 'em
the nun & St. Peter jokes 'bout to spin out
to the asphalt one more time, yeah, yeah

I think the weasel is waiting for you,
leave me the rope, doncha worry
'bout a thing, jus smooth your way out
by yo'self, whistle up

with yo' tiny crooked musical faces
thass your existence, Bobo Chango boy,
thass it.

Fuzzy Equations

Humility + oppression + a Virgin – territory = Latin America
Democracy + annihilation by color × 12 = Education
The idea of love + a lost glove ÷ Hollywood = Popular marriage
Rape + smooth talk – a door and a cheekbone = Love at first sight
Shaky lips – stiff legs × oblong punch to abdomen = Commitment
Doña Cleta's samba ÷ mal de ojo + 2 joints = Calle Revolución, 11 P.M.
Chile powder soup^2 × onions & palm grease = Romantic guy
Baked bread × Zen thought – hands on her hips = One hand clap
Militarization of Brazil + Xingu extinction × deforestation = Money
Black boots × black lipstick gloss^3 × a knife = The corner
Crack + St. Martín Caballero × 2 needles = Blue skies
Man with briefcase – accent + big watch = Equal opportunity
Roped face × chained hands + free ankles = New democratic country
Ice + seashell × shaman hand over the mountain = PR Love letter
Castro Street × Wall Street ÷ 7 straight boulevards = Here
Two kilos of corn tortillas × roped luggage boxes = Latin promo
Bad accents^2 × 3 altar boy genuflections = High culture
Silent dinner ÷ stiff corset × big mustache = Dante's 13th ring
Snipped chicken head × chopped cactus + fried pork eye = Diploma
Foucault × lover with tiny red pants = Long walk to the clinic
Hard-core Chicana writer ÷ hard-core Latino writer = Fried race

Letanía para José Antonio Burciaga

October 13, 1996,
at the old Victoria theater in San Francisco
on 16ᵗʰ Street where I used to
see Clavillazo & Luis Aguilar movies
while eating lobby chicharrones
in the early sixties

Ese Burciaga,
      vato de la divina tórica, vato escuadra
ruega por nosotros
ese vato muralista, con delantal de panadero,
      hacedor de pinturas y nuestras historias en paredones ilegales
ruega por nosotros
ese Tin-Tan del Chuko,
ruega por nosotros
      buzo del Segundo Barrio, Casa Zapata y de Menlo Parque
ruega por nosotros
ese poeta de la plebe bilingüe,
      escritor de milpa, misterio y esmelda
ruega por nosotros
ese tarjetero, cuate de vecindades
      en firme comunicación, cercos sueltos y campesinos en la libre
ruega por nosotros
ese vato, compañero de la Cecilia
      jefito del Toño y la Rebecca, hermano en la onda bronca
ruega por nosotros
ese cholo de Monterey
      con lápices y acrílicos y mantequilla y esperanza en la brocha
ruega por nosotros
ese Burciaga,
      tirador de botellas de colores contra los fiscales y sus changos
ruega por nosotros
ese Cantinchuko,
      de bolsa tijuanera, sacos de chiles chicanos y chistes de lobo
ruega por nosotros

ese Tony,
 profe del tomate, de la sierra en protesta y de los jarochos
ruega por nosotros
ese vato apasionado
 con letras locas, los nombres de los olvidados y
 movimientos por la justicia
ruega por nosotros
ese compa de los compas,
 con los burritos mochos y las tortillas frisbees pa' lonche
ruega por nosotros
ese silk-screen beret,
 tomando cultura y corazón en vez de Coka-Cola
ruega por nosotros
ese carnal con el fonazo político,
 con la voz urgente y las tardeadas en tu cantón al lado del 101
ruega por nosotros
ese homey del sol total,
 trozo de pan familiar y luz naciente sobre la mesa del barrio
ruega por nosotros
ese jornalero de tinta,
 voz para el pueblo, voz de oro y conciencia, voz del pobre
ruega por nosotros
ese cura con la corbata al revés
 sembrando letanías y amores, milagros sociales y flores
ruega por nosotros
ese poetazo de adobe,
 de pinole y pozole y curaciones y marchas a medianoche
ruega por nosotros
ese vatín alivianado
 de camiseta tipo camaleón, ascendente de Juariles
ruega por nosotros
ese vato machín con la guayabera tucked in,
 jalando con estudiantes y hermanas carmelitas hasta el amanecer
ruega por nosotros
ese Burgie,
 armando tertulias, rondallas, barbequiadas y lunadas de hermandad
ruega por nosotros

ese Tony con Tony Lamas del Río Grande
     en el Bracero Bar, en Madera Roja, dibujando las verdades
ruega por nosotros
ese jacalero de mi cora, cantando
       "San Antonio" en vez de Santone,
       "El Paso del Norte" en vez de El Pasowe
Sabes qué, carnal José Antonio, la verdad es que
    me canso
    me canso de no verte
       me canso de no escucharte
    de no sentir tu ternura a mi lado
    pero yo te recuerdo
    y no me olvido, la verdad es que
    no sé más que no olvidarte
    no sé más que siempre escucharte
            en esta vereda aquí

ese Burciaga, ese padrino del divino bolo, ese alacrán buti suave
    aquí te cantamos, en caló, en calor y puro amor.
Amén, Awimin
y Con Safos.

Marlene Dietrich, Rita Hayworth, & My Mother

Rita María Magdaleno

Salzbergwerk: The Salt Mines Tour

At two, our bus leaves Mirabell Platz,
heart of old Salzburg, "Salt Fortress,"
city surrounded by *Kurgartens*, castles
and Mozart's little birth house, the Salzach
River running deep, gray blue. This route
will take me through the Bavarian Mountains
and Obersalzberg, Hitler's mountain retreat,
his second headquarters. Here, I am traveling
alone past the Königsee Valley, farmhouses
and ruins. Here, I am crossing wet green
land and moving back into Germany, tour
to the Salt Mines of Berchtesgaden,
450 years old, this journey back
to my Mother.

At Berchtesgaden, I will put on miner clothes,
the muslin pants, the coarse black jacket.
There, I will follow the movement of Anna
Karolina Sohr, my grandmother who came
to these salt mines in 1938 with Sep,
her young son who would become a soldier
and die in Potsdam in 1945, a final stand
against the Allies. At Berchtesgaden, I will
travel deep into the salty tunnel. There,
I will take a 100-foot-long slide into the grottos;

there, I will ride a raft and glide inside
the glistening womb of rock and salty water;
there, I will learn about the origin of salt.
And I will begin to understand that it takes
at least one year to drill into a good spot,
to make careful preparations, to probe
and to analyze each sample
before any drilling begins.

Always, there is water: to draw out
the salt, to wash and to cleanse.
At Berchtesgaden, I will know
that salt mining takes time and patience,
takes so much tapping, carefully
tapping to make sure a new spot
is stable and capable of releasing
the salt—"White gold"—
from that womb
of rock and black water.

Cue Lazarus

Carl Marcum

Light Show

Sometimes I think of that brick house on the busy road,
where traffic was a constant funeral procession.
The room I rented there—the beat-up
springs of the used-up mattress, that half-covered
the dark stain (we never could identify), on the carpet
where she thought twice about treading barefoot.

I think of how there, in that bed with her
at night, we would watch the bluish slants
—the passing headlights—cast photo-positives
through the venetian blinds: across our bodies,
the mattress, the dirty carpet and up the bare walls . . .

until the ebb and flow of asphalt faded in distance,
                              and the room grew dim and quiet.

Then, we would coo like kittens, pausing only
to let the lights play over us, merely for the pleasure
of not feeling their touch.

A Prayer for My Brother

When my brother becomes a man, let him find something small,
maybe metal—a wristwatch or swizzle stick—in a shoebox
he's forgotten about. And this small monument he once held
onto, and has perhaps considered tossing out at the end of each
lease, will whisper to him of wind and martinis and the city.
Will whisper to him like the lips of a man he once kissed. And let
him remember how once he couldn't live without this small token
—grant him the memory of signing the credit receipt or slinking
the swizzle stick up a sleeve in a crowded bar. How he smiled
with the weight of possession, a small want satisfied. And let him
smile again as he holds this cold memory, allow him to set the dead
red face of the wristwatch to 3 a.m., or slide the swizzle stick
across his tongue and taste the metallic gin, the lovely sour-salt
olive as it broke, ripe between his back teeth. Confer on him
the moment he was convinced he would always remember, how
he said it out loud, twinkling and drunk. Let this all come back
to him like a dream-song half heard in a winter's sleep.

Breathing Between the Lines

Demetria Martínez

Discovering America

for P., 1992

Santo Niño on a
bedroom desk,
holy water in a
mouthwash bottle
Grandma had the
priest bless,
this house,
a medieval city
you visited,
what you sought
was not here.

Not in wrists
oiled with sage,
Chimayo earth
sprinkled on sheets,
nor San Felipe bells
that pecked away
the dark,
Cordova blanket
we hatched
awake in.

To prove love
I shed still
more centuries,
rung by rung
into a pueblo
kiva where
you touched
the *sipapu*,
canal the universe
emerged from,
brown baby glazed
in birth muds.

You thought
America
was on a map,
couldn't see it
in a woman,
olive skin,
silver loops
in lobes,
one for each
millennium
endured on this
husk of red earth,
this *nuevo méjico*.

Last night
I dreamed
a map of the
continent,
the train
that took you
from me whipped
across tracks
like a needle
on a seam
somewhere
near Canada.

It took me
four years
to heal.
Have you?
Have you
discovered
America
or at least
admitted
a woman grew
maiz here
long before
you named it
corn?

The Devil's Workshop

Demetria Martínez

Remedios

Each cough is an underground nuclear explosion,
Unraveling your body's hard-won peace accord.
It's back to the bargaining table: garlic, C, zinc,
Oshá root, a five-day course of antibiotics,
And a glow-in-the-dark vaporizer, UFO among the mists.

You quiet your mind, that well-stocked pond of opinion.
You meditate on your lungs, failed sails.
Herbs from Uruguay float in a teapot like lashes.
The package reassures: you are saving the rain forest
With each new bout of respiratory illness.

Your body starts a fever, a controlled burn.
You fear you will go up like Los Alamos,
But your brain is an underground lab,
Oblivious to the flames, busy with equations:
You are too sick to be in one place at one time,

Much less ten places at one time.
So when friends call, you say, "No."
No. No. No. No. Then you just let it ring.
Already you are shaking this thing.
Like the Mayas, you discover the Zero:

The Buddha-you the wind blows through.

Class Action

New York, Oaxaca: you promised trips.
For years I worked the late shift in your
Heart's sweatshop, assembling

Parts that make love tick.
Not even a raise, much less a union.
Rumors of a strike and you knock

At my screen door bearing fine
Wine, but my hurt is too vast
To fit inside a bottle like a ship

Where you are still at the helm,
Too proud to ask directions,
This time promising India:

Hennas and mantras,
Saris and tablas . . .
Sweetheart, I'll have to pass

On nirvana. I've seen so much
Light I need sunglasses.
The other huarache

Has dropped.
The redwood you hear falling
In the forest is you.

World to World

Valerie Martínez

Heritage

I hear sounds unlike my own.

Coo of syllables. Coo-cradles.

The red earth moving beneath.

Avalanche of history, with blood.

A mother-house, father-house.

The five plus one, cacophonous.

A girl's deft fingers, ever so.

Polite, *sin* intuit. Belying it.

The man infamous, car dangerous.

Now he has no voice, no cock, no hands.

Marauder. Plunder of marauders.

Adolescent of the wails-cum-words.

Belly-gone-convex-gone-concave.

The crave, crave and starve.

Secret books. The looping black marks.

Where the silence, silence was:

a rocky noise.

World to World

For Tim Trujillo
1951–1991

I discover the Buddha in the back yard,
    black paint on wood, head tilted,
smile so tranquil. Then the dead come
    over the grass, the garden stones,
a bed of wildflowers, without sound,
    mouths silent as under-earth.
We needn't have any words,
    the dead and I, just holy imagery,
the message *they come*, the secret
    passage under the wall, the creature
who climbs through, the sky
    over the clouds over the air over the earth,
world to world, this afternoon,
    someone I am someone I knew,
the layers beneath the layers.

Bowl

Turn it over and look up
into the sphere of heaven.
The tracery is lucent,
light seeping through to write,
white-ink your face, upturned.

Swing it below
and it's a cradle of blue water,
the sea, a womb.
A mixing bowl
for Babylonian gods.
Here, they whirl up the cosmos.

Pick it up and your hands
form a pedestal,
and all who drink
contain the arcs
of body and the universe—
and between them,

no imaginable tear or distance.

Wish

Everything she wants she sees
in the dark coin of this child's eye.

Desire lives in her like the secret
of the statue-goddess, when man
mistakes her for a fetish.

It isn't that she's had nothing
in those hollows: heart and pelvis.

Just that the orphan is asking her
with a look of wanting,
a mother-look, desiderate.

It could happen anywhere
but does so, finally, here

in the sugar fields, among the stalks
where she finds him sucking cane
in the harvest season.

And everything is gathered
for one second, endless.

He calls to her—his eyes go blind
in the sun. And every absent meal,
vicious cane snake, wish for beauty,

wish for beauty's reprieve, enters her
with sweetness and riches and thunder.

How Long She'll Last in This World

María Meléndez

Backcountry, Emigrant Gap

I thought we fell asleep
austere and isolated—

two frogs calling across Rock Lake.

By morning, deer prints
new-pressed
     in the black ground between our tents—

      more lives move beside us
      than we know.

In Biruté's Camp

Suppose God is looking for a good
     piece, who could be you with that bare
        strip of scalp parting your long hair,
    braided loose and looped up in the swamp heat,
sweat curling around your small, bristly eyebrows,
     your hands gleaming with juice and pulp
        as you hammer fruit on the feeding platform.

That strange orangutan,
the human-raised one called Pan-gan,
    who throws men off the dock
        like an overzealous baptizer, may
    be a god and here he comes
        padding side to side onto your platform in the swamp.
    If he curves the ridiculous length of his
tendon-riddled arms around your waist
and wrestles you down to the wooden boards,
    scream—he'sbitingyouhe'stryingtokillyou—no,
he's pushing up your skirt—

        become limp below the waist and make your torso
    a flexible branch for him to squeeze
        as he swivels from one world to the next;
    (now he is calm and deliberate,

                        now his eyes roll upward)—

    When he finally moves off
        the feeding platform and into the trees,
            rise into this loss, which is relief:
    his seed will shimmer out of you, unrecognized.

Why Can't We All Just Get Along

Think of pink pickup trucks.

And picture dead Americans
Doing their Vietnam-era combat dying
In neat ethnic proportion.

All hail, the proportional dead!

Visualize nonperishable respect
Handed out in paper bags to neighbors.

A Dignity Pantry open 24 hours.

Then, I suppose, we could each
Have a friendly lick
Off the other's cone.

But this is your real Mother
On Public Assistance talking:

Is the salt in all these crackers
And canned goods
Not supposed to kill me?

Why can't I use these vouchers
For organic cheese and milk?
Why are the wealthy allowed to be healthier than me?

* * *

Deep, cleansing breath everyone.
Oppression isn't rocket science.
It's easy enough
To ignore the torso
Of Evelyn Hernandez,
Afloat on the shore of the Bay
A year before Laci.
Her maternity shirt a billowing
Jelly-fish crown animated by waves,
Her case rejected from the rolls
Of *America's Most Wanted*.

SF Homicide tried spreading the word. . . .

I'm sorry to say, Evi, that without any
Lacey-white wedding photos to show,
Newsmakers thought no one would care much.

You were only 24, and being Salvadoran,
Maybe no one had shown you yet
How the gods of public opinion
Get fed around here.

The days of Good News are behind us;
Now a group of elites claiming expertise
On the whole Christ thing
Assures us He was way more uptight
About two men trying for wedded bliss
Than the brutal dismemberment of women
With names like "Hernandez."
     Sorry, señorita,
     The Bible's pretty clear on this one.

You don't need a PhD to see
This is a slap in the dead face
Of an entire chain of mothers,
Knotted and tangled together,
Circling down through history,
And coming to rest on the knifepoint
Of the present, as rosary beads circle down
To Christ's nailed feet.

       ❋ ❋ ❋

While we're on the subject
Of murdered muchachas,
Could someone please
Ask the slaughtered
Daughters of Juárez
Not to shriek so loudly
At night? They're bothering
Some nice people in Texas.
Would they mind not being so *political*
All the time?
     (Say the p-word as though invoking the name
     of a hated vegetable, e.g.,
          "Could you not be so *lima bean* all the time!")

Everyone knows that only a few Texans,
Only a few Americans,
Get to be political.
And then, only on TV.

* * *

I'm not an angry person, really.
I've never yelled at the snow for
Melting,
Or cursed a grasshopper
For disappearing into the weeds
When I wanted to catch it.

A river killed a man I loved,
And I love that river still.

Rough treatment from the Great Beyond?
I've come to expect it.

But someone—who?
The Son of Man?—
Told me I could expect better
From the hands
Of humans.

In all fondness for the grasshoppers, I say
My neighbors and I
Are no better than insects.

* * *

May the peace of legally recognized newlyweds
Be with us all,

And may Evelyn's broken breath,
As recorded in the Bay waves,
Fill our ears until we're deaf
To the Call for Complacency.

Adobe Odes

Pat Mora

Ode to Readers

Bien amados,
    hoping you won't slip away,
    and fearing your reluctance to
                    leap

into the web
    of language,
I offer odes simmered for years
    without knowing you.

To lure you,
I've devoured cookbooks
    written en español
by women with a weakness for blue
    roots, canapés garnished with slivers
    of light.
I've gathered what I could reach,
    stirred, concocted,
tasted
    in considerable anticipation.

Try the blood
    of prickly pears,
a woman's silver tears,
rose petals gathered by Sor Juana.

Snakes slept on my used books,
occasionally offered advice on appetizers,
all starting with the letter
S.
The recipe for guacamole
came from a crow.

Without you,
what I've prepared will whither
into dust.

Tempt you?

Ode to a Book

When I open you,
letters from a stranger
bound for my hands
from some distant place,
leafed treasure,
sturdy box
scratched and scarred
by my journey,

a breeze
wraps around my shoulders,
pulls me
to a grandmother dancing
with her shawl in the dark,
a man eating only carnations.

Like smoke,
a swirl of gray hair
    unravels
its canciones amorosas,
  its mysterious romance,
and a hummingbird dozes on a tiny
cotton puff
  while whirring crimson through its dreams.

Mirrors flow into the street
      spilling
gossip and beauty secrets.
  Wine-sipping syllables
    chuckle
  over their rhymes.

  Pearl of petals,
mi libro, un mundo,
  you open your mouth,
      a bud unfurling,
un canto viejo, fresco, dulce,
sonoro,
  canta, canta.

Ode to El Paso

  Stubborn mountain,
rock anchor,
  you grew from cuentos carried at night
in the wind's dry hands,
  seed pebbles
that became your wide-hipped,
unmovable contours, curves
where finches and secretive
  spiders nest.

Poet of ancient seas
and baritone fossils,
    of trilobites and cephalopods,
lyric cantadora of horn corals,
    ammonites and crinoids,

    impatient, gray historian
lured by the whir of a pen,

    its tip, a top whirring,
dancing on the page,
    you write until your fingers cramp
and your shoulders knot,
    weary at the echoes of grief
still moist beneath the boulders
of prejudice.

    You wake
stung, eye pierced
    by an angry, red thorn,
        burning struggles,
embedded in your pupil.

    Stern mother,
venerable sentinel, impervious
    to sand thrashings,
you close your face,
    head thrown back,
        you rise rooted in memory,
and when the storm limps away,
            hoarse, gasping,

you hum, unpack your rose shawl
and again toss the lace
    over your bare, wrinkled shoulders,
wear your rippling silver
    bracelet, el río grande.

Poised to protect,
you sleep standing,
    wrapped in your black rebozo.

    Cada primavera,
lizards play between
    your toes and young again,
you sip the yellow breeze,
    desert fountain of youth,
your breath soft as dawn. You blush
    at the wind's whispered invitations,
at the feathery caresses
    of ruby-throated hummingbirds
    and begin your slow spin.

Your skirts ripple for miles
    encrusted with cactus pads,
magenta cholla flowers, needle-gold spines,
    poppies fluttering like glorious sunsets.

At night, your long, glinting hair streams
    skyward, among the stars.

Ode to Women

Listen to the place where life grows,
        the inner seedbed
of music
            that curls and branches.

Women's hum of hope
        careens down canyons,
            skims the tops of pines,
the sound of luna's long fingers stroking
        a child's cheek or pouring
clear tea into the fragile cup
        of an old woman.

Listen to the hum
                that sweeps despair
into a battered dustpan
                and flings the gray
tangles out the door,
that simmers a wild abundance
                of summer pears.

The twilight lullaby sways
        forests, mountains, cactus,
homes struggling to stand in the dark;
            the hum
sways women weary from holding
                    together a family
of elbows and sighing skin.

Listen to its jazzy improvisations
                    luring, pulling
reluctant hands across borders,
        shore to shore carrying bodies
over choppy waves of fear
                on its sturdy song.

The hum soothes wounds
    with a mysterious melody that nestles
        in the soul and harvests discarded
stories, knits their threads
           into a shawl.

Listen, for when mujeres gather,
    O when women gather
to hold hands together,
    their hums rise and ripple, sway
like candles, a symphony
           of light.
The polyphonic harmony
melts bruises, guns, locks
rusted for centuries,
    the hum of hope swells,
            sails
across restless seas,
gathers and rocks the globe.

    Women,
the world's stubborn, triumphant hum.

Blood Mysteries

Dixie Salazar

Piñón Nuts

We begged him to teach us Spanish
but he wouldn't. Here in the heart
of America, skin tones
and tongues were homogenous
as milk from purebred cows.

We heard Spanish once a year
in Colorado where Grandpa
sold used cars at the Rainbow garage
after the Depression wiped out
a city block of his stores

and left him bitter as the juice
of venison strips he gnawed,
escaping into his camper
with its false bottom for hiding deer
shot out of season.

Ignoring postal regulations,
he mailed us deer meat, bleeding
in a bed of piñón nuts,
telling Bella, "¿Qué tiene Ud.?"
then, "Shut up" in English.

Bella went off to Mass
in their newest Chevy
and a velvet dish hat
chosen from over a hundred,
one for every fight they had.

His father died with the sheep
in a blizzard, Grandpa saved
by stuffing his feet in a foxhole.
His namesake, my father, got whipped
every time Grandpa saw him.

'59, snowdrifts high as frozen waves,
forced to turn back two miles past
timberline, they found Grandpa's name
and date of the day before carved
on a tree, his last deer at seventy-three.

After Bella died, he slept
on the broken spine of the back porch,
wouldn't eat or take his insulin,
telling her photograph or anyone
who'd listen, how much he loved her.

Each letter began, "Corazón
de mi corazón," a courtship
in a graveyard, words poured out
again later for her picture.
In between were all those hats.

Rainbow trout swimming in fat,
empanadas, flaky and sweet, a bowl
of piñón nuts, Grandma making faces
behind his back. "Montaña, huevos, sal,"
bits of Spanish she taught us . . .

and a swish of hats on a wall—
all that's left. In Spanish class
today, I learned "piñón" meant pine
and rolled the word in my Anglo mouth
like a sweet, round nut.

Why I'm Not Someone Else

This is an old story.
If my mother hadn't let
that soldier buy her a Scarlett O'Hara
in the Sweet Gum Lounge,
and if those two nervous molecules
hadn't bumped together
in the great cosmic elevator
neither you nor I
would be reading this now.

If your grandfather had been
an archaeologist, mad about Homer,
he might have christened you
Agamemnon, by laying
a copy of the Iliad
on your head, instead
of the cranky feed salesman
who married the muscular gym teacher
and called you Northrup instead.

And if my grandmother's
first suitor hadn't been struck
by lightning, and she hadn't fallen
for the used car salesman
who courted her in the cemetery
then I might have been
the famous Australian soprano
a shy French chef named his peach dessert
after, or the identical twin

who almost killed you, boring
a dart smack in the center
of your back when you were ten.

And if the gypsy who turned
your palm upward
to the Mona Lisa sky had seen
that slice of moon hooked over
the eaves like a secret smile,
she never would have dared predict

your mother's amazing luck,
the conversation overheard by the nurse
on the bus, and our story wouldn't be
our story, and we might be
like Cary Grant and Deborah Kerr,
passing in separate taxis
missing train connections because of a goat
you going up in the elevator,
while I'm going down.

elegy for desire

Luis Omar Salinas

The Luxury of Darkness

I live the life of a stargazer,
watching the leaves fall off the trees
as I doze off reading Agamemnon again.
I do have the luxury of darkness,
which clothes me like the Paris
of my house—dressed in green velvet,
I have nothing golden or otherwise
to offer to the stars. But the lucent
stars cheer me, and the eminence
of the brooding landscape I enjoy
before I lose my temper, and the nymphs,
intent on ruin, jump into a pool darker
than their hearts. A bit confused,
I try to make sense of my tragic kingdom
and the fierce clouds as I name
the hazy constellations, one by one.

The Disappearance of My Wife

for Heather

I must be part magician.
Things seem to disappear on me.
I lost my handkerchief this afternoon,
And my wife, if I had one?
But to have a wife is to swim
With her, and if you lose her
In the water, there's nothing
For it.
        When I first met you,
I knew nothing—your autumn—
Colored hair and gentle eyes
Spoke a language beauty knows.
Your small breasts must have
Been persimmons, I did not see
Them. You were close for a while.
Now I'm as far away from
Your heart as the ocean in this
Late spring, with the wind
Raising its voice down the length
Of this inland valley. Still,
The flowers in the garden
Recall your radiance, and though
I just met you today, I miss you
The way I always miss the sea.

Elegy for Desire

Never borrow money
To buy flowers—
There is an exquisite aroma
To beauty, you can spot it
In the garden amid
Plenty of hyacinths.

I am Omar, the intrepid
Romancero who climbs
Balconies to ladies
Who are beautiful
And dangerously
Within reach . . .

*   *   *

I'm merely making a statement:
I've done away with
My rancor—my mind
Is pure, the night
Darker than my thoughts . . .

A poem is a poem,
Regardless of the color
Of her eyes
That capsize the moon's
Light across her cheeks,
That subdue the wind,
The intrigue of the sea.

*   *   *

I turn in for the night,
But your lips, your eyes,
Breasts and etc. twitch
On my tongue, and sprout
The impetuous gardenias
Of my heart. All night
I stand in the garden
And watch as you
Lay your slip by the pillow
And slowly comb your hair.

*   *   *

There's a full moon out
And I didn't even look at it—
I was carried away
By your dark eyes
As you sat there
With notes on your hands,
Musing, preparing a song,
Your lyrics glowing
With your lipstick.
And as the shadows
Darken and curl
Beyond my hands,
I turn and point
Out Venus . . .

＊　＊　＊

When I'm a little drunk
With desire, my brown eyes
Are aggressive as the blue
Jays on the grass.
And all day I lectured
Robins in the heat
Who told me to go
Inside where it's cool,
where I am reminded
Of a summer—your cheeks
Of peach, and lavender
Dresses on the clothesline.
I think of your lovely ears,
The crush of the sea sound
Where I smell the sweet
Air, and this elegy
Almost brightens me.

Palm Crows

Virgil Suárez

Animalia

As a child, the games to break boredom included a certain cruelty
of which only children are capable. Plucked wings from flies,
caught lizards & geckos, trapped fireflies in jars. I kept my distance
from the frogs, which the other kids in the neighborhood, aware of my terror,
insisted on putting down the back of my shirt or pants. We caught

lagartijas with long grass stems & noosed them around their necks, then lowered
the lizards into the black recess of a spider's hole—like fishing, the spider
bit the lizards & dragged them down. The trick was to pull the spider out
of its hole; then one of us would smash it with a rock. We hated
everything that crawled on so many hairy legs. Ants we fried using

a magnifying glass & the power of the sun. We encircled scorpions
in a ring of kerosene & set fire to the ring to watch the insect sting
itself in an act of suicide. Once, I slashed the tires of my brand new bike
(a bicycle my father had stood in long lines to buy) & made a double-banded
slingshot, the best the kids in the neighborhood had ever seen or held.

They envied, all right. A group of us went into the backyard to shoot
sparrows. I killed my first as it perched on the clothesline, preening
its feathers. The pebble from my slingshot broke its breast-
bone, & it plummeted to the ground. Fueled
by the violence of those days, I became an expert at killing—I learned

from watching my father & uncles slaughter so many animals in our backyard.
    Pigs, chickens, goats, rabbits, turtles. The pigs my father knifed in the heart
        while they ran. "It's the only good way," my father would say,
    "so they don't squeal." The goats bleated & kicked as they hung by ropes
from a roof beam, necks about to be slashed in one swift motion,

their throats opened & so much blood flowing. Then the countless chickens
    & ducks & guinea fowl whose necks my mother wrung, lending meaning
        to "running around like a chicken with its head cut off." Rabbits, turtles,
    pigeons, turkeys, fish, from both the rivers & the ocean—all killed & gutted
in the eyes of so many children. Stray dogs followed me home from school, mangy,

filthy & hungry, but my mother wouldn't let me keep any as a pet. In those days,
    as now, people would kill & eat anything in Havana, Cuba, & I think she feared
        the temptation. We raised & kept animals in our yards. So did everyone else
    in the barrio. Even after severe sanitation laws and fines, people took chances
& hid animals in their bathrooms, bedrooms,

closets. One time the military came to our neighborhood & confiscated
    all the animals, rounded them up & led them to a huge pit dug by a bulldozer.
        All the animals were herded into this pit & set on fire.
    Ah, the carnage & the wail of so many burning animals. On school field trips
they took us to the chicken hatcheries & showed us how male baby chicks

were ground up to make feed for the zoo animals. My father was a *gusano*
    then & made to work against his will as a killer of horses to feed the lions
        & tigers at the zoo. He never confirmed the story about the baby-chicks-
    ground-up-as-feed. He did tell us about the monkey that played & teased
a cage full of tigers until one day it slipped & fell, & the tigers quartered

it immediately. My father smuggled home some meat from the horses
    he killed. There also were sexual-perversion stories told
        by neighborhood punks—with goats, pigs, dogs, even chickens.
    My father told me that when he was a kid & his uncle wanted to get him out of a
conversation, he'd send my father to *tentar las gallinas*, which meant that my father

went into the chicken coop & stuck his pinkie into the chicken's cloaca to feel
 for the next morning's egg. I had a bunny which a couple of fierce
  neighborhood dogs caught & mauled. Cats, too, suffered
 in our neighborhood. They died regularly in jute sacks hung from trees
& beaten like piñatas or left in bags on the railroad tracks.

Such cruelty makes the mind's-eye burn, the heart flutter . . . We fished
 the rivers, roamed the woods for everything & anything
  edible—doves, quail, even rats. When my parents sent me off
 for the summer to San Pablo in the province of Las Villas, to my maternal
grandparents, it was no better, no escape from people & their slaughter

of animals. Within the context of a farm, the killing made sense,
 became less disturbing. I witnessed the castration (in cold blood) of pigs
  & bulls. My grandmother chopped the heads off guinea fowl.
 She set me the task of plucking the feathers & cleaning each bird. In 1970,
the madness stopped when we left for Spain, where the only animals were those

that people kept as pets. Of course there were the carcasses at the markets,
 but humans no longer killed & ate their pets—they didn't have to. I too kept
  my first animals as pets: goldfinches, goldfish, hamsters, a turtle.
 I kept them throughout my youth in Madrid & later when we moved
to Los Angeles, California. After so many years I came to appreciate creatures

well-kept & alive. These days I have a dog (more on him later) & a garageful
 of canaries. I've become quite a canary culturist. During the breeding season
  it sometimes becomes necessary, because of genetic disasters,
 to dipose of a canary chick. Often, if things go wrong, a chick might be born
without a limb, or, as was the case recently, without eyes. To have to cull

is to return to the violence I experienced in my youth, but to leave
 such a creature in pain is unpardonable, so I cull, which means I push
  the chick into a glass of water. Recently, at a bird show I asked several
 bird keepers what humane methods they employ. The discussion turned
into a heated argument about the best way being no good at all, but the majority

of us agreed that to kill a bird quickly is to, like a chicken, snap its neck.
   The process by which this is done varies from the cruel & macabre
      to the quick & painless. Now about the dog, our basset hound, Sir Mongo
   of Tallahassee, who, though AKC registered, is far from being a
champion. Our dog. Our dog which has been howling & crying at night since

we brought him home as a puppy. His nocturnal whimpering & wheezing
   are enough to test anyone's patience, & I won't mention his lack
      of intelligence. Sometimes when he can't stop crying, I get out of bed,
   naked or clothed, & I walk to the kitchen to plead with the dog for a little
silence, a little rest. But it is no use. He whimpers & cries more. We keep him

behind a gate in the kitchen, & when he isn't making noise, he is busy making
   mischief. He will search & destroy almost anything he can reach, from cereal
      to fruit, from thawing meat to coffee. It's worse when we have visitors. He
   once stole David Kirby's glasses & chewed, possibly ate, glass & plastic—we
found only half of the frames. But the nighttime is the worst,

& so there's nothing to do but rage. Once I let myself hit Sir
   Mongo of Tallahassee with a rolled-up newspaper, & he stopped,
      but only briefly to catch his breath. It was during this moment that I
   glimpsed a reflection of my half-naked self in the window—a creature
nocturnal, like any, driven mad by lack of sleep. When I looked across the dark

expanse of yard, I saw a light in my neighbor's kitchen window.
   I imagined a person there, awake at the same hour, up for a glass
      of milk, & then, the same image I saw on my kitchen window, a big naked
   Cuban, rolled-up newspaper in hand, threatening to beat up his dog. No, not
easy to explain, the many years as witness & participant in the slaughter

& cruelty to animals. What would you think?

El exilio

White birds over the gray river.
Scarlet flowers on the green hills.
I watch the Spring go by and wonder
if I shall ever return home.
—Tu Fu

After his accident in Hialeah where he worked
        as a coffee packer, my father returned home
from the hospital and sat by the window
        of the room where my mother sewed,
and he watched the world through the two-inch
        window bars, *su prisión,* he called it,
this catatonia of spirit, he sighed,
        breathing with difficulty in the air-
conditioned apartment he shared with my mother,
        and we would talk on the phone once during
the week, and then on Sundays, he spoke little
        of how he felt, often repeating yesterday's
news or how gray the weather hovered in Miami,
        these cumulus clouds of surrender, a bad
omen for those crossing the Florida Straits on makeshift
        rafts, all trying to get to freedom,
and my father would chuckle his ironic laugh over
        the telephone line as if to say few made it,
and indeed when they made it, *pa'que,* he'd say,
        to lose life in the United States, too much
work, not enough money, too little to show for it,
        but he believed in freedom, in how he came
and went out of his house and had no soul
        ask him for papers or where he was going,
like his old life in Cuba, and the language,
        El Inglés, he never learned, only chewing
on a few necessary words like "mortgage,"
        "paycheck," "punch clock," "bills," . . .
the rest all sounding like the barks of mad
        dogs in an alleyway, the rest

like the poetry he lacked in spirit. *El exilio*
    he sighed, did this to him, his life,
and my mother would sew a dress's hem
    and she would stop long enough to tell him
he was wrong, their (our?) lives here
    had been a blessing, even if hard,
even if they were now alone in this apartment
    in Hialeah where my father watched
the children arrive in the yellow buses
    at the school across the street.
He was there when they came, and there when
    they left, his visions of a daily routine,
like clockwork, beyond the barred window,
    his sedentary life without the use
of his hands, and often, he looked at his thin
    fingers, he thought of the crows he ran
over by the roadside in Cuba, when younger,
    where he knew bad luck when he saw it,
the way these scavengers of the earth
    flocked over a rotting carcass of a killed
animal, the way he wanted to scream out
    his bad luck in English now, say "Fuck You!"
to his life, to this life of sitting and waiting.

Naked Wanting

Margo Tamez

First Choice

You ask me which shovel I want to use,
give me first choice.
I pick the one with a worn handle;
its length suits my height.
I know I won't get splinters—
the wood, seasoned with years
of your skin and sweat.

Our first garden, a second marriage.
We feel what we want, shy to say it all.
This is like making love,
the first time conceiving.

At the gin, we fill a truck's bed high with mulch,
some laughter, mostly wordless labor,
the slicing sound of the blades in earth,
our jeans dusty up to the knees.
The repeated arcs of quiet arms,
your eyelids.

We unload it all into our field.

For Keeps

for Milagro

In the opening petal of your eye, my face is a head,
a large face, larger than the rest of me.

I tremble at the reflection I cast—
distorted in your cornea, my head is colossal,

my chest a tapering stem. I reject my
diminished chest. I want to

be naked, unafraid,
to show you my defeats, the wanting

when my body was an oily slick
in thin water, no merging

between me and language,
me and the never heard, never known,

restless pulses that cut me away
and would not vaporize if wished for.

How loud the silences really are,
piling on each other,

with faces showing regrets,
the undone, or the pushed away and

once-believed-in attachments.
Like thin-throated specters, they quiver

their accusations, mount each other,
dig in hard, and rock in the genital ooze.

All the things I let die, or killed,
getting screwed.

I never knew
this hunger against silence

would resurrect my dead,
lay down the genealogy between fear, denial,

clumsiness, disregard,
the sweet breath between our lips,

ropy flesh between mother and child,
one's grief, the other's mutiny,

we gamble away each other's promise,
and promises, then fear when we have to pay

for the damage we commit,
keep telling our children

we can change
we can change

ourselves, this world
and make it a promise to keep.

what i'm on

Luis Humberto Valadez

dear reader: this is what i thought on easter day

this work wrestles with itself, despite the temptation to project tar.

I give you what I have to give.

Of utmost importance, the environment taught me that this work didn't have to be a platform from which to extract revenge against my existence.

search for the intention behind the initial sentiment.

illuminate the possibilities of existence to a young man who saw the world as merely black, white, brown, and without redemption.

What is presented in these pages chronologically displays this young person's progression of understanding.

present it despite fear of hindsight

rally against an inflated self-conscience looking for gratification in the form of striking out against an audience.

This, I would learn, was not the case.

There was a time in my life when I believed that merely scraping off the mildew of my visage and writing about what I saw underneath was enough to emancipate myself from the unfortunate events that comprise an existence that shaped my perception.

Section 7

gangsters and yogis and vegetarians
    cannot confirm
    they can't form a whatnot
    a vet ran rest

gangsters and yogis and vegetarians
    are not the lone ocean
    won't mess with sonnets
    can't rent love

gangsters and yogis and vegetarians
    forget the righteous like a set son
    hit sweetly and make sure
    no con forgets

And my subjective "eye" versus this collective "we"
    messes wit he
    sees debt to hit
    is a beggar who
    rants what he can't
    and asks
    "did He let 'em die
    to let my go to me?"

radio

list ad/ makes you/ self what
en akes/ possi/ wor change/ urse
don veto hat/ sor at it
feels/ air less/ blade need be
at akes hir round rip/ sel bade/ mote
with place/ where more/ radio alone
a feed tri limp/ til ant be let/ faath
cing wit less
pit very/ get lace/ lit heed
can vile/ see the dai son/ hil rey nel
reyn on
vile can
very lace
les faath
be let
mote feed
akes
change
wor
veto
rip

if you listen to the radio
it makes you feel impossible
as if you were the challenge to yourself
you don't have to like what it says or what it does
or what it feels
none of that makes the air around you less crisp
less of a blade
or promotes less of a need to triumph over impossibility
you still want to be a bullet
unfathomably piercing the air
spiting everything in its place
until you die where you can't live anymore
because the radio is on while you're alone

esau past love

i saw past love
        Esau passed love
and wasn't happy
        san wand
i saw passed love
        Esau past love
and was lustful
        lul

caring eyes run rotting
        Esau past love
rig constructor's matrix
        he saw passed love

my matrix is thinking
        about your matrix
and how your matrix
        perceives my matrix

neurosis is a doorway
        me saw passed love
but not to no where good
        me saw past lust

don't understand we other

on Tuesday, when the homeless disappeared

Marcos McPeek Villatoro

The Deer

Nicaragua, July 1985

From tiny villages
Of morning tortillas,
Where a man bathes in the river
Before leaving home
For the day, where a woman
Stands at his door, her shiver

Scarcely hiding worry;
Where pigs ignore fences
And a soldier ignores his fear
Of the mountains
He left last night, shuffling
Toward a mother angered to tears;

Upon the stony road
That runs through wet jungles,
Past smoky thatched shacks
And simple, one-room churches
Where an elder man packs
Clay into bullet holes;

Through early morning dew
The truckbed bounces south
Kicking us off our feet.
A baby almost flew
Out of her mother's hold.

A boy laughs. He rolls his eyes
At this world. He stands
To my left. He has much to prove,
Passing death in such stride,
Leaving her in church walls.
He stands right next to me.

I ride in the middle.
The thin fog penetrates
The woman's shawls. The babe
Sucks at warm milk. The rest
Rub the bumps into our arms
And contemplate the harm:

Our eyes follow the fog
Through pine and malinche,
Beyond a silent bog
So recently disturbed
By boots. The snapped reeds
Bend in forced genuflection

Toward the mud. They were tired;
The sole explanation
To leaving blatant clues
Out of broken stems.
We take consolation
In their absence.

A woman contemplates
While gazing at the mire,
"Or maybe they rushed away."
The truck grinds to slow our day,
To miss a rock, or perhaps
To rouse her desire

Concerning the living.
The arrogant boy
Stops laughing. A young man
Clutches a girl's fingers.
They glance toward the forest.
The truck turns left, then right,

Cutting a crescent moon
Into the billowed road.
A man lets go his hold
Of the truckbed's railing.
He opens a small sack
And hands us oranges.

We smile at his kindness.
Though it means to appease,
We take the fruit and listen
As he fakes the ease
Of accepting Eternity:
He mentions many names.

Some of those names I know.
We carried them all
To the town plaza,
Placing the larger pieces
In a bloody row
That families passed, collecting.

"Pues sí . . ." that peculiar
Affirmative, ". . . pues sí."
Passengers let go their breaths.
One woman crosses herself
To bless those recent deaths
Or perhaps to bless the truck.

The trucker's sudden brake
Jolts us toward the cab.
He steps onto the road
And stares into the fog.
We also see the beast
Stepping over a log.

The deer stands at attention.
Its rack towers into two
Wooden laurels. Their tips
Almost touch. Its neck
Holds the crown still. Its eyes
Hold our crowd still.

"Qué bello," someone whispers.
We nod our heads, a herd
Of mammals in a cattle truck.
Even I forget the reeds,
Broken, until a word
Snaps over the trucker's lips.

He rushes a step forward,
Lifts a hand to the deer.
"No." Then he stops, knowing
his movement will cause movement,
his warning will create flight.
Where he turned left, then right

Is where one hoof now stands,
Right in the crescent moon
Of the billowed road.
The trucker whispers
Curses like a prayer
And turns away.

We do not understand.
We learn quick enough
As he turns the motor
And a sharp, kicked puff
Follows a wire's click
That our driver avoided

With a crescent moon.
The deer cannot be seen,
Except for shattered laurels
That snap through thicker fog.
Then there's the acrid smell of deer
In the fog's gun-powdered sheen.

El Salvador, 1932–1981

I

Witness

Before the trumpet sounded, before
Anyone needed to lift their skulls, before
There was a reason to mention any of this,
God touched the head of a fly named Martínez.
A bug that wore laurels. It confused the folk.
So they called him El Brujo, for only a witch with balls
Could get away with all this.

He announced La Limpieza.
"Papá knew nothing of The Cleansing. He
Rushed into the room
To scoot us out the door.
We hid in a cornfield
Where mamá kept a finger
In my baby brother's mouth.

Then the rattling, it began.
I first thought those were cornhusk dolls
Kicking over the tassles, leaping
At a full moon.
My family huddled between two rows.
I crawled to the edge to watch
The dolls become bodies and drop into a ditch.
Women leapt over the bank
To join their husbands.
Children jumped to follow their mothers.
Soldiers sat on the bulldozers.

"I crawled away to other stalks
Across from the plaza.
Two soldiers played soccer with skulls.
Five soldiers worked to make more balls.
They grabbed clumps of hair, drew machetes, and chopped.
They grabbed clumps of hair, pulled back,
Chopped, flung heads, snatched hair,
Chopped tossed snatched,
Chopped, tossed, and
Snatched again."

Should this be told any other way?

"This is too fucking slow!"
The rattle beat against my cheeks.
I heard one end, another begin,
Like thick chains falling on the plaza.

"I saw the children.
They trembled five feet away from my stalks.
If I could reach through the corn
And touch their shoulders, if I could grab
The waists of their pants.

"'I can't kill kids,' a voice said.
The commander slapped the soldier,
Snatched a baby by the neck,
Tossed her up like a heavy coin
And held the rifle erect.

"Papá's whisper wished to scream
At me. His hand
Flapped between corn at me, at me.
But I mowed down the stalks,
Snapping down a row an acre long.
Water woke me.
I slept.

"To my left moved
The hump of a woman's back.
Her shoulders pushed against the ground.
I could not see her head.
She had survived decapitation.
I yelped when
The shoulders lifted from the earth,
Hauling a face from a hole in the ground.

"She whispered, 'Don't scream girl.
Don't cry. Don't scream.'

"A warm arm wrapped my shoulders.
She pushed my head into the hole.
I could not see the morning light.
I smelled the humid earth.
I heard her gentle commands
Repeated above me, '*Now child,
Go ahead. Cry. Scream, child.
Right in there.*'"

II

The Phoenix of the Guanacos

I saw her in the distance, in her time
As she snatched at wind, gathering whispers
In a canasta of dried beans and corn.
She barely smiled my way, so busy,
Knocking sunshine into the frying pan.
She spoke her language, and though I did not know
The meaning, I recognized the cooking.
The tortillas raised up in hot protest
Like nervous clams. The blood, up to her knees
Couldn't trip her dance. As the brown vision
Whipped away I wondered if she listened
To a rhythm of hope or madness
Echoing in the hollow wind that passed
Over the lips of nineteen thirty-two.

Guanaco: The nickname for the people of El Salvador.

✳ Fiction ✳

. . . dig up black dirt on the trail in the forest, carry twisted wood and leave it at the edge of the road with good words between you and the squirrel behind the trees, go back and find seed-voices, the ones that raised you, the letters that arrived in your red-green spirit, the ancient songs way deep inside.

—*Juan Felipe Herrera*

excerpt from

The Region of Lost Names

Fred Arroyo

Part I, Chapter 3

The sun had dipped below the horizon, the lake a charcoal blue, the sky smudged with pink bleeding into an azure that slowly darkened the farther I looked away from the horizon. Boogaloo stopped, his purple scarf fluttering up near his left ear, its color deepening all the blue we stood amidst.

Boogaloo said, I don't know what you do . . . I mean for work, Ernestito, I don't know that kind of work. But I have a feeling that some days you think it is too easy, you don't feel good for all you do.

We stood just short of the water, the waves white and loud, rushing with sand and stones. Two children, their heads covered by their yellow slickers, ran along the edge of the waves, a flock of seagulls swerving up above them, screeching. Their father threw an orange float tied to a long white rope out into the sea, a black Lab running into the waves and paddling out to retrieve it. The children ran away into the darkening blue, their mother following close behind.

Don't feel this way—don't feel bad, Boogaloo told me.

I nodded, turned my head down, dragged the tip of my shoe through the moist sand, tracing an *E*, scratching it out, and following with half an arc.

Good work is good work. And remember that your father is now going into the dark. He needs to see some light, no?

We stared at each other.

Escúchame, hijo: don't forget your father . . .

Boogaloo stopped, his hand raised to his mouth.

How you say it, ante de memoria? You know, after memory?

Yes, after, but you might also mean *before*, or maybe *more*. No?

Seguro. You know what I mean. We have to live ante de memoria . . . We live with more than memory.

My stomach was full and warm; I felt like a child who had filled himself with a scrumptious meal before bed. I liked how Boogaloo called me hijo; for once it felt right, not mean but filled with concern, perhaps even a kind of respect. I repeated to myself what he had said: *Don't forget your father.*

I remembered then the time we couldn't find any work. The days were cold and wet, too cold for summer, and July seemed to pass in a silver mist. Boogaloo drove us farther north than we had ever been. Finally, Boogaloo stopped at a blueberry patch. We—Boogaloo, my father, and me—were paid thirty-five cents for each pound we picked. Boogaloo and my father could bring in five dollars after a fast day of work, their pants soaked to the knees from walking down the rain-filled paths, brushing against the bushes, the patch bathed in a thick fog. I was lucky to make a dollar fifty, maybe two; it took me forever to pick a pound of blueberries. I worked with a water cooler at my side, trying to stay in the patch as much as possible, peeing when I needed to, drinking water and eating blueberries so I wouldn't lose any time. Everything was wet, water everywhere I turned, my hands red and raw from so much water, so that I suddenly came upon an idea: I could have a pound of blueberries much faster if I poured a little water from the cooler into the tin of blueberries. No one seemed to notice, and for a few days I left the patch with a dollar or so more.

One day I slipped on the muddy path and cut my right hand on the thick, gnarled trunk of a bush, my hand wet with blood and mud when I arose from the path. I wiped my hand on the front of my pants. I started filling an empty pail with water to soak and clean my hand when the manager of the patch, a short heavy woman in a green rain poncho and red boots yelled out, Well, I think we found the one who's putting all the water in the berries. She told me to get my things together and come up front. They called Boogaloo from the patch; my father was asleep in the car, shivering with fever and too much drink. We stood on the edge of the patch, the manager pulling off the hood of her poncho and talking to her husband, who weighed the blueberries and packed them. Boogaloo stood next to me, a half-filled pail of blueberries in his hand. She explained about the water, handed Boogaloo and I a dollar, and then she told us we had to go. She and her husband turned and walked down the lane toward the small lean-to where the berries were weighed.

Boogaloo pulled his pail back and flung the blueberries out into the air, a stream of blue cutting through the mist—his gesture quick, light, and with such grace that I didn't understand how he suddenly stood in front of me. He swung the pail and struck me on the side of the head, and my ears filled with the bright tin and my face was hot and pulsed with a sharp pain. Boogaloo looked at me with great disgust, his jaw clenched, his lips turning up, his eyes black and deep. He said things; I couldn't hear anything for the ringing in my head. And then he punched me in the stomach, and when I doubled over I heard *¿Tú me entiendes?* Never, never give up work, Ernestito. Work is work.

I closed my eyes for a moment, my fist crumpling the dollar tightly. When I opened my eyes, Boogaloo had disappeared. My head was hot with sweat, my shoulders beginning to shake in the wet, cold air. I tucked the crumpled dollar into my pants pocket. When I raised my hand to wipe away the sweat from my face, I realized I was shaking with tears and my hand was soaked with blood.

Now Boogaloo touched the side of my face with his open palm, his dark work-worn hand soft.

I am sorry, Ernestito.

I thought, I'll never forget what happened, and just at that moment the side of my face felt like it was on fire. I wanted to tell him: *You had no right or reason to hit me back then, Boogaloo, and I'll always remember the taste of that tin pail.* But instead I said, Thank you, Boogaloo, thank you for everything.

He tried to smile, held up his hand as if to push my thanks away, a big tear dropping from his right eye.

No, *listen*: thank you, Manuel Perez.

And before he could say anything I raised my hand up to his neck, tucking the fluttering end of his scarf under the collar of his coat. In that moment I had to let him know I knew his name; that Manuel Perez was not lost in all that blue.

Ernestito, no matter who we believe we were, or what we think we have done, we have to live . . .

He took hold of my hand and kissed my palm.

I squeezed his shoulder. I wanted to say, *I forgive you, Manuel.* Those words never came, and instead I said, I find many days, many, many days, where I don't know what to do. I looked down at the sand, and then looked him in the eyes. I haven't talked to them in so long . . . What can I say? Why will they want to talk to me?

My nose filled with sharp pain as my eyes filled with tears. Boogaloo held my hand tighter, and I didn't cry.

Maybe no one will have anything to say or do, Ernestito. But you never know. You can only do what you can do.

There was a dark blue streak of sky behind Boogaloo, then both our heads turned toward the bass tremble of a distant foghorn. I felt the darkness of the sea beginning to rise all around us.

Boogaloo said, You have your daughter to think of now.

I jerked my hand away, hugged myself tightly, bit down hard on my teeth.

My daughter?

Yes, Isabel, he said, without any hesitation or wonder. Magdalene's never loved anyone but you, everyone knows that, hijo. How can you not know Isabel is yours?

Boogaloo touched my cheek briefly, shrugged.

Isabel would soon turn five . . . My legs trembled and I could only think of the years that had passed, of my not knowing, even though Isabel and Magdalene were never that far away from me. And then, *Magdalene took Isabel to Puerto Rico because she knew I was her father, and now they are miles and miles away.* The dog down the beach barked, and then the children laughed, followed by the deep bellow of the foghorn and the waves crashing into the shore. I had tried to stay in touch with Magdalene. One day, out of the blue, after I had gone into the world on my own, she wrote to me and asked if I would meet her on Mackinac Island. We spent a wonderful weekend together, one of the best times of my life, and after I left her up there I wrote Magdalene a letter or a card once a month for the next nine, and when she never answered I tried to call her. I tried and tried; I wanted deeply to be a part of her life. She never called back or wrote. She seemed to be ignoring me, and though I couldn't understand why, I finally left her alone.

I took Boogaloo's hand again; I needed it; I was confused, the swirling blues and grays of the evening causing me to shake and swerve as I tried to walk. I had to find a new path—*how could I cross the distance that kept me and Magdalene and Isabel apart?*

Just in front of his cabin Boogaloo stopped. He said, If I could do it all over again, I'd do anything to know my daughter.

Your daughter?

Yes. She never knew me. And it's probably too late for me but not for you, Ernestito.

My daughter, Isabel. What will she know or say of me? And then I saw her and Magdalene standing under a mango tree, their legs and feet streaked with red dust; and when they turned to me, hummingbirds in purple and green circled around them.

We took a few steps closer to the cabin. I said thank you once again, and when I went to say more, Boogaloo put two fingers up to his lips to quiet me. I heard sand striking the porch with a small yet sharp sound. Boogaloo pointed to the sea with his hand, his fingers sweeping back the waves, almost as if he could stop or part them, and then I understood he was saying *Go, go away.*

He told me, Your father and I never got it right; we didn't know how—or were never given the chance—to be fathers. You have to learn for yourself what that means, Ernestito. But you can make a lot fewer mistakes than us.

His hand was still in the air, and once again he pointed to the sea, his fingers waving me backward toward the waves. Boogaloo opened the door to his cabin and stepped inside. A light came on, gold behind the curtains. The wind picked up strong and shook the rum bottles hanging on the porch, their clapping along with the sound of the foghorn, and I heard the blues of this evening, the surging melody of a newfound feeling: *Isabel, Magdalene.*

Boogaloo had waved me away. Go, go away. He wasn't saying good-bye; he was telling me, showing me: *Go, go away across the sea. As fast as you can—go.* Boogaloo's figure, outlined by the golden light, was seated next to his table. I heard him turn on the radio, a soft trumpet sketching a ballad.

I turned back to the sea. Boogaloo had offered me the chance to go, but back then on that March day the sea seemed so dark and wide, stretched by miles and miles and miles, and though I should have run as fast as I could and jumped in, I turned away from the sea, and the waves continued to crash with its memory and remorse, and Magdalene and Isabel were still thousands of miles away, across an even vaster sea.

Part I, Chapter 4

Boogaloo's ashes were housed in an eight-by-ten cardboard box. Gently rocking it in my palms, I felt Boogaloo dancing, heard the sweet sound of salsa, *Ay, que suave,* Boogaloo's strong, hard torso black and shiny in the sun, his shirt wrapped around his head, Boogaloo dancing on the edge of a potato field, golden dust springing from his shoes and powdering the air. Ever since I had claimed his ashes, I had this need to keep Boogaloo close by, safe, while I figured out what to do with his death.

I placed the box on the windowsill next to an empty canning jar. Shadows fell through the window, the sound of feet running through the grass. The walls of this migrant shack were bare, the wood cracked and stuffed in places with bright pieces of wool and balled-up newspaper. On the floor, a twisted mattress, half of it wet, the other half torn open; its insides puffy, pouring out into a thick yellow mound. A single bulb hung above a table, the outer figure of the bulb black with soot. There were no chairs, or a refrigerator, or a stove, but there were three blue cups, a white plate, an empty coffee can, and a small trail of crumbs on the table. A milk crate sat on the floor just off the edge of the table, almost as if someone had recently eaten here. Out in the orchard, voices, laughter; inside, the floor creaking in places and turning soft, then becoming hollow and hard as I stepped into the doorway.

I looked up, squinted, following the blue sky beyond the trees, and then I found the sun beginning its slow descent.

Children zigzagged back and forth across the orchard lane, yelling under the trees brimming with blossoms. There was music in the air along with the distinct smells of cherries, cinnamon, coffee. Migrant workers, farmers, city folks, tourists—all had gathered to celebrate May Day. John Lindquist stood on a makeshift stage presenting red and blue ribbons to students from the local schools. The crowd clapped. A boy waved a ribbon over his head, smiling. *Renaldo Lacasa.* He waved the ribbon higher, with more flair, ecstatic with accomplishment, and I smiled and waved back, stepping from the doorway onto the orchard lane. I nodded to Mrs. and Mr. Lacasa, both of them filled with pride. I slid my hands into my pockets, turning my head downward, the orchard lane worn smooth and bare. Renaldo rushed over to me.

Standing there in short pants and sandals, a striped purple and yellow T-shirt, Renaldo shyly held the ribbon in his palm. I crouched down, took the ribbon from him, and pinned it to his T-shirt with the ribbon's small golden clasp. I stood and shook my fist in solidarity, a gesture that always elicited a response.

First place, Ernestito, he said. He lifted the coarse vanilla paper.

Excellent, Renaldo. I held the paper at arm's length as Renaldo and his parents looked on. Renaldo had painted the landscape as if he had stood above the countryside looking down on the city, the streets, his school, the freshwater sea, the cannery his father worked in.

Pointing at the watercolor, I said, Renaldo, and this little bay, the road, the boy on the bicycle . . .

Yes, here—Renaldo pointed with quick excitement, the bodily shift of recognition—my blue harbor and my sea road. I love to ride this way and look out on the boats, the sea, the harbor.

He laughed, then suddenly stopped himself, perhaps self-conscious of my understanding. I immediately heard memories of another sea road, some other blue released into our *now*.

Ah, yes. I see the blue is its own. It is a blue different from all the rest. It's *your* azul, Renaldo.

I unfolded the thick white paper dusted with cinnamon, the paper smudged and flecked with brilliant henna highlights, vivid in the late-afternoon light.

A colleague and I spent our Thursday afternoons at a local arts center helping elementary and high-school students with various projects; she often shared diverse forms of art and music; I, an array of literary works and documents. Out of all the students who had worked over the winter and spring to get their projects ready for the festival, it was Renaldo who had created countless drafts, who always had a sense of beginning again, who waited for something to appear, for something to happen. Renaldo seemed to relish the depth of a page; he followed the bold letters and lines, traced the strange curves of blue and red, and the squiggly ornament of green and black lines on the top edges of letters he studied in old volumes. Sometimes we simply left the arts center behind, left books upside down or open to the sun, left our brushes wet with paint, our hands streaked and splotched, a whole group of students walking out into the winter afternoon, the air freezing the paint hard on our hands. We walked into the woods looking at the light take shape on the snow, listening to the creaking, ice-covered trees. I stopped on a ridge, the sheen of the distant, open sea blue on the horizon, knelt down, showed Renaldo the silver fur of a rabbit torn and fluffy on the snow, the little drops of blood, the imprint of a hawk's wing.

Renaldo had taken all this in and waited for something to swoop down on him—and, now, I held it in my hands. The paper unfolded like a map, into four panels revealing long whitewashed walls. Around the borders of the walls he had painted lavender flowers, tall stalks of cane, and thorny pineapples. Then the imprint of something swooped down on me. Magdalene had been teaching before I ever started; I never told her this, but she was my model, my hero, and what she accomplished helped me to imagine my possibilities as a teacher. If she were here, Magdalene and I could have worked at the arts center together. Isabel could have said: *My father works with books. My mother too.* And Magdalene and Isabel could be standing here with me now, looking at Renaldo's work.

Marvelous, Renaldo, just marvelous. I squeezed his shoulder, Renaldo's face reddening with embarrassment and pride.

Inside the border of flowers, cane, and pineapples, Renaldo had created walls where he had written poems. He had composed the poems himself. He had composed them in the words he had heard from his mother and father, from his memories of Cuba; they were poems inspired by the words of those poets who had most moved him in this first winter here, this first year away from his island home. And between two poems about his abuela, Renaldo had placed a photograph: Renaldo and his mother and father standing on the edge of a runway, a white plane behind them. Fat, heavy-looking bags pulled down his parents' shoulders. Their faces were mournful, composed of severe smiles as they waved. Renaldo stood between them, his eyes staring wide and hard, filled with dark fright, a small book cradled in his arm.

I carefully folded the paper. Mrs. and Mr. Lacasa came closer.

You have a great talent here, I said, looking into Mrs. and Mr.'s eyes. *Es un poeta.*

They nodded, smiling. Mr. Lacasa shook my hand. Mrs. Lacasa put her arm around Renaldo.

Will you sit with us, Ernest?

Sure.

I turned to give Renaldo his walls of poetry, his watercolor.

He shook his head.

No . . . No, Renaldo I can't . . .

I want you to have it, Ernest, for helping.

Mrs. and Mr. Lacasa told me with their eyes that the gift was mine.

Thank you, Renaldo, thank you.

Renaldo took my right arm, his mother my left, his father's hand on my back, and like a small parade we marched off toward the crowd gathered around the stage. There were bowls of cherries, plates of cheeses, bottles of wine and juice, and blankets spread across the field in a confetti of colors. The crowd looked up toward the frame of purple curtains that adorned the stage.

We sat down. Mr. Lacasa handed me a short glass of wine. We clinked glasses. We shared sliced mango, strong goat cheese, crispy French bread.

Would you like some rice and beans? Mrs. Lacasa asked.

Yes, I nodded, my eyes widening.

A short man in a dark green khaki uniform walked to the front of the stage, a blue blowtorch in his hand, a long orange and yellow flame rising just above his head. Tree warmers brought in from the orchard lanes were placed around the perimeter of the crowd. The man in the green uniform bent down in front of one, and then there was a loud *wooofff*, followed by flames appearing in the warmer. People clapped. He lit another. *Wooofff.* More clapping. And then another. The heat from the warmers pushed in toward us, barely visible clouds of warmth beginning to take shape in the air and to surround the larger field of memory we were sitting within. Out here, in this orchard, families had gathered into a community of work, wages, food, and celebration. Some picked cherries. Some stirred vats filled with cherries. Some stacked cases of cherries. To some, I was much better off and quite different than these families. I was an oddity—a solitary man, unmarried, without friend or family, a rare bird who almost always walked around in a black suit (perhaps the most casual memory someone had of me was of a warm evening, my shirt sleeves rolled to my elbows, my tie tucked into my breast pocket, pitching a softball in the bottom of the seventh inning, my white shirt and black pants streaked with red dust). I was extremely fortunate; I had been given the opportunity to teach writing at a small fine-arts school, but somehow I had also become a part of the larger life of this community: a man who worked as a teacher, who sometimes helped workers fill out forms, sometimes helped to organize events for this May Day festival, sometimes started a softball game in an orchard.

I wasn't that alone, though. I had Boogaloo. What to do with him, I thought, is something I still need to come to terms with. *I must live with Boogaloo a little longer.* Then I can tell my father, I can tell Magdalene all I hope for her and Isabel—for them, within my life.

Mrs. Lacasa asked, What about your family, Ernesto? You were born here, no?

I watched the shifting orange flames of a heater for a moment, heat rising up into the air, and then I crossed my legs at the ankles and held my knees.

Yes, I was born in Michigan. My father answered a call for work and came here to work at a mushroom cannery. That's when he met my mother.

I rocked back and said, About fifteen years ago they moved to Puerto Rico; it was always my father's dream to go back.

How are they doing?

Okay, I guess.

You say that as if you don't know, or don't talk to them, Mr. Lacasa said. He was lying on his side, his head propped up with one hand, Renaldo leaning back on his chest.

You are right . . . I don't talk to them. I . . . I stopped, looking up into the darkening sky that still held blue and was tinted with the orange of the evening's sun.

You think you are the bad son, Ernesto? Mr. Lacasa asked.

I guess so. They moved far away. I was happy for them, but I think, too, I have a hard time understanding their choices, or even my own, I said. And then: They had some hard times. I don't know how they can still be together, why their love stayed so strong.

Hmmm . . . Mr. Lacasa took a drink of his wine, and I raised my glass to my lips, looked at Mrs. Lacasa, and then said, I'm the bad son because I avoided them, I tried to forget them, and now I'm too ashamed to . . .

There was a small pocket of silence, as if the warmth of the burners had surrounded us, quieting our voices, our thoughts.

Nonsense, Mrs. Lacasa said. Everything you might have done may seem the acts of a bad son, but all you are doing now might be that of a good son.

Sí, sí, it is true, Mr. Lacasa said.

We all turned, and four children walked out across the stage, big silver stars tied to the front of their bodies, their arms raised high in the air. They had brought out the night, and in their brief presence we were to experience the unfolding darkness within the sanctuary of their brightness. Mr. Lacasa raised Mrs. Lacasa's hand, palm open, to his lips.

My brother went away to England for almost twenty years, Mrs. Lacasa began, and without a word except maybe a postcard every five years or so. One afternoon, after a heavy rain, the trees still wet and the red road full of mud, Papí points, screams, Ay, mijito. We saw a man walking next to the cane field, his arms and face pale like a ghost against his yellow guayabera. My father and mother walked, almost running, as fast as they could toward my long-lost brother, Javier. Tears were streaming down their faces, but they were so happy, she said.

Everything quieted. She wiped her face with the back of her arm, and Renaldo came over and sat in her lap. She hugged him and kissed the side of his neck.

I remember Papí kept saying Javier must have walked for days, mile after mile, pointing to his feet, and we couldn't see Javier's boots because they were caked in hard red mud, and his pants were soaked and clung to his knees.

The stars began walking off the stage, and I saw underneath those stars an evening when Mrs. Lacasa's memory would become part of a story we would return to because we needed to tell it to one another—a story I would tell, hoping Isabel and Magdalene would come and sit by me.

White paper birds suddenly appeared on the edge of the purple curtains, fluttering above us. Following the birds was a young boy who was the sun, who helped everyone see the new morning of this play.

Excuse me, I have to go for a moment, I stood up, and then, caught in the heat of the tree warmers, I glimpsed my own arms, no longer pale but reddened by the sun of this May Day.

I'll be right back.

They nodded. I turned away, rolled my shirtsleeves back down, buttoned them, and found a path through the crowd, my eyes intent on the shack, on going to get Boogaloo.

excerpt from

Samba Dreamers

Kathleen de Azevedo

Chapter 20

O Ano 1978

Ten Rules for Latin actors (or how to behave like one):

1. You must be named Pancho, Pepe, José or Rita, María, Rosita.

2. You must have a Mexican accent; even if you don't have one, get one.

3. You must always want sex.

4. You must never get sex.

5. You must dance or play guitar, or, failing that, you must know how to play cards and gamble.

6. You must always make shady business deals without a contract; if possible, seal all deals with a kiss.

7. You must live with the notion that the blond girl will be the star. Realize that your only function as a Latin actor is to return the blonde back to her Americano sweetheart.

8. You must have a hot temper.

9. You must be willing to play Argentine gauchos, Mexicans, Cubans, Brazilians, East L.A. riff-raff, and sometimes all of them at the same time.

10. You must realize that the good Latin parts will go to non-Latin *blanca* actors. Remember, you will be interesting enough for them to make a movie about you, but never good enough to play who you are.

Rosea's parole officer sat at his desk, him with his suit and striped tie, trying to look so hip with longish hair that curled behind his ears in two hooks. He was young, but not as young as he wanted to be. He was holding the *L.A. Times*. He flipped the paper over, showing her the headlines: DEAD MAN FOUND ON VAUGHAN ESTATE. "Did you know this?" he asked. "Amazing the guy would get shot just as you were on parole. Nobody even thought much about the Vaughan mansion, except it was a bit hard to get to, and all of a sudden you're out, and all hell breaks loose. Do you find that strange, Mrs. Millard?"

"Please call me Ms. Socorro Katz."

He didn't respond except to blink his dotlike eyes.

Rosea trembled inside but modestly smoothed her hand down her skirt. "Why would I blow it? I have such an excellent job."

Her officer handed her the newspaper, got up from his desk, and went through a file drawer. DEAD MAN FOUND ON VAUGHAN ESTATE. Rosea read the article while eyeing her parole officer at the file cabinet. The dead man lay there overnight until the production office got nervous and sent the LAPD onto the estate—with some dogs. That's a relief, the news about the body being there for a while. Rosea prayed no one had seen her escape.

"Did you know Mr. Driscoll, the victim?" the parole officer said as he found the file—*her* file no doubt.

"Never."

"Seems like he works in the movies. I think he was thinking of using the place for a film. Do you know anything about it?"

"I'm not in the movies. I hate the movies. Don't even ask me."

So the man who had gotten in her face was a Hollywood hoo-haa. The man who had seemed so distant, a zero, a nothing. A bad dream. He was probably trying to make sense of her mother by drifting through her property. Just some no-name drifting through. What did the man expect? What big secret was he looking for?

Her parole officer sat down and folded his hands over the file he had pulled out. "Have you ever visited the garden since your release?"

"Why should I?" Rosea snapped, "My mother doesn't live there. What good is it? Hollywood killed her off and left nothing but her platform shoes."

"Well. You work at a tour company. And one of the things on the tour is the houses in Beverly Hills, so it stands to reason I should ask."

"I have a desk job." Rosea tossed the newspaper back to him.

The man stared at her for a long time and twirled one of his wingish curls around a finger.

Rosea caught herself rubbing her forehead. She stopped and dropped her arm down. Why don't people just shut up about everything? She looked beyond him to the window, one of the old ones where the bottom half slid up. At five floors, Rosea wondered if anyone had ever leaped out and landed on the street in front of a lunchtime crowd. She'd take a leap if she had the courage. Or run away with Joe to Brazil. Wouldn't matter if they lived in a hut somewhere. They could go by plane or ship, wouldn't matter. If the plane crashed, no problem. If the ship sunk, she'd pull him down into the water and watch his dark eyes widen, his strong arms flail as he desperately tried to clamber out of the air bubbles. Then she'd clutch him as her hair floated and spiraled like an eel, and they'd tumble on the powder of the long undisturbed sand and rest their heads among the clams. Dead and forever innocent.

"You might want to be careful," the parole officer said finally. "You've got a rap sheet—no murders or anything, but . . . you know what I'm saying? I mean—I'm no federal judge. I'm just looking at you and thinking 'She's a big girl. A really biiiig girl with a lotta anger.'"

Rosea lunged at him. He flinched, and she pulled back. "Look. I've been straight. What do you want, a martini? If I wanted to break parole, I would have gone into the house and stolen the TV! You can't connect what I did before! My marriage was totally different! I mean, everything was different. Jeremy Millard was strange. He even slept with a monkey! He was asking for it—" She stopped.

He looked at her admonishingly, narrowing his eyes. "I hope you're through punishing people for all the bad things you think they've done to you."

Rosea bolted up, whirled toward the door. "What in the hell do I have to see you for if you're going to say shit like that?!"

The parole officer ignored her, opened the file, and started filling out her parole report.

Rosea thumped her palms against her temples. "I can't believe this," she muttered, "everyone here is nuts." She paced in front of the beveled glass door that blurred and buckled the bodies of people moving up and down the hall.

Her parole officer was still writing. Writing a lot.

"Jesus," Rosea moaned, "you writing a book about me or something? A man dies in my mom's yard, and you think I wouldn't be a little crazy?"

The parole officer finished writing, then spun his chair side to side, eyeing her.

Rosea looked away. The other two desks in the room were empty. She felt like the only one in the world on parole. Then she gazed out the window again, imagining herself plunging down to the sidewalk. Keeping her eye on the other building across the street, she finally said, "If that movie man was looking for some tropical thing up there, he'd be wasting his time. The last toucan was roadkill a long time ago. Ended up just a splat on the road with its beak sticking up like a dick."

As Rosea crept to her office, she touched the wall to steady herself. She heard talking and laughing from the crowded reception area, but something was different. Chucky wasn't haw-hawing like a gangster, Tom Mix had dropped his stupid cowboy accent, Mickey was acting like an adult, and Bogey wasn't mouthing off. It almost seemed normal; they were acting like people from this movie decade of *Network* and *Deer Hunter* and of Brit actors doing nude scenes, not like the usual funny bunnies from the Silver Screen.

Desiree in her usual floral dress stuck her head out of the crowd, spotted Rosea, and beckoned her. Rosea grunted and instead slid into her office, lowered herself down in front of her appointment book, and massaged her temples as if her head would split open. Desiree appeared at the doorway and asked if they could talk. Rosea shuddered. Desiree took it as a yes and sat down on the chair beside the desk, crossed her skinny arms, and gave her perpetual cold shiver. She started rattling on like a half-wit about how Chucky was the friend of someone's agent who was representing someone doing a film based on Carmen Socorro's life, but who needed advice.

Rosea squinted, "Who?"—feeling sick as hell—"Who needs advice?"

Desiree gave a little "oh," realized she was prattling way too fast, and started more slowly, explaining that Chucky was a friend of Nancy West's agent. "You know Nancy West, she played the girlfriend of Jason Hart in the movie *Honey Hill*? She's young? Blond? I think she's dating Brandon Kahn, who starred in *Gunfire at Point Zero* with Vaughan Peters—you know, the one shot in Guatemala? You know the Nancy West I'm talking about?"

Rosea groaned and closed her eyes. She didn't know a Nancy West. She hated movies, and she'd been chanting "I hate movies" to people over and over again like a psychotic Buddhist monk. She heard Desiree's voice in a haze: "They're making a film about your mother's life. You know, Carmen Socorro? Chucky has offered you as an advisor to Nancy West. She's the star."

Rosea heard the last line but couldn't believe it. *Someone* named Nancy West is going to play Carmen Socorro, and she, Rosea Socorro Katz, has to give advice? She shifted in her chair, her stomach in pain.

Desiree came back into focus. "Isn't it fantastic? After all those violent serious films, we deserve something to cheer us up. *Carioca Craze.* That's the name of the movie. What's a 'carioca,' Rosea? I forgot. But no one forgot your mother. She was always so happy. So much happier than most. Ohh, ohh," Desiree gasped, looking at the wall, at the calendar, at anything instead of at Rosea, "how exciting for you. I would have done anything to be in the movies."

Rosea reeled over to her, flaring, "WOULD YOU HAVE GONE BUTT NAKED?!"

Desiree sat there red-eyed, her hair in the two aggressive, 1940's-style hair rolls. Her pointed chin quivered, and her boxy shoulder pads made her neck and arms look like sticks coming out of nowhere. "Oh, Rosea, that's beside the point. My career never got that far."

Rosea slammed back on her chair. "I gotta work."

Desiree got up and left. Rosea held the edges of the desk and breathed hard. She thought she'd faint right there. Desiree came back, tossed a screenplay on her desk, and hurried out. Rosea stared at the manuscript. *Carioca Craze.* She was repulsed but a bit curious. What would they say about her mother? She wondered how she herself would be portrayed and who would play her. Someone kind of pretty? Would the film have a scene where her mother brushed Rosea's hair and talked of the Amazons thundering through the jungle on their horses? Would the film include her mother's crushing saudade in which she wandered down the hall calling for her Brazilian gardeners? Who knew enough about Carmen to make a film?

Suddenly from the waiting room came an explosion of conversation about the murder. Rosea listened. Someone went on about the "one who was shot," some location manager, as if he were the star of the show. Bogey hollered, "Whoever shot that man should be shot himself!" and the cowboy added, "Maybe hung, pardner, maybe hung!" Rosea rubbed her tight and painful stomach pushing up against her lungs and stared at the script's faux-leather covering. Some guy died for this? All that's left of him is this screenplay, one of the millions of screenplays in Hollywood usually ending up as doormats or being handed back and forth like old whores?

Carioca Craze. She turned to the first page and passed her hands over the paper. It felt cold. The words blurred until she couldn't read. The letters were like ants that swarmed out of cracked and rotten coconuts. Rosea narrowed her eyes. The room started to spin; the words began to crawl up her fingers and inside her sleeve. The white pages liquefied and churned in her stomach. The room had a sharp, rotten smell. Rosea bolted, that white-chalk feeling rising up in her throat. She rushed to the bathroom and kicked the door open as if she were the police. Her stomach heaved, and she made a horrible gagging sound, producing only a spider thread of saliva. The bathroom walls were pink like human insides. Another wave hit her head, and, too big to sink to her knees over the toilet, she grabbed the edge of the sink and the toilet-paper dispenser and hung there, trying to bring up the poison guilt that had settled in her bones.

Rosea lurched out of the bathroom and collapsed back in her chair. Beads of cold sweat crept on her hairline. Desiree bounded in again—

"I have to go home, I don't feel well—" Rosea snapped. She shouldn't have said that. Desiree would suspect a nasty case of nerves. But instead Desiree pealed, "How sad, I'm so sorry." Rosea rolled up the screenplay like a club. She let Desiree advise her to go home and drink tea and watch *General Hospital*. And of course—Desiree winked—do some reading. Rosea slowly stuck the screenplay in her purse. Then she rose and carefully lifted her purse to her shoulder and staggered down the hall.

Rosea drove east to her old hang-out bar, Nuestro Lugar, to read the screenplay. She didn't want to be near Hollywood, where everyone who saw you with a screenplay craned their necks to check: Who are you? What are you reading? A spec or under contract or sold or what? Who's your agent? Are you very good?

A few boys strutted past her and hooted—"Hey vieja!" A shopkeeper tossed out old mangos and tomatoes into a cardboard box while his assistant dumped a shipment of fresh oranges into an empty bin. Once in a while a fry cook would step out from a restaurant, lean against the wall, and light a cigarette. Old Impalas thumped by, the bass on their radios turned up, crystals twirling from the rearview mirrors and making small rainbows on the windshields.

The bar seemed bleaker than ever. The dull glint from the naked bulbs shining under red-glass lampshades reminded her of prison at night, where there was always the throb of a light. Joe was right. This is a sad place to be. She slipped away to her usual back table. The men looked up from their beer, and one group had the energy to play pool. The balls clashed together like knocking heads. A Mexican *norteño* song went on and on about *corazón y calamidad*. She ordered a beer and listened to the men's heels clicking as they went around the pool table. She heard a dime sliding into a pay phone. They say these guys are dangerous, knives in their pockets, guns hidden underneath their jackets. But here they looked innocent and lost, not knowing where else to go. They probably never killed anybody, probably couldn't even handle a knife or a gun; it would be too overwhelming to attack or kill someone and change their lives forever. They probably did nothing but drink in the morning and sit on their doorsteps in the afternoon, tottering to and fro while their wives went shopping and gossiped with friends about the old drunks they had married.

She sat with her beer and lit a cigarette. The smoke curled like a small fist, then spread out as a gray haze. She began turning the pages, creaking past the title *Carioca Craze*, past the character descriptions. Then she began reading . . .

Ten Lies from the screenplay that did not happen in Carmen Socorro's Real Life:

1. American Pete Shinsky discovers Carmen singing in a bodega in Rio.

2. He offers her money and a career in the United States, not like the cheapo Brazilians who offer her only a free beer.

3. She has a Mexican accent.

4. She always wants sex with her servants.

5. Her lovers play guitar, but are into gambling and making bad business deals that involve drugs.

6. Her Americano friend Pete Shinsky straightens her out, says she's talented and can make it. He books her into various nightclubs. A lot of them. Including Broadway. Numbers involve big hats. Monkeys, bananas, and, on one, dancing zombies.

7. Thanks to Pete she is a hit. They get married.

8. She has a hot temper. Still.

9. Pete, her inspiration, is killed in a car wreck.

10. In her grief, she lights candles, somewhat mystically. She wanders topless around her garden (drums pound in the background). Then continues her career triumphantly. (Fade out.)

Rosea finished the manuscript and slapped it shut. The beer and cigarette thickened in her empty, upset stomach. The music played in the background, and at the pool table someone started a new game, smacking a set of balls. She heard a voice, "Otra cerveza?" She leaned over the table, crossed her arms, and lay her head down. No revelations on why her father, after his brief stint as her mother's cha-cha man, left for Miami to swindle chlorine-smelling ex-movie stars. No story of what happened in Brazil to cause her mother's heart to explode in flames. Nothing about a daughter making the plot too messy, watching everyone doing dirty things to each other. The only thing clear was that Mr. Pink Polo Man was where he wasn't supposed to be. Hollywood sticking its nose in everything, what's new? She wasn't sorry she had killed him. Not one little bit. She almost wished he would come back to life so she could kill him over and over again. Ah hell. She created in her mind ten Mr. Polo Men and lined them up against the wall, then took a machine gun and blew them away to bloody splashes. That's how the ending should go. End with a revolution. *Viva.*

Chapter 21

Women were brought to us for our pleasure. Lima informed us of the Petiguar custom, that we could request any woman, for if a man is to die, they deny him nothing, not even a wife of the chief. First, the old women were brought to us. They had full stomachs that hung over their loincloths. Many had cicatrices and scars from war and rashes from ringworm. We refused them. Bring us the younger ones, we demanded.
—Diário de Carlos Manoel Teixeira da Cunha, O Ano 1643

O Ano 1978

Joe and Rosea laid a blanket on the ground away from the water's edge and removed their shoes. Rosea shoved her shorts farther up her thighs as if she were ready to wade through mud. She said something under her breath as she plunked down and made a big deal about rubbing the sand out from between her toes. Joe eased down on the blanket—not too close to her, but not too far either—and leaned back on his hands. The ocean waves smeared a membrane of foam on the surface, and fleas bipped around piles of washed-up seaweed. The dilapidated lifeguard towers were spray painted with letters that looked like inky bird claws. In the distance, someone set up a motion-picture camera on a tripod and did nothing but film the ocean. It looked like some experimental Cinema Novo movie made by a crazy art student.

Rosea had wanted to bring him to the beach, and he had agreed to go, as much trouble as it was. They came to talk about what to do next about this guilt, growing so large Joe felt as if he had killed thousands. How do you think about something like this? Joe wanted to ask her, but when he saw Rosea clutching a tote bag tight between her knees, then rifling through its contents, he knew she was ready to erupt again. Then she yanked out what she said was a screenplay.

"Ah no," Joe grabbed the screenplay from her and shoved it back into her bag. "Nothing like this. I want to talk serious."

She snatched the manuscript out again and slapped it down on her lap. "It's serious, alright. You need to know what the end of the world might look like."

"I DON'T want to talk about the movies."

"Joe. They are making a movie about my mother!"

"I don't care. I want to talk."

"We are TALKING ABOUT LYING!" Rosea glared at him, her nostrils flaring. The wind ruffled the pages. She deliberately turned to the first page, and her eyes slowly dropped as she began reading.

He refused to listen; it wasn't important. He closed his eyes and willed the memory of Sonia; he did not wrestle with the memory; it did not come as a flashback, in a jolt of violence, but with sadness and pain. He let himself remember Sonia running toward the waves, her long hair down her back, hair so wiry, like wool mixed with air. He let himself remember how her bikini revealed the small of her back, a perfect place to put his thumb. *É prohibido prohibir.* It is forbidden to forbid. These words, the cry of the Tropicalistas, became the music of love. During this time, lovers split up, ran away, disappeared, and their cars burst into suspicious flames. It was a lot to go through for someone. But it was not forbidden to forbid. What the Tropicalistas meant was that *era prohibido amar.* It was forbidden to love. But nobody could follow the rules; the longing was always there. It hadn't gone away.

Rosea tossed the manuscript off to the side with a "whack!" Joe looked up.

"You insensitive motherfucker, you aren't even paying attention!" she said with fury. Suddenly she bolted into the ocean and ran into the water up to her thighs.

Joe sprang up. "For god's sake, Rosea! Don't be so strange! Come back!"

Rosea turned once to cast a look at Joe, her hair undulating in a long snake down her back, then she lunged forward, jetting into the water. She sank and rose like a large fish, her hair unraveling in the tide. Joe ran in after her, water up to his knees, then his thighs; he dived in just as she propelled herself forward through a loaf of water. "Come back! Come back!" he croaked as Rosea swam steadily away from the beach. He saw his hands dipping down into the water, first pale and glimmering, then disappearing as his body surged forward, over and over again. He screamed out Rosea's name, but his voice was muffled as the water lapped around his ears.

My God, was she crazy, trying to swim back to Brazil? Was he crazy to follow her? She wouldn't even make it to Panama. He found himself bobbing in the dark waves, watching her swim farther on. The ocean stretched around him, hopelessly remote, and the water underneath him swelled, then let go. He lunged toward Rosea and got hit with a mouthful of brine. He coughed, and his lungs burned. Thick ribbons of water flowed through his kicking legs. Rosea was out too far for anyone to catch her. He looked toward the rim of the sand and thought of Jeffy and Keffy waving, of Sherri waiting for him with a bag of sandwiches, of his Brazilian family calling him home, telling him how it would be worth it to be in love again, if he could.

He knew he could not save Rosea. He had caught a current and was being taken back to shore; he wouldn't fight it. He imagined women with sunglasses and amazing hairstyles, standing around him and teasing: Why did you swim after someone so crazy, and why are you in so much trouble, José? How can you resist the look of our sunglasses when you used to love them?

His knees scraped on the sand, and he scrambled up onto shore, the water spilling from inside his shorts. Rosea had made it to shore farther down the beach, and she was stumbling and running toward him. She began crying as she got closer to him, and she rushed and clutched him hard, embracing him until their wet clothes popped between their chests. "I want to go home," she wailed.

Jose nestled his face into her hair. A small piece of seaweed had gotten caught in the tangle. "É nada," he whispered as he combed his fingers through her hair, "forget everything." A tiny spider made its way out from the depths of her black wet mass, scampered up, then dropped downward on a fine strand.

Joe let the door swing open and stood at the threshold to the living room. His wet T-shirt clung to his chest, the legs of his soaked shorts flapped together, his dry arms bristled with goose bumps, and his spirit was so low it felt like a dream. Everything was happening in slow motion—the kids running, stopping with a lurch, a toy truck slowly falling and making a complicated clatter on the floor. Joe told himself to act normal and held his arms out, beckoning to his sons. Only Keffy came, waddling cautiously, looking over at Jeffy. Joe lifted Keffy, watching his son's face rise, then he placed Keffy on his hip. The boy set his warm fat legs against Joe's wet clothes and started to cry. Joe held him close, the crying sounding like from another time. Keffy's stomach tightened and puffed, his fat legs tried to wiggle away. Joe pulled Keffy closer, a bit more roughly, wanting to feel his son's aliveness, but Keffy struggled harder, then flung his body back and bawled, showing the mean little roof of his mouth.

Sherri ran from the kitchen to check out the commotion. "My goodness, what happened?"

Joe set the baby down, and the crying stopped immediately. He walked past his sons, cupping his hand hard on top of Jeffy's head. The twins cooed and shuffled together like pigeons. Joe continued to the kitchen, not saying a word. Sherri hovered, her mouth made a pop as he passed, and she finally said, "For god's sake, Joe, you're wet!"

Then Joe saw him. The old man, sitting at the table. Joe said nothing, but went over to the refrigerator and pulled out a beer. He imagined himself saying, "Watch how to drown your sorrows, old man. If you even have sorrows." But instead, his mind went blank, and he held the cold bottle in his hand, trying to think of what came next. Sherri swooped open a drawer and quickly pulled out a bottle opener. He opened the bottle and took a gulp.

Part of him wanted to say he felt glad he was alive. Part of him wanted to tell Sherri that he swam out to save Rosea, then decided not to and swam home. But he couldn't.

Sherri waited for an explanation.

"I fell in the water," he said simply.

Sherri moved closer. "What water? Where did you go?"

"The beach."

"The beach? We would have gone with you."

Joe didn't answer and took another drink.

The old man shifted in his chair but didn't take his eyes off him.

Joe felt a bite of bitterness. "Hey, velho, I bet you notice I'm wet, too."

Melvinor wavered a bit, then said, "You didn't fall into the water; you jumped in. And you jumped in because you wanted to drown."

Joe slammed the bottle down hard on the table, and beer erupted out of the top. "Cala a boca! You stupid old man!"

"Joe!" Sherri cried.

Joe wiped the foam from his chin and hurled the bottle into a corner; it hit the wall with a clatter, the rest of the foam spilling from the neck. "Stop thinking you know things about me! You know nothing!"

"Joe! Slow down!" Sherri cried.

Joe didn't care; he lunged at the old man and grabbed his shirt collar. The blue vein on the old white neck fluttered. "You are not part of this family!" Joe yelled and gave him a jerk. "You hear! You cannot be over here a hundred times a day!" He felt Sherri hovering, peeping, pecking at him with pleas and pleases. Joe brushed her away with his foot and grabbed Melvinor's shirt harder and tried to lift him, but the old man would not get up, stayed sitting, making himself damn heavy. Sherri pulled on Joe's arm, crying, shrieking. Joe ignored her and shouted into the old man's face, trying to drill the words through his skull. "I don't want you over here! This is my family! I am the man here!"

Joe let Melvinor go and hurled himself at his wife. "Either I'm the husband or he is! You can't have it both ways! Choose! If you choose him, next time I *will* drown!"

"Joe, of course you're the husband, but what is all this about drowning? Did you try to drown yourself, Joe?"

"There are some people in this world that need to be killed! Some people could use a gun shoved down their throat!" Joe didn't know if he was shouting at him or at her.

"Stop that! I'll have my friends over if I want! At least I'm not sleeping around like someone else I know!"

Joe snatched both her arms and shook her. "I am not sleeping around! I am not drowning!" He heard his voice catch, and he gave a small whimper. Sherri's small lips moved, and the lower lip pushed out a bit, defiantly. "You hear me?" He shook her again and saw her blue eyes snap shut.

Everything was crying around him. The kids threw their small bodies against them, bumping their foreheads on Joe and Sherri's knees, their wails so loose and wide. Melvinor got up and dug his fingers into Joe's shoulders, trying to pull him away from Sherri.

"Leave me alone!" Joe cried, still hanging onto his wife, "don't take her away from me! Don't take her away, God." Melvinor slipped away, and the twins fell on their seats and cried, yet the noise seemed far away. Joe took a deep breath and quietly smelled the grilled-meat odor on her shirt, then sniffed at her neck for a tingle of sauce, hanging on to her so she wouldn't run over to the old man. "Sherri," he said. "I'm sorry. I'm sorry, Sherri. I'm so sorry."

She held onto him and soft-voice kissed his neck with sweetness.

"Sinto muito," he whispered into her ear, "tenho medo." I am afraid of what comes next.

excerpt from

If I Die in Juárez

Stella Pope Duarte

11

Ofelia's husband was not home when Petra's family arrived in Juárez on a cold damp Saturday morning. Petra noticed the air was hazy, as if there was a cloud of smoke over the city. Traffic on the busy streets sounded like the rushing of water to her ears, so used to the silence of mountains and deserts. She tried to shake off the fear that had spiraled inside her when Tío Alvaro's car had rounded the corner of the highway into Juárez. Something had happened to her that she couldn't explain to anyone. An unknown *something* was hanging in the air, suspended, threatening, and it made her shiver and rub her arms with her hands for warmth.

Ofelia was standing at the window and pulled aside the curtain, peeking out at them. In the gray morning, she was only a shadow seen for a few seconds before she opened the door. She was wearing a long dress, with socks and huaraches, and her gray, windblown hair fell to her shoulders. She had draped a flannel shawl over her shoulders, plaid with bright colors, red, green, purple. Flor opened the car door and ran into Ofelia's arms, and the two women hugged and cried, holding onto each other tightly. Estevan couldn't sit up and had to wait for Tío Alvaro to help him out of the backseat, looping arms with Petra for support.

"We're here, Papi, we're here. Ofelia's house! Everything will be all right."

Her father mumbled something that Petra couldn't understand. Ester and Nico woke up and climbed out of the car, yawning and stretching their legs, staring at everything in amazement. Estevan got out of the car and walked balanced between Flor and Tío Alvaro, with Ofelia rushing ahead, her old huaraches flapping on her feet, leading them up three stone steps and into a small entryway to the front door. Petra looked at the house and wondered how they would all fit inside. Then she looked down the narrow dirt road, crowded with houses and storefronts, and thought of the desolate roads leading to Montenegro, with only a few scattered ranches in sight and with horses and livestock competing at times with cars for use of the road.

Ofelia had a room prepared for Estevan at the back of the house, bare except for a bed, an old wooden dresser, and a kitchen chair. From the kitchen, Petra smelled coffee brewing, fresh tortillas, and chorizo with eggs cooking on the stove, and suddenly she felt as if she was starving and remembered that none of them had eaten since they had left Montenegro.

Flor and Alvaro led Estevan to the bed. Flor asked for a glass of water, giving it to her husband so he could take more aspirin and antibiotics, which he swallowed in one gulp. Petra watched as her father closed his eyes and lay wearily on his side in the fetal position that had become customary. Then he startled everyone by opening his eyes wide and staring at his wife, grabbing her hand, and holding on until his fingers turned white.

"Flor, promise me, if I die in Juárez, you'll bury me in Montenegro."

Flor searched her husband's face, then lowered her head.

"Did you hear me?"

"Stop talking about death! We're in Juárez now. You'll see a doctor, you'll get well."

"I won't let you go until you promise me. Why are you so hardheaded! Caprichosa! Promise me!" The whites of Estevan's eyes had turned yellow, and his face showed the bony ridges of his cheeks. Flor looked at him in fear, knowing this was her husband's death wish. "And you, Petra," he demanded, staring hard at his daughter, "convince your mother—if I die in Juárez . . ."

"Papi, por favor!" Petra said, tears starting, as her father's passionate plea reached them all.

"I promise you," Flor said, lacing her fingers gently through her husband's hand. "Te prometo."

Estevan smiled, something he hadn't done in months. He could already see his grave and himself resting peacefully under the huge cottonwood trees in el camposanto close to their ranch.

He turned his face toward the wall. "I'll feel better once I rest," he said, gasping for breath. The walk into Ofelia's house had wearied him. Flor covered him over with a blanket and patted his shoulder gently. There was a look of relief on her face in spite of Estevan's wish for death. She knew there were doctors in Juárez, hospitals. Tomorrow something would be done for him.

As everyone sat down at the kitchen table to eat and drink coffee, Prospero walked in. He was still boisterous from a night of drinking, his clothes and hair disheveled, his belt hanging loosely at his waist. He reeked of the smell of hard liquor—tequila, cigarettes, and an unwashed body. He pulled off his tattered jacket and walked in confident that Ofelia would not fight with him in front of her family.

"Compadre!" he shouted as he clapped Alvaro on the back. "How long has it been since I've seen you? Too long, too long. But here you are in the flesh. And your hair—what happened to your hair? You're bald!"

"It happens to the best of us," Alvaro said. And both men laughed, clapping one another on the back again in a gesture of affection.

Prospero turned to Flor. "Flor, I swear you get younger by the year!" Flor got up from her chair and Prospero hugged her, though Petra could tell her mother wished he wouldn't. She pulled away politely as Prospero looked around at all of them. Meanwhile, Ofelia ignored him and served everyone more coffee and small glasses of orange juice.

"Somebody needs a bath," she said loudly.

"No!—a kiss!" Prospero said playfully. He tried to kiss Ofelia, but she turned away in disgust.

Prospero looked at Petra. "This can't be Petra!" he said, staring at her in amazement. Petra was standing with Ofelia at the stove, warming tortillas. Prospero rushed toward her and grabbed her in his arms, making the warm tortilla in her hand tumble to the floor. He lifted her up slightly as he hugged her, and Petra felt his arms around her back, bony yet strong. She was conscious of her breasts pressing against his chest and pulled away.

"This can't be the little girl who used to visit us and always wanted a paleta. She could never get enough ice cream!"

Everyone laughed. "You can have all you want here in Juárez," he told her, holding her hands. "What a beauty! I would lock her up for safety and throw away the key!" Everyone laughed, and Petra felt herself blushing.

"Ya, Prospero, you're embarrassing Petra," Ofelia said. "She's a young lady now, not a child."

"Of course, you're right." He released Petra and turned his attention to Ester and Nico. "And these two fine-looking children? Don't tell me they belong to you Flor? No, it can't be!"

He hugged the children and kissed them on the cheek. Petra noticed that Nico smirked slightly but allowed Prospero's kiss. Flor watched Nico sternly for any signs of disrespect.

"You don't know this viejo, because you weren't born when I last saw your mother and father. A beautiful family, don't you think so Ofelia? We should have had more children, hundreds of children, not just two. And now they're old and married and never visit us." He frowned as he looked at his wife.

"Don't tell me what we should have done," Ofelia said. "You should have been here last night; worry about yourself." Tension rose in the room like an electric current. Tío Alvaro put an end to it as quickly as he could.

"Estevan's also here," he said, "and glad you've opened your door to him, sick as he is. We're all grateful to you and Ofelia."

"Where is he?" Prospero asked, his bloodshot eyes softening. "My heart aches for him, and for any man who is so ill he can't provide for his family. God knows, a man has to provide. I've had my share of illness, and my poor wife has helped me through the bad times."

Ofelia received her husband's compliment in peace.

"We've helped each other," she said. "La lucha, always, the battle to live is before us."

Tío Alvaro walked with Prospero as he moved unsteadily to the back room to greet Estevan. Flor followed. From the kitchen, Petra heard Prospero's shout as he greeted her father and then his loud sobbing as he saw Estevan's condition. Ester and Nico sat quietly at the table, their food untouched.

"Eat," Petra told them. "Drink your juice." She felt tears run down her cheeks.

"He was always so strong, your father, so handsome," Ofelia said.

Petra looked out the small living room window at the street in front of Ofelia's house. The day had begun. There were people and cars passing by. The houses across the street were built one after another, some with iron grills around their windows and doors. It was strange for her not to see the open spaces of Montenegro and the blue sky overheard.

Very quickly, Petra found out that nothing would be as Ofelia had said. Her house was so small, they couldn't all stay with her. Ofelia said the problem had been resolved, as one of their cousins who lived in a colonia nearby had said she would help out. Petra and Nico would stay with Brisa Reynosa, Ofelia's comadre.

Ofelia talked privately to Flor and Petra while the children and the men were helping unload the car.

"I'm madrina to Brisa's daughter. You remember your cousin Evita, don't you Petra?"

"Yes, of course. We played together when we were children." Petra remembered holding Evita's hand, running in and out of the house, twirling and playing together. Twins, Evita would say. She wanted them to be twins.

"And her mother, Brisa?" Ofelia asked.

"Brisa?" Flor frowned. "I never got along with Brisa. Wasn't she a drinker? She's from my father's side of the family, and some say she was adopted by one of my aunts and nobody ever knew who her father was. I remember her—a talker, chismosa, and nobody could stand her."

"Well, that's true, but she's changed. Why, just the other day she was here, crying over Evita. Evita's had problems with her mother and has run away from home several times. She's supposed to be at her sister Lety's house, but no one knows if she's really there at all. I tell her not to be out on the streets, but she doesn't listen. It's dangerous for women with all the violence in Juárez."

"This city's always been violent," Flor said. "That's nothing new."

"Yes, and now more than ever. They've uncovered the bodies of women, raped and murdered—young women, left out in the desert to rot. And of course, no one is talking."

Flor put one finger to her lips, looking in the direction of the room where Estevan was resting, and she leaned toward Ofelia.

"Please, I don't want Estevan to know too much about all this. He knows Juárez is violent, but if he knows details of all that's happening, he'll make us leave—and you know we can't go back! He'll die on the way, and I—"

Ofelia interrupted her, putting one hand gently on her arm. "I know. Of course, we'll keep as much as we can from him."

Petra looked at Ofelia, fear in her eyes. "Don't worry," Ofelia whispered, "they say the girls were prostitutes, living a double life, ya sabes, working during the day, then at night running around in bars, I'm sure without their parents' permission. Decent girls are safe."

Then she told them that one of Brisa's children was born an albino but had died when he was only two years old, drowned in a bucket of water. It was truly a tragedy for Brisa.

"I still have the story from *El Diario* about him, if you'd like to see it. She has another son, Reynaldo, but he rarely comes to Juárez. He works in el otro lado, in El Paso, and doesn't stay long when he visits. I've already spoken to Brisa, and she says Petra and Nico can stay in Evita's room."

Ofelia didn't tell them about Brisa's new man, Alberto. She was afraid Flor wouldn't let Petra stay at Brisa's, thinking the man would be a danger to her daughter. Nico could stay with Petra—he was twelve years old, and that would be a protection for her. Ofelia felt bad for her cousin, but there was nothing she could do. She had little money and no room for them.

Flor seemed to be spinning in circles, talking rapidly, moving quickly, clearing the dishes away from the table, washing them, sweeping. She was already nervous about staying with Ofelia, and it was worse now that she knew Prospero was a drunk. She'd be separated from Petra and Nico, even though Ofelia told her Brisa's colonia was only twenty minutes away by car and less than an hour by rutera. As she repacked a suitcase, taking out items that belonged to her, she leaned close to Petra.

"As soon as we start working in la maquiladora, we'll start saving money," she whispered. "You'll see, mija, we'll have plenty, and we'll get us a house. A room for you—all by yourself—and dresses, new shoes." She looked deeply into her daughter's eyes and saw her fear. Petra wanted to grab her mother in her arms and cry, plead for them to go back to Montenegro.

"Watch Nico," her mother said. "Take care of each other at Brisa's. If there are any problems, call me. It's not far from here. I'll be there every day if I can. And I'll find out what school Nico and Ester will go to. I have some money for their uniforms and books. Your abuela gave me some money she had saved up."

When Petra heard Abuela Teodora mentioned, her throat ached and tears surfaced.

"Don't cry Petra. Gustavo Rios will keep his promise to get us work."

The mention of Gustavo Rios sent a shiver through Petra's body. At any moment she expected him to walk through the door with information on Western Electronics and when to report for work. In the next room, they heard Prospero arguing with Ofelia over his clothes not being ironed. They heard something thump on the floor and found out later that he had thrown the iron at Ofelia because she didn't have his clothes ironed and ready for him. Flor looked up at the ceiling, her eyes closed, and whispered a prayer.

"Tomorrow," she said, "your father will be seen by a doctor at the hospital. Pray that he'll get well."

As Flor embraced her, Petra smelled her mother's hair. It smelled like the shampoo they bought in Montenegro, inexpensive yet perfumed with various fragrances. Her mother's favorite was a sweet lemony smell, and suddenly Petra felt herself a child again, sleeping with her mother in bed, one arm looped over her back, her nose buried in her mother's fragrant hair.

Tío Alvaro drove Petra and Nico in his car to Brisa's house. Once on the street, Petra was conscious of everything. It was as if she was floating everywhere. There was so much to see, people walking, a small band of musicians playing at the corner, food stands with smoke curling up from grills packed with carne asada and vegetables. There were children, some riding on old bikes, two and three to a bike. People called to each other from one side of the street to the other. There was a vendor walking slowly down the street with a cart filled with drinks for sale—soda pop, juice, and paletas—with the name *Mi Amigito* painted boldly in bright blue letters. Men gathered at street corners talking, smoking cigarettes, and staring at them as they drove slowly by looking for Brisa Reynosa's house in la colonia Quinto Sol.

Brisa was as old as Ofelia but dyed her hair black. She pulled it back behind her ears in a short bun held together by a hairpin decorated with rhinestones, and wore slacks, a flowered blouse, and black pointed shoes. She greeted them politely, and Petra picked up the fragrance of the perfume she was wearing—sweet, almost like candy, maybe meringue. She was light-skinned, and in spite of the wrinkles on her face Petra could see that she had once been a very attractive woman. She said she was delighted to have them stay with her, as they were all family and should always help one another.

"Come in, please, make yourselves at home." She helped Tío Alvaro bring in their bags, even though Petra told her Nico could help.

"But you're my guests," she said. "I'm at your service." She smiled sweetly, and Petra noticed her teeth had been worked on by a dentist many times. There were silver fillings in almost every tooth, reminding her of the mines in Montenegro. So, this was one of the things they sold the silver for, to fill holes in teeth like those in Brisa's—her father's life hanging in the balance because of holes in people's teeth.

"Is Evita here?" Petra asked her.

"Oh, that one! She's at her sister's house. You'll stay in her room. It won't be any problem. Evita comes and goes, and most of the time she's gone."

Brisa was especially attentive to Tío Alvaro and offered him coffee and cookies. She served coffee to him at a small round table set in front of a sofa and brought Nico and Petra glasses of lemonade. She arranged small sugar cookies on a glass dish: triangles, squares, rectangles, and circles. The sofa was vinyl and the seats worn, but it was still in good shape. There were fancy pillows set up on the couch, crocheted beautifully in bright colors—blue, yellow, orange, and purple. Glancing underneath the table, Petra noticed a small carpet with designs that looked oriental. She had never seen a rug that looked oriental and studied the designs closely.

"Nice, isn't it?" Brisa said, noticing Petra staring at the carpet. "I got it from a Chinese family I worked for. They owned their own store, and I helped sew for them. They liked me so much they gave me the rug as a gift. Now I run my own business, sewing bedspreads and tablecloths, even those pillows you're leaning on. Some of my things sell for lots of money, but by the time the money gets to me, it's almost gone from the shops taking their cut and everybody wanting something. Rich people can afford the best. There are rich people in Juárez. You know that, don't you Alvaro?"

"Oh, yes, very rich people. Those who own the poppy fields that produce heroin, for example, that sells around the world for billions of dollars, not to mention la marijuana—that's been around since the world began. A weed, can you imagine—meant by God, I'm sure, to be used for good and not for evil."

Brisa said every word was true. Drugs ruled the world, and those who fell into their power were bound to end in destruction. Of course, drinking was a part of life, she said. A drink here, a drink there, never hurt anybody. She told Petra and Nico to sit on the sofa next to Tío Alvaro and pulled up a kitchen chair across from them, smiling and making jokes, laughing with Petra and Nico and serving Tío Alvaro another cup of coffee. Petra and Nico snacked on the cookies and laughed, trying one of each shape, and all the while Petra was thinking that staying at Brisa's might be good for them after all. She watched Nico enjoying the cookies and Tío Alvaro talking with Brisa about the stupidities of the Mexican government and the hopeless condition of the people in Mexico.

"We need another Benito Juárez," he said. "We need a revolution to rid ourselves of the rich once and for all. The soul, you know, does not feed on money, not at all! It lives on truth and hope, faith and love."

"Beautifully said!" Brisa told him, and she smiled broadly, the silver in her mouth gleaming.

Then, Tío Alvaro got serious, asking Brisa what she knew about all the violence going on in the city.

"Do you mean the murders?"

"Of course, I mean the murders. I saw the story in *El Diario* about the two young girls murdered and found in el Lote Bravo. The man I met in Montenegro, Gustavo Rios, promised my sister and Petra jobs at one of las maquiladoras, but he never mentioned anything about the murders. Now, I'm wondering if this was all a big mistake, and we should all go back to Montenegro. I tell you, if Estevan knew about all this, he'd make us go back tonight, sick as he is and almost dying."

"Oh, no, there's no need for you to go back! I know it's very frightening, and no one is safe. But it's always been that way in Juárez. La policia know more than they tell us. And money silences everyone, las mordidas. But women must also find ways to protect themselves and not put themselves in danger. It's girls who run on the streets that get themselves in trouble."

"I heard the girls who were murdered were maquiladoras—they worked at an American factory."

"It is believed they were—unless they were leading a double life and spending time at night at the cabarets."

Petra looked intently at Tío Alvaro as he discussed the murders with Brisa. When he turned to her, his eyes softened. "Don't be afraid, Petra. If it's all that bad, I'll take you back to Montenegro tonight."

"Don't be afraid for her, Alvaro. Really it's girls who run away from home who fall into the murderers' hands. I tell my daughter, Evita, to stay home, and does she obey me? Absolutely not! I worry day and night that someday they'll find her body—God forbid!" Brisa made the sign of the cross over herself and shuddered. "I tell you, Alvaro, I have no way to control my own daughter."

"Estevan won't rest once he hears this. I'm sure he'll find out what's going on here, very soon," Alvaro said, shaking his head.

"The girl from across the street, Yvone, works in one of las maquiladoras," Brisa explained, trying to lift the sense of doom that had descended on Petra. "Petra can go to work with her. If she always walks with someone else, and tells someone where she's going, she should be perfectly safe. She isn't the type of girl to go off in the middle of the night—are you, Petra?"

"No, of course not. My parents don't allow me any freedom, and besides, I would never go out alone at night."

"And that's so wise! I only wish my daughter was as obedient as you are! And, besides all that, you have your brother here for protection—right, Nico?"

Nico sat up straight in his chair. "You can count on me!" he announced. Petra reached over and put her arm over her brother's shoulder.

"Said like a real man!" Tío Alvaro said. "Nico will keep an eye on Petra, qué no, mijo?" Nico nodded.

Brisa stood up and put her hand on Tío Alvaro's shoulder. "Alvaro, you're welcome to come back at any time."

Petra could tell that Tío Alvaro was suddenly uncomfortable with Brisa's offer and the attention she was giving him. She wondered if her mother was right. Maybe Brisa had been adopted and wasn't their cousin at all.

"Gracias for the invitation, but I have a friend who lives here. He has only a shack, but I can share it when I come to Juárez. I have to go back to Montenegro tomorrow morning. I run the Gonzalez ranch in Montenegro, and it's big, with acres of land, cattle, and crops to harvest."

"But you'll be back won't you?" Brisa's eyes narrowed, then became huge again. She turned her head to one side, almost as if she was a young girl flirting with Alvaro. He stood up and laughed, which was his way of ending anything uncomfortable.

"Oh yes! My sister, Susana, has a phone in Montenegro, and Petra here knows the number. If anything goes wrong, any little thing whatsoever, I can be reached through my sister. And of course, I'll be back to check on Estevan's condition. The poor man needs medical attention as quickly as he can get it."

Then he put his hand in his pocket and took out money and handed it to Brisa. She refused it, and he insisted. She refused again, even though it was obvious she wanted the money. When he insisted again, she finally accepted the money, saying it wasn't necessary, not at all. Then she reached over and hugged Alvaro tenderly, as if he was a son she was saying goodbye to.

On his way out of the house, Alvaro wiped his forehead as if to wipe away sweat and whispered to Petra, "I'm glad I'm not staying here! That woman is a flirt!" He held Petra's hand tightly. "You heard, Petra. Absolutely do not ever walk out on the streets alone—and of course, never at night. Take Nico with you every chance you get."

Petra held onto Alvaro's hand as they walked out, feeling his warmth, the calluses on his hands, hard and dry. It seemed to Petra as if she was letting go of Montenegro completely when she let go of Tío Alvaro's hand. She had not known what he meant to her until she had to say good-bye. Then she knew she'd miss his kindness, his funny stories and jokes.

Alvaro sensed Petra's fear, saw her tears, and put his arm around her. "Petra, all will be good. Any problems, call me. Yes?" He lifted her face in his hands and brushed her tears away. She wanted to tell him to greet Antonio for her—tell him she was already dying in Juárez without him. As if reading her mind, Alvaro said, "And don't worry about Antonio. If he really loves you, he'll wait."

Brisa directed Petra and Nico to the room they'd share. It was cold and damp, and Brisa had stripped it of everything except the furniture. She didn't want anything to remind her of Evita, she said. There was a chipped dresser in one corner with a mirror and a closet where Brisa said they could hang their clothes. Nico could sleep on the floor until Flor was able to buy him a cot he could use. She'd give him an extra blanket, she said, but no pillow, because she had no other pillows except the ones on the sofa, and they were decorations, not to be used as real pillows.

"You're from a ranch," she said, "and I know you don't have things like this out there. But you'll get used to it. This is the city, and we try to keep our houses looking nice, even if we are poor."

Petra was surprised to hear an edge in Brisa's voice, as if she was mocking them. She wanted to tell her that Abuela Teodora crocheted beautifully and had made them bedspreads and sweaters and all kinds of doilies for tables and chairs, but decided Brisa didn't want to hear what she had to say.

"Oh, and Nico, you dropped some cookie crumbs on the carpet, so get the broom and sweep them up. I fight cockroaches here every day, and it won't help if you leave crumbs for them to eat." She looked sternly at Nico, and he hesitated, not knowing what to do.

"Did you hear me?"

"Yes," Nico said. "And I'm sorry about the crumbs." Petra could tell Nico was afraid of her.

Brisa ignored his apology. "Well, what are you waiting for? I tell you, children of today need to be told over and over again, when everything's so simple. But then, of course, you are from a ranch. You've never learned how to do things the right way." Petra stood behind Nico and put her hand on his shoulder. She sensed her brother's back stiffen. They both looked at Brisa in silence.

"Now, what's this? The two vagabonds looking at me like they don't have to do what I say." Her face turned into a dark scowl, and she raised her voice and pronounced each word, as if spitting it out of her mouth.

"Get the broom! Are you that ignorant?" She saw Petra's face go red with anger.

"Angry, Petra? Already? And what will you do? Tell your sick father, and your mother—and worry them?" Then she turned her back on them.

"If Evita comes back, tell her you now have her room," she said, and walked out of the house without another word.

Close to midnight, Brisa came home with a man. As they stumbled in, Petra heard his voice, loud and angry. His name was Alberto. She knew this because Brisa called him by his name many times, trying to quiet him, but he wouldn't listen and continued to argue with her.

"No!" he said. "It wasn't that way at all. I should have killed him was what I should have done. I owe him nothing!"

"You owe him nothing, but he'll charge you anyway. You idiot—you know what that means!"

They argued back and forth about someone Alberto was fighting with. After several minutes, their voices turned to mumbling and the sound of muffled laughter. Petra heard Brisa's bedroom door shut with a bang. Then there was silence.

She looked up at the ceiling, watching dark shadows appear. The crouching figures on the mountains of Montenegro had followed her to Juárez. She stared at them, comforted, and drifted off to sleep.

12

Petra woke before the sun rose, feeling as if she hadn't slept at all with all the trouble at Brisa's. Her body had recorded the early morning hours of Montenegro, and she couldn't go back to sleep, even if she had wanted to. Abuela Teodora's voice spoke in her mind, *Sing, Petra, sing to the morning.* She looked out the window and discovered that Evita's bedroom faced west, not east. She couldn't see the rising sun unless she went out the front door and found a place where she could look east. She watched the room's shadow's turn from dark to gray in the early dawn and whispered the ancient song to herself.

Iwéra rega chukú kéti Ono
Mápu tamí mo nesériga ináro sinibísi rawé
Ga'lá kaníliga bela ta semáribo
Si'néame ka o'mána wichimoba eperéame
Népi iwérali bela ta ásibo
Kéti ono mápu tamí neséroga ináro ne

Né ga'lá kaníliga bela ta narepabo
Uchécho bilé rawé mápu kéti Onó nijí
Ga'lá semá rega bela ta semáripo
Uchécho bilé rawé najata je'ná wichimobachi
Népi ga'lá iwérali bela ko nijísibo
Si'néame ka mápu ikí ta eperé je'ná kawírali

Uchécho bilé rawé bela ko ju
Mápu rega machiboo uchécho si'nú ra'íchali
Uchécho bilé rawé bela ko ju
Mápu ne chapiméa uchécho si'nú 'nátali
Népi iwéraga bela 'nalína ru
Uchúpa ale tamojé si'néame pagótami

Echiregá bela ne nimí wikaráme ru
Mápu mo tamí nesériga chukú sinibísi rawé
Echiregá bela ne nimí iwérali ásima ru
Mápu ketási mo sewéka inárima siníbisi rawé
Népi iwériga bela mo nesérima ru
Mápu ikí uchúchali a'lí ko mo alewá aale.

✳   ✳   ✳

Be strong father sun,
you who daily care for us.
Those who live on earth are living well.
We continue giving strength to our father,
who fills our days with energy and light.

With great joy we salute our father
with one more day of life.
We are living well following one more day on earth
as you light our way.

One more day to learn new words,
one more day to think new thoughts,
giving you strength you in turn
give energy to your brothers.

Thus I will sing
to you who daily care for me.
Thus will I give you strength
so you will not be discouraged.
With all your strength
care for those you have created
and given the breath of life.

Petra thought first of her father, wondering if he had his appointment
to see the doctor. Next, she thought of Abuela Teodora, who at this early
hour must be getting the stove ready to make breakfast for Susana and the
children. Antonio should be getting up at this very moment and getting
ready to go to church. She had put the ring he had given her in the pocket
of one of her jeans, still in her suitcase. Someday they'd be married, and
she'd wear it on their wedding day.

Petra's head and stomach ached, nerves she thought, from being angry
with Brisa for talking to her and Nico as if they were idiots. She walked
quietly to the bathroom that smelled of sewage and found out the toilet
wasn't working and the shower was nothing more than a box constructed
of moldy wood and broken tiles. A trickle of water came out of the fau-
cet at the sink when she tried to wash her face. Seeking another toilet,

she walked out into the backyard, where there was an outhouse next to a shack. Rushing into the outhouse, she latched the door, all the while thinking that at any moment Brisa, or her lover, would come pounding on it.

In the kitchen, Petra couldn't find anything she could cook for breakfast. The cabinets were bare except for cans of food and sacks of beans, flour, and sugar. She was wondering where Brisa kept everything else when Alberto walked into the kitchen. He was a fat man with a heavy dark moustache. He reminded Petra of a homeless person, with his hair stuck to the side of his head and his legs still unsteady from last night's drinking.

"I didn't know Brisa had angels living with her," he said. "And to think, she didn't tell me."

Petra walked past him and back to her room, sensing him staring after her.

"I'm not good enough for you, am I? I imagine a queen like you would be used to a king!" Then he laughed and grabbed a bottle of liquor and poured himself a drink.

Petra heard Brisa yelling for him and telling him to mind his own business and get out of the kitchen. Alberto only laughed louder, taking another drink.

Nico was up, and Petra told him to get dressed so they could go out to buy a cup of coffee and get something to eat. Petra got a jacket for Nico and a sweater for herself, to keep them warm in the cold morning. When they walked out, Petra noticed an old pickup truck parked along the side of the narrow street across from Brisa's house. It was painted bright orange except for its rusty hood, which looked like it had been added to the truck after it was painted. Two men were sitting in the back of the truck and two more were standing outside by the cab door, smoking. The two men outside the truck puffed on cigarettes and laughed. One pounded his thigh in a sudden burst of laughter. Petra was conscious of them as she and Nico got closer, and she held Nico's hand tighter, remembering all the talk about the murders. There were other people on the street, two children and a woman with a child at her hip. All of them were hurrying along, bundled up in coats, sweaters, and shawls. A car turned a corner and sped by, the music from its radio blaring. The driver of the car shouted at the two men standing by the cab of the truck, and one of them, the one who laughed the loudest, chased the car for a short distance and then returned.

"Idiota! Someday he'll run over somebody, and I for one will be there to give him a good beating." The man stood in the middle of the street, then noticed Petra. He whistled through his teeth.

"Finally the neighborhood is looking good! Looks like we have company. My lucky day!"

Petra felt her face turn red and walked faster, but the man hurried to catch up to her and Nico, while the men at the truck commented loudly on her looks.

"I haven't seen anyone that beautiful since Inocenta got married," one of them said. "Now, that was a good-looking woman—but this one is even better looking!" They laughed and passed a cigarette back and forth, cheering their companion on.

"Ándale, Luis, let's see what you can do."

The man quickly caught up to Petra and stood at her side. He was stocky and muscular and wore a blue baseball cap, which he pushed up over his eyes to look at her. She noticed the man's cheeks were red and raw, dry skin showing in places where his skin was peeling.

The man shifted from one leg to another, awkwardly, as if trying to keep his balance. He was polite, apologetic. "Forgive me, señorita, but I believe I'm your neighbor—that is, if it's true that you have arrived in Juárez to live in this God-forsaken colonia. Are you the people from Montenegro?" Petra nodded and looked into his eyes. She sensed that he wanted to please her. There was a shyness about the man as he stood in front of her as if he was her servant. It soothed her to know he genuinely wanted her approval.

"A sus órdenes," he said. "I'm at your service. My name is Luis Ledezma." He shook first Petra's hand, politely, then Nico's. "It's rare that we have someone who is, how shall I say, as beautiful to look at as you are señorita, and please forgive me if I'm offending you."

When Nico looked hard at Luis, Luis teased him. "Don't worry, hermanito; I'll mind my manners!" His courtesy and humbleness moved Petra. "No, of course, you're not offending me," she said. "I'm here, it's true, to stay with la Señora Brisa Reynosa for the time being. I'm here to work in las maquiladoras."

"Ah, sí, you and hundreds of others. Is Montenegro close to Chitlitipin?"

"Very close."

"Ah, well, that's far, over four hundred miles away. So I suppose you won't be going back soon. I'm also from a village, not too far from

Montenegro, but I've been here since I was a boy. And your name, señorita, if I may be so bold."

"My name is Petra de la Rosa, and this is my brother, Nico."

Luis put his hand up to his heart, as if he had just heard a poem. "A beautiful name, señorita—yes, music to my ears. A pleasure, señorita, a great pleasure to meet you. And welcome to la colonia Quinto Sol."

Petra smiled when he said the name, remembering Abuela Teodora had told her they were living in the era of el Quinto Sol, which would end in earthquakes. She wondered if Luis knew the story.

"You like the name?" he asked.

"Yes, I do. It's ancient. It belongs to the world of our ancestors."

"Oh that, yes, it goes back to the Aztecs." He smiled broadly, happy to have impressed her with la colonia's name.

"If I can be of service to you, señorita, I know this place. I have sisters, cousins, who can also assist you. There are also friends."

"Gracias, Luis, for your kindness, and certainly we will be calling on you if we need to." Then she asked, "Do you know anything about my cousin, Evita?"

"Evita? Yes, I saw her the other night."

"How is she? I've heard it's dangerous here, and I—"

Luis interrupted her. "You musn't worry for Evita. She knows how to take care of herself. Her mother's always fighting with her over one thing or another. But don't concern yourself with these things," he said, smiling. "I'm here if you need me."

Then Petra asked him to tell her where she and Nico could get something to eat, and he walked with her the distance of the street and pointed to a stand nearby with hot coffee for sale and burritos. She asked him for a church close by, and he pointed to the east, telling her that only three streets away she would encounter la Capilla de la Ascención. They had services there—not big ones, but simple ones, twice on Sundays.

Petra looked at Luis, waiting for what would happen next. She asked him if he would like something to eat, and immediately he realized he was intruding on her breakfast.

"Of course not! Señorita, forgive my bad manners. There's no need to buy me a thing."

Luis's companions at the pickup truck whistled for him noisily and called out to him, telling him to shake himself away from the vision and give them a ride back to town. Luis excused himself, apologizing for taking up her time, telling her his companions had no manners and would she please forgive them for being so crude? She nodded and smiled, feeling lucky she was talking to him and not to the other men. Luis walked back down the street, climbed into the driver's seat, and started the pickup's engine, driving slowly past Petra and Nico. The men sitting in the back of the pickup laughed and waved good-bye as they drove by, and Petra could hear Luis scolding them, telling them they were all uneducated brutes who had no sense of how to treat decent people. Petra and Nico walked up to the food stand, where the man behind the small counter said, "Don't pay the least bit of attention to any of them, señorita. They're on the streets all the time, making trouble for others." Then he added, "If I may be so bold, may I ask your name?"

Petra told the man her name and asked him for directions to Ofelia's house in la colonia San Fernando. He was more than happy to oblige, describing each step of the way, gesturing with his hands for emphasis. One rutera, he said, then another rutera, and she should be there in less than an hour.

Brisa had coffee brewing on the stove when Petra and Nico returned but didn't bother to tell Petra where she hid the coffee. She was in a better mood, as if she sensed Petra was already making plans to leave as quickly as possible. She invited them to eat breakfast and acted disappointed when Petra told her they had already eaten. Alberto sat at the table drinking coffee, pretending Petra and Nico weren't in the room at all.

Cleotilde, Brisa's neighbor, stopped by to say that Petra's mother had called at her house, wanting to talk to her daughter. Petra's heart raced as she grabbed Nico's hand, and they ran down the street to get to Cleotilde's house, only three houses away. She was thankful the woman had a phone and was worried the call was bad news about her father.

Petra found out from her mother that her father couldn't get into a hospital until Monday morning. She asked Petra how they were doing at Brisa's, and Petra lied to her and said things were going well. Her mother knew the truth—she could hear it in Petra's voice—but she was unable to do anything about it. She only said: "Promise you won't walk out on the streets alone—no matter what—remember there's danger everywhere. We'll be working soon, and we'll go together in las ruteras to la maquiladora. God knows, we both need to work to get us through all this!"

Then she told Petra that Gustavo Rios had stopped by and told her he was almost certain they'd start work at la maquiladora by next week, the same one he had mentioned to them in Montenegro—she couldn't pronounce the name in English. In spite of Petra's distrust of Gustavo Rios, she was relieved that soon they'd be working, and she'd be that much closer to leaving Brisa's house. Flor told Petra that by next week, God willing, Ester and Nico would be attending the school, Primaria Benito Juárez, in San Fernando, Ofelia's colonia. Nico would have to get on las ruteras to go to school every morning, but he was old enough to do it and it shouldn't be a problem.

"And mi papi? How's he feeling?" Petra felt tears surface as she thought of her father curled up in a ball, wrapped in a blanket, suffering intense pain.

"He's noble and brave. He'll be well soon." Flor sighed deeply, and Petra knew the truth—her father would rather die than stay in Juárez. As she walked back to Brisa's with Nico, she sensed herself floating above the dirt road and over la colonia Quinto Sol, which in her mind was a huge puzzle made of tattered, broken pieces, everything confused and sticking out at the wrong ends. Juárez was unreal to her, a chain around her throat, tightening.

Brides and Sinners in El Chuco

Christine Granados

A Scenic Night

Legs up on the dashboard, bare feet making toe prints on the windshield inside a banana-yellow Chevette, Sandra and Yvette giggled, making the car bob up and down. Whenever Sandra got in a fight with Chano about his visiting their three-year-old daughter, Alma, the girls took a trip up to Scenic Drive. They drove up the mountain at least once a week. At night, the view from atop the Franklins always lifted their spirits. They saw where the yellow lights of El Paso stopped and the high glow of the white lights of Juárez began. A perfect line running east and west that divided the two cities and people. In the daytime, the line disappeared, and both cities looked like one looming industrial plant.

"No, seriously, Sandra, if you want to stop the nosebleeds, you have to shove your middle finger up your nose as far as it'll go." Yvette flipped the bird at Sandra, with her chorizo-sized finger.

"Does it have to be Vaseline? Can't you just use crema," Sandra said. "Vaseline is so thick."

"That's the point, it'll coat your nostrils," Yvette slapped her hands on her fat thighs. "If you want your wedding dress ruined when you get a nosebleed, then do it your way. You'll have to pay chingos of money to the photographer to touch up the pictures."

"Whenever I get married, I'm wearing black anyway, so it don't matter," Sandra said.

"You'll pass out from the dehydration before you even make it to the altar." Yvette tapped her foot on the glass in front of her. "You know, I read where some scientists from Cambridge did a study on heat and what it does to the body."

"You read?" Sandra tapped back.

"You're so funny." Yvette's foot tapped faster on the glass. "They found out that the heat can make people crazy."

"Does it even get hot up there?" Sandra's bare feet were still.

"Where?" Yvette said. "What are you talking about?"

"In Cambridge." Sandra squeezed her toes into the window until they were white. "It's in Connecticut or somewhere, right?"

"That's not what matters." Yvette put her legs down. "What the point is, is that they found out that the heat makes people nuts and they can't think straight."

"I believe that. I've seen you around guys and you can't talk, let alone think."

Yvette said, "Ay, it's no use trying to be smart. You're just too dumb. Change the subject."

Sandra lifted an eyebrow. "Remember when I'd give you free drinks at the bar?"

Yvette sat up in the car seat. "Yeah, those were good times."

"I knew it was time to split when the drunks I served started asking me for money to buy beer," Sandra laughed.

"How old were you?" Yvette said, poking the glass in front of her with her big toe.

"I was fifteen. Remember, I lied and told them I was nineteen." Sandra jabbed her foot in the air. "That fucker . . ."

Yvette interrupted, "Who? Chano?"

"No, stop, I don't want to think about him." Sandra sighed. "Steve, Steve, my manager, Steve. He told me I wasn't pretty enough to be hostess. I'd make a better waitress because even though I wasn't too pretty, I wasn't so bad that men didn't want me around."

"And you stayed?" Yvette asked, incredulous. "Why didn't you ever tell me that?"

Sandra shrugged.

Yvette snorted out loud. "I remember your first day. That fat fucker," Yvette sucked air into her mouth so that her cheeks were round, then said in a low voice, "'Sandy, you're going to have to raise that hem line.' The look on your face!"

"I'm so glad you were there. No one would have believed me." Sandra moved the knob on the broken radio.

"I would've." Yvette took Sandra's hand. "Men are capable of anything," Yvette said.

Sandra sang in a falsetto, "But it's above my knees." And she pointed to her legs.

Yvette boomed, "We're trying to sell liquor here, we're not playing ball!"

Both girls laughed and stamped their feet on the windshield. They stopped when they heard a crack. After inspecting the glass for damage, they giggled some more.

"You would have looked so good if you would have just let me hem the shorts up to your butt like I wanted," Yvette said, with her hands in prayer position.

Sandra slapped her best friend's hands, not wanting to read the green letters below her knuckles. "Yeah, it was when I was pregnant with Alma." Sandra pointed to her seat. "But I didn't want my ass all hanging out while I was working. I wouldn't have been able to serve shit thinking about it. I still have the scar from where you poked me with the needle. Sí tú, Miss Seamstress."

The girls slapped at each other then stopped.

When their panting was the only sound in the car, Yvette spoke up. "Why don't we go out?" She pointed toward Mexico.

"We are out." Sandra raised her hands in the air so that her palms faced the windshield. She dropped her hands. "*He'll* be there, and I got to get back and put Alma to bed."

Yvette whispered, "You know your Mom's already got her down. It's Friday, no school tomorrow. Come on, let's just go. We'll go all spontaneous."

Sandra shook her head, then she gripped the steering wheel and looked straight ahead. "All right then, vámonos."

Inside the adobe room, was a blitzkrieg of lights, drinks, chatter, and dancing. The girls had to scream into each other's ears to talk. They sat at the plywood bar, and the bartender poured them drinks without asking what they wanted.

"Red light, green light," he said, then passed the girls a red and a green drink, and he took a yellow one for himself.

Sandra kept one eye on the door, waiting for Chano, and the other one on the dance floor. A man asked Yvette to dance. The minute she stepped onto the dance floor, Yvette nuzzled her pelvis into the man's crotch. He held her waist. Sandra watched Yvette tease the man, who looked like he was about to pass out from all the grinding.

"Your friend likes viejos?" the bartender yelled in Sandra's ear.

"Yeah, I guess we both do," Sandra yelled back.

"Is twenty-five old enough?" The bartender pointed to himself.

"Not old enough," Sandra screamed and looked at the doorway to see who was arriving. She saw Chano walk through the door with a young girl. Sandra spilled her drink. The bartender handed her his white towel.

He leaned over the bar and said, "You know him?"

Sandra nodded and watched Chano pull out a chair for the teenager, who was several years younger than Sandra. He looked up and caught Sandra's eye, then grinned.

She smiled and turned back to the bartender, who used his index finger to tell her to come closer. When Sandra leaned into the bar, he kissed her. She was grateful, sad, and excited. When she opened her eyes after the kiss, Chano was standing next to her. Not looking her way, he just tried to order at the bar.

The bartender slapped his towel down. "You'll have to wait; I'm taking a break." The bartender walked around the bar and took Sandra's hand, then led her toward the door.

Outside Sandra felt nauseated. She stopped and crouched near a truck to put her head down, waiting for the sick feeling to leave. The bartender opened the truck door, lifted Sandra and set her on the seat, then he got in with her. Inside, he pulled her pants down to her knees. Sandra did not resist. She did not move. She did not make a sound. He groped at his pants, found what he was looking for, and then came before he entered her.

Sandra laughed. "You really are a viejo."

"Shut up, bitch," the bartender said pulling up his pants. "That's the last time I do anybody any favors."

"Hey, I didn't mean anything. I'm just playing around. Don't leave."

He opened the truck door, got out, then slammed it shut. It felt like a slap on Sandra's face. She sighed, used a dirty pair of socks on the floorboard to wipe herself off and then pulled up her pants. When she got out of the truck, she saw Yvette scanning the parking lot. Sandra waved.

"Where you been, bitch?" Yvette said. "When I saw Chano, I thought you left me."

"Don't call me that!" Sandra said. "I'd never leave you."

"Huh," Yvette said. "Let's go home, yeah?"

The two girls walked side-by-side. They passed a liquor store and a taco stand, and stepped over men lying on the sidewalk, who smelled like lime and vomit. Nearly at the tollbooth to cross back into El Paso,

Yvette tripped. Sandra caught hold of Yvette's tattooed hand to keep her from falling. She grabbed the tips of Yvette's brown, stubby fingers and squeezed them together. The rings on her own hand scratched, and Sandra wanted to let go, but she kept her grip.

Sandra was there when Yvette got the tattoo on her fingers. She wanted to tell her to stop, but Yvette was so angry, drunk, intent. She watched as Yvette's step-dad defiled and scarred her best friend. The hands that were Sandra's comfort during thirty-six hours of labor were no longer the same. Now, whenever Yvette made a fist, her right hand read F-U-C-K and the left read T-H-E-M. These were the same hands that had touched, poked, prodded, slapped, or caressed Sandra every day of her life since the second grade, except for the two weeks in junior high when Yvette had the chicken pox.

Yvette stayed upright then giggled—her breath a puff of smoke.

Sandra turned her head to look into her friend's hazel eyes—eyes that were lined with her charcoal-colored eyeliner on the inside of the eyelids, and on the outside corners, like Cleopatra.

"These fucking sidewalks, man," Yvette said, the tip of her purple fingernail pointing to the uneven cement.

Sandra nodded her head north, "Yeah, you'd think they'd know how to pave sidewalks, as many of them that work over there."

After a few steps, Sandra let go of Yvette's hand. "That bartender came all over me."

"So that's where you were," Yvette said. "I was wondering."

"I didn't really want to," Sandra said.

"Why'd you go?" Yvette asked. "Nevermind. Stupid question."

"I couldn't stop," Sandra said.

"You really love him?" Yvette said.

Sandra closed her eyes, and tears streamed down from the corners.

"Ay, Sandra you got to stop." Yvette made a fist with one hand. "My step-Dad told me this after my Mom left him, 'You know, chula, some people watch life pass them by y otros, they take life by the balls and squeeze every last seed out of it.' Of course, the motherfucker was leading my hand toward his balls as he was saying it, but I never forgot the meaning."

"I know. I know," Sandra snorted and wiped her eyes. "So which kind are you?"

Yvette showed Sandra the palm of her hands, which were callused and dry from her work at the hotel, scrubbing floor and toilets. "How do you think my hands got this way?"

Their laughter filled the night air. The two girls looked drunk.

"You got a dime?" Yvette pointed to the tollbooth.

"No, just a quarter." Sandra stepped toward the turnstiles and set the quarter on the counter. "I got to go on with my life." A dark hand with grime under the fingernails shot out from underneath the clear plastic window, covered the quarter, the slid it inside.

"How old do you think that girl was?" Yvette ran her nails up Sandra's thin arm.

Sandra shrugged.

"She did look kind of young, no?" Yvette said.

Sandra had goose bumps as she said, "Nooooh! How old was the grandpa you were dancing with?"

"Maybe thirty-five," Yvette said.

"Válgame, Yvette that's almost as old as—" Sandra broke off. She frowned at the man in the tollbooth who was picking a nickel out of a steel box. He put his fat lips on the coin, then stepped outside. Sandra waited for her change. Holding the nickel between his thumb and index finger, the man pressed the coin into Sandra's palm and said, "Wanna come home with me?"

Sandra snapped her hand shut then walked past him.

"How about you?" he looked at Yvette.

Yvette moved the turnstiles with her hips and said, "You wish, viejo!"

He clucked his tongue, which made Sandra cringe and grind her teeth. Every man she had ever met or dated could whistle, cluck, and suck air through his lips louder than the cars they drove with no mufflers, she thought. Yvette's long nails tickled Sandra's back, and she sped up.

"Why do men do that?" Sandra sighed.

"Because they're assholes." Yvette turned back to see the man looking at them. "Plain and simple."

Sandra closed her eyes in disgust. "She must have been thirteen."

"No, I don't think the girl even started yet," Yvette added.

"It might as well have been Alma."

"Don't say that!" Yvette shook her head. "Don't ever say that about your own daughter. Chano's a mamón but he'd never."

"All those fucking Juarenses like 'em young," Sandra said, waving her hand in the air.

Three boys surrounded the girls as they left the turnstiles.

"You got any change?" a boy with a harelip asked.

Sandra said, "What?"

"Hey, baby, got a quarter?" an eight-year-old boy said as he pulled on the hem of Sandra's shirt. "Come on, Miss, give me some money. I'm hungry. I haven't eaten all night."

An older teenage boy, about Sandra's age, stood next to the eight-year-old boy but didn't say a word.

Yvette waded through the rail-thin boys and kept walking. "I hate those dirty—"

"You little shit get away—from—me!" Sandra yelled.

She held the forearm of the eight-year-old behind her, while the older teenager tried to put his hands inside the front pockets of her jeans. Sandra kicked at the teenager as the boy with the harelip cupped her breast. Sandra let go of the eight-year-old, who immediately tried to put his hand back into her pocket. She balled her hands as much as her long nails would allow and shot her fists in front of her, hitting chests, the tops of heads, arms, whatever she found. The boys kicked and punched back. The boy with the harelip had a bloody forehead, cut from one of Sandra's rings. Yvette stepped into the scuffle, grabbed the eight-year-old, and pushed him to the ground. The boy with the harelip tried to get his hands in her pockets, and she slapped him away. The older boy grabbed hold of Yvette's long hair so that she was bowing to get out of his grip. After slapping at him several times, he released her hair. She grabbed one of Sandra's flailing arms and pulled her forward. Sandra stumbled a bit, regained her footing, and like Yvette started to run up the urine-stained sidewalk of the Santa Fe bridge toward El Paso. The boys did not follow but yelled, "¡Putas!"

Sandra and Yvette did not stop running until they made it to the middle of the bridge. Winded, Yvette sat on the concrete marker that showed the boundary between Texas and Mexico. Sandra leaned her backside against a chain-link fence and breathed hard.

"You look like you're smoking," Yvette panted.

"I could use a cigarette about now," Sandra said, rubbing her hands together. "I'm cold."

"Me, too," Yvette looked up at Sandra.

"You'd be warm right now if you had let me bring my jacket, stupid!" Sandra frowned thinking about her windbreaker lying over Alma's crib. The red lipstick Yvette wore, the same color as on Sandra's lips, was smeared across the right side of Yvette's face. Sandra chuckled.

"That ratty jacket don't keep anything warm," Yvette tossed her hand in the air. "Besides, who needs a jacket when we're just going for a cruise?

You probably would have left it somewhere, and right now you'd be dragging my ass back to the other side, and we'd never get home."

"No, those little shits back there would have stolen it!" Sandra pointed south.

Yvette laughed, "Yeah, probably."

"I told them to shut the fuck up and leave me alone," Sandra said.

Yvette put her hands on her hips. "No wonder. Why'd you say that?"

"I don't know," Sandra waved her hand over her head. "I just got sick of 'em, you know?"

"I know." Yvette sat in silence.

The fight near the turnstiles had reminded Sandra of circus clowns. Arms flying everywhere but missing all the other clowns. She always felt that way. Like she could never connect with someone. She had remembered one of those silly painted-faced men coming right up to her and giving her a balloon. It was one of the first things she could ever remember having gotten from a man. It wasn't one of those round balloons but one shaped like a dog, a little curly-haired dog, like rich ladies own. She still had the dog. It was just a long balloon, not any shape now, but she had it tucked away in her Bible under her bed. The balloon and Alma were all men were good for, she thought. Yvette's smeared face struck Sandra as funny, and she laughed. A blast of white smoke shot out of Sandra's mouth, and this made Yvette smile and rub her hands together for warmth.

They both laughed, and they both dabbed underneath their eyes with their middle fingers upwards and out. Yvette made fists and put them together in front of Sandra's face. Sandra looked down, not wanting to see, but mouthed "Fuck them." Sandra and Yvette continued to walk down the bridge and leaned into one another for support.

"Why is it so cold at night?" Yvette rubbed her arms together.

"I read somewhere that these Alaskans did a study and found out that it gets cold here at night so that all people who have gone crazy in the daytime will say, 'El Paso's not so hot,' and stay."

"You read?" Yvette slapped Sandra's arm.

Small Time

These potted palm trees, escalators, staircases, and tiled water fountains are as familiar to me as my own bedroom. It is inside this two-story sanctuary, in line at the lemonade and hot-dog stand, where Mom passes on her secrets. I listen, arms crossed in front of me.

"Pick the men cashiers; they usually don't know what shoes and dresses cost," Mom explains with dramatic hands gestures that everyone in the Davilla family uses. "When the clerk isn't buying it . . ."

". . . ask for the manager. Ya, I get it."

"What's wrong with you, Teresa?" She points at me with the plastic bag she is holding.

After a few moments of silence, I say, "I think I'm going to cut my hair."

"You've got a short neck, and short-necked women should never wear their hair up. It makes them look stubby," Mom says, slapping the underside of my chin with her fingers.

I slip the pencil out of the bun in my hair, and it unravels and falls to my shoulders.

"That looks better. Did you wash your hair? It looks oily, not shiny oily, but dirty oily," Mom says, while brushing strands of hair away from my face. "Ay, mija, with your hair down like that you have to wear more makeup."

"I'm wearing lipstick," I say, pointing to my lips. The gesture is so familiar that I stop and let my hand fall to my side and clap my thigh.

"Yes, I see your lipstick." She pinches my chin with her forefinger and thumb. "I guess you do listen. I can thank God for small favors." She lets go of me, and her hand falls to her side and hits her thigh. "I just have to repeat myself over and over. But, the color—pink? You're twenty-two, not nine. Your lips fade away with that color." She hands me the bag and digs a compact out of her black leather purse to reapply her lipstick. "What would happen if Revlon discontinued it?" she says, pointing the red color at me. "I'll stock up next time."

After buying a lemonade and corn dog, Mom sits on an iron bench to eat. I stand several paces away from her, opening and shutting the bag. A little girl, walking on tiptoes, drops an ice-cream cone nearby. And older woman leads her away by the hand, and the little girl looks back and cries. Seconds later, a man steps in the slush as he bites into a cinnamon roll. A woman in a suit, wearing tennis shoes, swings her arms high and huffs past us.

"You have to sacrifice comfort for beauty," my mother says, laying her food on the bench so she can slip off her new shoes. She places a Band-Aid on her raw heel. "Like I said, make a big escándalo, and they'll take it back just to get you out of the store."

I look down at my tennis shoes—the same kind the woman in the suit was wearing. Mom stands with a sigh, leaves her food on the bench, grabs the bag from my hands, and we take off for the store. Remembering the blisters on her feet, I slow my walking pace. We stroll past boutiques and fine department stores, listening to the Muzak version of "Mandy" over the loudspeakers.

Plastic, soap, and pine fumes attack my nose when we step onto the shining linoleum of the department store. The same crushed velvet couches that are in our living room are somewhere in this store, I think. My brother, Anthony, can do no wrong since the new living room set was delivered. This store brought the loveseat and matching couch right to the house. Anthony had used our cousin's credit card to buy the sofas. When cousin George had put two and two together after coming to our house and sitting on the new furniture, he and my brother got into a fistfight in the front yard. Gravel was scattered everywhere, and George got a raspberry on his cheeks where Anthony used his foot to grind our cousin's face into the ground. Our next-door neighbor had to pull the two apart. He ran barefoot across the rocks that covered our lawn, while Mom and Dad watched. I had made fists with my hands and then opened them, "Come on! You can't be surprised that George is upset. Your son, Anthony, who doesn't have a job, can't just show up at our doorstep with the couches you've been dreaming about since before you were born." I had pointed at my mother. Mom and Dad were silent. They just picked Anthony up off the ground and helped him wipe gravel off of his arms. Since then, my cousin hasn't come to the house.

Mom's pumps clack, and she straightens her round frame and walks to the return desk. There are two people behind the counter, an elderly woman and a young girl. Mom takes a deep breath and heads straight for the young girl. The elderly saleswoman leaves. I hang back, hear steel scrape against chrome, women's voices, and my mother's high-pitched voice.

"Are you telling me I don't know where I bought this dress? Is that what you're telling me?" Mom leans over the counter and shakes the teal dress she has in both her hands. Lupe Davilla will not take no for an answer. "You think I'm stupid?"

"No, ma'am, I never said that. I just wanted to be sure you bought the dress here because, it's just that, this dress looks worn." The tiny, dark-skinned clerk pulls on her nametag, with its big bold orange letters that spell "Esmeralda." The minute the words come out of her mouth, I can tell by the way she steps away from the counter that Esmeralda is sorry she said anything. She reminds me of Anthony when he was six years old, sitting up in bed, trying to keep his eyes open. Afraid. Afraid to sleep because he knew that when he woke up, all the money he had made pulling the weeds that grew between the bright gravel and cactus in people's yards would be gone. Taken in the dark by our mother. My head aches from hunger, the bright lights, and the inescapable smell of plastic.

"Oh, so now you're calling me a liar." Mom jerks the dress off the counter. "I want to talk to your manager."

I cringe. My mother looks radiant. Cheeks flushed. She gets a thrill knowing she'll soon have cash in her hand. Mom can make money out of anything. She lifts books from the shelves of our neighborhood library. She enjoys making up stories about her dying mother, while gushing real tears, just to get her hands on quick cash. Her credit cards are maxed. The banks, her brothers, mother, and father won't float her a loan anymore. She's nothing like her brother, Carlos.

"I'm a liar, you say?" Mom shakes the dress she holds in both hands and then slams it onto the orange counter top. "I shop in this store every week." She taps the counter with a red manicured nail. "And you can bet that after treatment like this, I won't be shopping here again." Mom points the finger she had tapped on the counter toward Esmeralda, "You know what, you can just take my credit card right now." She digs in her purse for her wallet.

"Ma'am, you don't have to do that," Esmeralda says, glancing behind Mom at the line that is forming.

Mom turns and winks at me. She has the same crooked smile as tío Carlos.

I roll my eyes thinking of tío Carlos, because he's someone I respect. He tried to rob the Credit Union. Would have walked away, free and clear, if his wife hadn't been upset. Tía Yoli had driven off and left him in the parking lot holding a sack load of money because she was still mad at him for cheating on her. He spent two years in prison, all because she was pissed. I remember how nervous Yoli was while waiting for him at the bus station in Huntsville. We all were. When he saw her, they ran to each other and hugged for the longest time, and just like that, all was forgiven. Carlos doesn't set his sights low.

"I've been shopping here since before you were born. This is the thanks I get for being a loyal customer?" She waves the white credit card in the air. Her close-cropped auburn hair bounces softly. "You know what? I'm sick of arguing with you." She points the card at Esmeralda, and my mother's coiffed hair moves in perfect sync with her actions. "Where's your manager? Let me talk to the manager."

Purple blotches form on Esmeralda's dark face. The English she has worked so hard to perfect becomes spotted with Spanish, "I cannot accept this dress, señora."

"Well, get me someone who can accept this dress, damn it! This is ridiculous, just ridiculous. I've been insulted and accused of lying. I'm not going to ask you again. Get me your manager."

I stand fast, in a fleeing, yet staying, position, feeling as nervous as I was waiting for tío Carlos's reaction to Yoli after he got out of jail. The week after he was out, he had driven up to our house in a shiny black Lincoln town car and had given it to Dad. "Those letters, ése. I looked forward to getting them every week," Carlos had said, then knocked fists with my father. I could tell Dad had wanted to hug him but held back. Dad washed that car every weekend. We'd all hop in and take a drive along the Border Highway, then park to watch illegals cross over. The car is history, just like this sales clerk is going to be. I look at the wrapping paper samples behind Esmeralda, then at the blotches on the girl's face. I match up the shade of purple to the square samples tacked to the wall, hoping no one I know would show up. Mom had worn that teal dress two nights ago to a quinceañera.

"Please let me see the dress. Perhaps I did not inspect it closely," Esmeralda says. She takes the nylon dress from the counter and asks my mother for the receipt, which of course she doesn't have.

Mom said before we got out of the car, "I don't need a receipt." Then she slipped the dry-cleaned dress out of its plastic, and we both ran inside the Mall because it had started to sprinkle.

Now, she empties her purse on the counter and inspects every stained, folded slip of paper she comes across, as the line behind her gets three people longer. She ignores the people, and unfolds the seventh and last square of paper on the counter, then says finally, "I don't have a receipt."

Esmeralda squints. Mom grinds her teeth then sighs. The air comes out through her nose, her shoulders lift then drop, and she never takes her eyes off the young clerk.

"How much did you pay for the dress?" The word "much" comes out sounding like "mush." People in line cough and sigh.

"It was one hundred and forty-eight dollars."

Esmeralda turns to look at the door behind her, then she looks again at Mom, whose argumentative eyes stare right back. She says, "Un momento, por favor," and walks through the door to find her manager.

I smile. Mom frowns. When the store manager arrives, he apologizes to my mother. She turns to me and smiles wide.

I frown. Thoughts of the Lincoln town car fill my head. After Dad had lost his job hauling chickens, my brother, Anthony, got his teeth kicked in in a fight. Desperate, Dad had called some friends to take the car from the Mall parking lot. They had driven it over to Juárez and parked it on the strip with the keys inside. "Leaving your chaqueta in the car was a nice touch, ése," Carlos had told my Dad. "But Chuy, you should have wrecked the car. There's a lot more money in damage claims. Shit, you could even sue Ford, where the real money is." Carlos is always thinking about the big picture. All Dad had gotten out of the deal was a nice satin windbreaker from the insurance money—the rest went into my brother's mouth.

The store manager looks a lot like the insurance adjuster who checked on the Lincoln. The manager fingers Mom's dress then scans a ledger that's three inches thick. He finds what he's looking for, then punches keys on the cash register. The drawer opens, and he tears a receipt off the machine, scribbles on it, asks my mother to sign, then hands her one hundred and seventy-one dollars and sixty cents.

I say, "But—" then stop when I see my mother's jaw muscles relax. She looks just like she did when she tried on that pair of five-hundred-dollar sling-backs at Neiman Marcus then walked out with nobody following her.

Her eyes become the charming eyes of a hostess at a party as she says, "Thanks so much. I'm sorry I was so upset. It's just that I bought this dress for my daughter's wedding but that puto never showed. I'm still a little . . ."

"I understand señor—," Esmeralda corrects herself, "Ma'am."

As we walk away from the counter, and as Mom puts the money in her wallet, I whisper, "I thought you said the dress cost one hundred and forty-eight dollars?"

"You're upset because I lied?" Mom holds her pocketbook to her chest. "Are you kidding me?"

I say nothing.

"Here we go. Esta Sandra Dee is trying to tell me how to live my life," Mom says to a teenager passing. The boy shrugs his shoulders. "Please, Teresa, enlighten me."

Before I can speak she says, "Well you know what, they're big corporations, they couldn't care less. You know how much money these people are making off people like us? Do you?"

I shake my head remembering the seventy dollars Mom gave me to buy the stroller for the quinceañera girl, who is four months pregnant. I stand taller because I still have thirty of those dollars in my hip pocket. The stroller had cost me one dollar and ninety cents. I smile thinking how easy it was to switch price tags. But still, my hands had been sweaty and sticking to the green handles on the shopping cart. I wonder if Mom ever gives a silent prayer like I did before I paid.

"They make more than we'll ever see in our lifetime," Mom says. "These pinche corporations even have money to cover shoplifting. They hire big fancy lawyers to get all their money back from the government. They don't pay no taxes—"

"You made a twenty-three dollar profit," I say.

Outside the rain makes the parking lot look freshly tarred, and the air smells like mud. Mom says, "Perfect."

Inside the car, I ask, "What's so perfect about rain?"

"The man is coming to see about our roof today."

"We're finally going to get the leaks fixed?"

"Better. We're going to get a check."

When we arrive, tío Carlos is under the eave of the house, where no rain can hit him, talking with Dad and Anthony. The cement driveway is dark gray. I smile and wave as Mom honks. All three men look at the car, and toss their heads back slightly.

Mom and I run to the door, and the men follow us inside the house.

"Get the ollas," Mom yells.

I walk into the kitchen to get the big pot Mom uses to cook menudo. I set the pot at the end of the hall to catch the water leaking from the ceiling. Mom, Dad, Carlos, and Anthony are huddled around one of the leaks in the dining room.

"You think he'll show?" Dad asks Carlos.

"Rain don't make them melt," says tío Carlos, then turns to me, "Hey, Teresa, clean out my car, yeah?"

"But it's raining."

"¿Y qué?"

I sigh but do what he tells me. His car is spotless, but I find fifty cents under the seat. I walk back inside, and all four of them stop talking.

Mom points to the pot full of water.

"Why do I have to empty it?" I say.

Dad walks down the hall, picks up the pot, water spilling onto the carpet, and dumps it in the kitchen sink.

"What's up with him?" I ask.

"He's nervous," Mom answers, real snappy, so I don't ask any more questions.

Ignoring me, Anthony asks tío Carlos, "You think the insurance will go for it?"

"Of course. Everybody in El Paso is getting cheques," Carlos says.

"God provides," Mom says.

"When's he coming?" Dad whispers. He sets the pot on the coffee table and sits in a chair.

"Soon."

When the doorbell rings, everyone is still, and Mom walks to the door to let the insurance inspector inside. The inspector says good afternoon, and Mom offers him some coffee. He declines and wants to get right to work. Says he needs a ladder. Dad jumps out of his chair to get him one. When Mom shuts the door, she gives two thumbs up to Anthony and Carlos.

"He's mexicano; we're in!"

I hear him walking on the roof. When he comes inside, Mom points to the leak in the hallway. I am sure he is going to touch the ceiling and feel the wet paint, which Dad applied only last night. Instead, the inspector asks, "Where's the attic?" Dad and Carlos take him into the garage. Mom goes into the kitchen and pours herself some coffee. She sits on the red couch and runs her fingers over the cushions. She stands when all three men walk back into the room. The inspector wants to know when the leak started.

Mom acts like she's going to sip some coffee but then says, "Chuy, you remember when the leak started?"

Dad smiles and shrugs his shoulders like he does before he's going to tell Mom why he came home late, "It was after that real bad hail storm. I remember having to get a pot so the water didn't ruin the carpet."

All four of us turn and look at the inspector. It's as if we're holding our breath. I hear drops of water sloshing on the carpet. The inspector says, "Yeah, I've been seeing a lot of that lately. I guess these roofers figure it isn't going to rain here so why bother making them right."

Mom exhales, her jaw muscles relax, and she finally takes a drink from her coffee cup. When he leaves, everyone talks at once.

"I'm going to buy the coffee table that matches my new sofas."

"No, Lupe, we need to buy Toño a car."

"I am nineteen." Anthony says.

"Don't forget me, hermana. I'm the one who hooked you up," says tío Carlos.

"A bottle of El Presidente for you."

"That's what I'm talking about," tío Carlos says.

The carpet in the hallway is drenched, but before I pick up the pot from the coffee table, I say, "I want a Revlon curling iron."

Inner View

Moist under my arms from my sprint to the building, I walk through the double doors, and a blast of cool air hits my face. Rather than refreshed, I am nauseated. After I sign in with the security guard, I jog down the cavernous hallway, find the glass door I am looking for, and step inside. I swallow and head toward the secretary, whose angular face and slender arms remind me of a TV news anchor. Her face, with its hard, porcelain-like veneer, shines under the florescent lighting. I squeeze the St. Christopher medallion in my hand, and her bored expression makes me more uncomfortable. I smile. The secretary's blue eyes give no warmth—all points and hard edges like a cube. She speaks before I do.

"You must be No-ella Boost-a-mont," she says, mispronouncing my name. "Mr. Richardson is expecting you. Please take a seat. He'll be with you in a minute," she says with her eyes already focusing on the computer screen in front of her.

I do as I'm told and sit on the leather sofa. The couch I rest on costs more than the car my father drives. I place my Naugahyde briefcase on my knees. The dark, rich textures of the room are gloomy and intimidating. I feel out of place, like I did in P.E. class in grade school, even a little ashamed of myself. I imagine the walls painted the banana yellow of our living room and think it would brighten up this dreary office, maybe give the secretary something to smile about. I remembered my mother's words as I got out of the car, "Pórtarte bien, Noelia, you're wearing a dress. Sit like a lady." I put the briefcase on the floor and cross my legs. The minute I do, the pointy secretary tells me Mr. Richardson can see me now. I stand as if to race.

The smell of coffee hits my nostrils before I see Mr. Richardson. My mouth waters, and I'm feeling comfortable despite the gloominess of the beige walls. Mr. Richardson is all roundness and folds. He reminds me of tía Ofelia's spoiled cat, Gertrudis. He walks around from behind an elaborately chiseled mahogany desk and shakes my hand. As he holds my hand in a stiff, tight clutch, he glances at me—from the diamante rhinestone barrettes in my hair, down to the discount-shoe-store loafers I'm wearing. Even though he doesn't say it, I feel it—cheap. He wants to get right down to business. Doesn't offer me a cup of espresso from the espresso machine behind his desk. He doesn't ask me about my trip. If I'm comfortable, hot, or tired. He wants me to tell him a little bit about myself. Why would I be a good addition to Richardson, Richardson, and Stoddard? Annoyed, I answer, "I've been the office manager of the credit union for five years. . . ." I can see Dad's car through Mr. Richardson's window. It's just behind the high-backed chair Mr. Richardson is sitting in. Dad has parked across the street, illegally. ". . . and before that I was a checker at Big Eight, and I'm bilingual . . ." I stare out the window because I see my sister, Teresa, get out of the car.

She's probably had enough, I think. Everyone in the family is inside Dad's blue Chevy in this 100-degree heat, and Dad turned off the air conditioner when he parked. As I got out, he was telling Teresa, "Eres escandalosa. No hace tanto calor." Titi just lifted her thick black ponytail and fanned the nape of her neck, which was drenched in sweat. "You're lucky you even have a car to ride in. I had to walk . . ." I slammed the car door and ran across the street toward the plaza, grateful that I didn't have to hear the end of the story again.

"Ms. Bustamante? Is there something outside?" Mr. Richardson asks.

"No, no sir," I say. I try to focus my attention on his face, but I'm distracted by Titi, who is waving her arms wildly, and now my father is out of the car.

I had tried to convince Dad to let me take the bus to the interview. He'd said, "I'll take you, no problem. When is it?"

"It's Monday," I said. "You'll probably want to rest on your day off."

"Rest? I can rest when I'm dead."

I cringed.

"Lunes, I'll take you to your job interview. We can all go."

"No, Dad, really I can take the bus," I said, desperately.

"N'ombre, you shouldn't take the bus for such an important day. We'll take you."

I poured him a cup of coffee, and as I handed it to him, I said, "I already planned to take the bus. It's no big deal."

"What do you mean, no big deal." He slurped. "You crazy? How much will it pay?"

"I think $28,000."

Dad whistled, "With that kind of money we can get a new roof for the house. I'm driving you, so you can have some support." He sliced the air with an open hand.

I turned to my mother, who was folding laundry on the kitchen table, and shrugged as if to say, "Help!"

"It'll be all right," she said, folding my T-shirt into thirds the way I like. "You're going to want someone to talk to after the interview. This way will be better. We won't worry, and don't you worry."

I rolled my eyes in defeat.

Mr. Richardson swivels in his chair, "Oh, I see—a family argument. Amusing, eh. I love the Mexican culture. That's why my wife and I moved here. Actually, my wife isn't too fond of this hot weather." He looks out the window. "They are such an emotional people."

"Yes I know," I say.

I was pretty emotional when Dad announced we were going to pick up abuela on the way to the interview.

"We only have twenty-five minutes to get downtown," I pointed to my watch. "There's no time for this."

"It don't matter if you're a little late," Dad said. "It's just an interview, not like you're going to actually be working."

When we got to grandma's house, Dad made us all get out of the car to greet her. I sighed loudly.

Dad yelled, "There's always time for manners."

I didn't want to leave the air-conditioned car but stepped out into the heat, and as I walked toward abuela's gated yard, I noticed the padlock shackle was closed tight. I turned to look at Mom.

"So what's the problem?" Dad called out. "Jump it."

I pointed to my business suit and shoes.

"Oh, forgot. Titi jump it and go get Abuela and tell her we need the key so we can come inside."

"No, Titi," I yelled, "Just tell her to come out because we're running late." I didn't dare look behind me.

Abuela shuffled outside with the key to the padlock in one hand and Titi holding her arm.

"Titi, get abuela's bag and shut and lock her door!" I yelled and got slapped on the back of the head.

"What are we late for?" Abuela asked, shaking as she tried to put the key in the lock.

One good tug would break the rusted chain that was cinched together by the padlock. I stopped myself from pulling and said, "Let Titi do it, abuela. I've got an important job interview."

Abuela said, "Titi, get my bolsa."

I loved my sister at that moment because she ran down grandma's brick pathway and was back a few seconds later carrying the large tote.

Dad said "¡Mira ésta! She has one job interview, and she thinks she can boss us around now."

"No te preocupes, mijo, she's just nervous," Abuela said. I looked at my watch and saw that we had fifteen minutes to get downtown.

Once we got abuela settled in the front seat, Mom sat in back with Titi, Joe, and me. I sat in the middle on top of Joe's lap. It was coolest there. The air-conditioner was hitting me straight on, and my makeup stayed in place.

"Would you move your fat head so I can get some air?" Joe moaned.

"Shuttup. I can't go to a job interview all sweaty."

"Why not?" Dad said.

Titi rested her hand on my thigh, but I ignored her. "Because it's unprofessional."

"Unprofessional? If you're sweating that means you're working hard. Any idiot can see that."

Titi rolled her eyes.

"I saw that," Dad said, giving her the evil eye through the rearview mirror. "You keep doing that, and I'll slap you so hard your eyes will roll back permanently. Malcriada."

"Dad," I said, and Titi started to place her hand on me, but stopped and sighed. "This is an office job. No one wants to walk in and see a sweaty woman inside an air-conditioned office. It doesn't look good for the company."

"At least they'll know you're working and not just sitting on your ass, drinking coffee."

"That's the trick, to make people think you sit on your ass—"

Dad said, "Watch you language."

"And drink coffee all day but in reality you're working, working very hard," I said.

"What's the point in that?" he said.

"It gives you more prestige."

"Prestige? ¿Qué es éso, prestige?" He waves one hand in the air. "Sounds like bullshit to me."

"Being late is not good either," I added.

Dad looked at his watch. "Ah, you're not going to be late, mija. We'll be there en punto!"

Grandma said, "I like my coffee with a lot of cream and sugar."

Titi and Joe laughed.

"The best coffee I ever had I drank with a gringa," Dad looked over at Mom, who smiled at him to go on. "My boss's wife. She had a shiny machine. Looked like it was made from rims. The good ones like at the car show Joe took us to. Remember mijo, the trokitas were my favorites and the bombs."

"I liked the girls the best," Joe said.

Titi punched his arm.

"It's true," Joe added. "And Dad didn't mind the view, either."

Mom hit his other arm, and everyone laughed.

"Ay, Dad, it's an espresso machine," Titi rolled her eyes.

"Yeah, yeah, one of those expression machines. The coffee was bien duro, but she gave it to me in one of those coffee cups you girls used to make me drink out of when you were little."

"Demitasse," Titi said, then whispered, "Idiot."

Mom reached over me and slapped my sister's thigh.

"Sorry," Titi said.

Oblivious, Dad said, "You were little, and you both wanted to make my coffee. You shouldn't be sorry. I loved playing with you girls. That's what the gabacha reminded me of, a little girl in a big house all by herself. She kept talking about this machine and how it was from France and what it did, when all I wanted was another cup of coffee, in a real cup."

We all laughed.

"Gabachos," abuela said, absently. "They love their things, and they're always in a hurry."

I tried not to look at my watch.

Mr. Richardson's watch was a gold Rolex. He tapped it every few seconds, while he spoke. "Tell me something . . . Are you of Mexican descent?"

"Descent?" He catches me off guard. "My grandmother's family is from Chihuahua, so, yes, yes, I am."

"I thought so," he says. "I'm sorry, please go on; you were saying you are bilingual."

My head is spinning. I wonder if what he asked was proper. If he just violated my rights. I look at this balding, pale man, really look at him. His eyes are the color of abuela's brass padlock. There's a spot of hair on his neck just above where his collar chokes him that he missed shaving. His shirt collar, starched stiff, is tinged gray with grime. He taps his Rolex, as if to remind himself he owns it. He seems sad. I wonder if Mr. Richardson's wife is alone right now—alone in her big house.

"Yes, I'm bilingual. I can type 100 words a minute and write in English and Spanish. Do translations."

I wonder why I tried to get here on time. I feel bad about my irritation at my father, who had grabbed my arm as I opened the car door.

"Remember mija, men don't like show-offs." He looked serious.

Mom added, "And don't bite your nails while you're talking to him."

My little brother Joe said, "Try not to fart like you do in your bedroom."

This got Titi laughing hysterically, and Dad slapped Joe on the top of his head, "Serio."

I was almost out of the car before my abuela said, "Wait mija. I forgot to give you this."

I glanced at my watch: 2 p.m., and I thought, "I'm going to be officially late for my interview," but still I waited. It took her a few seconds to unclasp the necklace that holds her St. Christopher medallion. I wanted to rip the thin chain off her neck, but I waited.

"This is for good luck," she said, and winked. "¡Qué Dios te bendiga! He'll help you charm your new boss."

"Thank you, abuela." I took it, slammed the car door, and ran.

"You can translate?" Mr. Richardson asks.

"Yes."

"And you're Mexican American?"

"Yes."

"You don't look it."

"Thank you," I say, ashamed.

He smiles and clears his throat. "Most Mexicans I know have an accent."

"How many do you know?"

"Well, the cleaning lady here, and my gardener."

"They're probably recent immigrants or illegals. I've been here for two generations on my father's side and three on my mother's," I say.

"Fascinating," he says, dismissively.

A buzzer goes off, and his secretary says, "Mrs. Richardson, on line one."

He presses a red button on his phone and almost touches his lips to the speaker, "Tell her I'm busy."

"She says it's important."

"I'll call her back in ten minutes," he says, agitated.

I try not to roll my eyes or pass judgment, but I do. My interview warrants ten minutes of his time. I prepared all weekend for this meeting, dipped into savings and bought a new outfit, even shoes, and got my hair done. My mind races, and I imagine this man sitting alone with his wife in a large house. He probably doesn't even tell her that he's interviewing someone for a paralegal position. I'll bet they eat their roast-beef supper in silence, speaking only when they're in bed and turn off the lights. "Night, I love you," they lie to one another. It's what I assume Anglo couples do.

"Sorry about that. My wife calls at least three times a day. Probably wants me to pick up some milk on the way home."

"Bored?"

"Yes, I think, you're right," he says.

"Where were we?" he says, and the buzzer goes off again. "What?!" He presses his lips to the speaker as he pushes the button.

"Mrs. Richardson."

"I'll take it," he hisses, then lifts one finger toward me as he picks up the phone. "Hello. Yes. How should I know? I only took two semesters of Spanish." He looks over at me and pauses, "Wait a minute. Hold on."

With the phone still to his ear he says, "Excuse me."

I picture a graying, slender woman on the other end of the line, wearing faded denim and turquoise jewelry. I can see her explaining to her friends that she wears rocks embedded in silver because she loves the culture. It's why she and her husband moved to the Southwest.

He snaps his fingers. "Can you tell me how to say, 'Please don't trim the rose bushes' in Spanish? My wife likes to trim them herself," he says sheepishly, "because the roses are Golden Wings from her Auntie Lem's yard." He covers the receiver of the phone with his hand and whispers. "She wanted to bring a little bit of home with her here."

I pause for a moment, smell the espresso, think about the secretary, the walls, the couch, how much translating I'd have to do for this man, my family sitting out in the car, and I say, "Sure. Here's what you can tell him: 'No riegue los rosales.'"

Snapping Lines

Jack Lopez

La Luz

When the snowflake fell, I'd almost laid out the entire house. It descended slowly, like a lost feather out of a down pillow, its form palpably magic. We didn't get snow this far south, this close to the ocean in California. But there it was, a solitary snowflake, changing form before my eyes, turning from a frozen crystal into a wet imprint on the wood.

I looked up. Everything was gray. And I could see my breath exploding before me in small puffs. Saws were going on other slabs, guys framing. The cutoff saw still whirred its hollow, reassuring echo, and farther back on the tract the plasterers' hopper droned as it spat "mud" on lathed houses. I could smell the aromatic scent of wet fir being sliced over and over as we fashioned three-dimensional puzzles in space, and I could smell the wild pungent aroma from the surrounding fields, even now smell the oranges from the grove. The trees drooped, laden with fruit, orange Christmas decorations sparkling against dusty leaves, glowing, almost, in the gloominess of the day. Putting my hammer in my bag, I saw the snowflake half disappear into the two-by-four on which I'd made my last layout mark.

From out of the orange grove, farther down the dirt street where only the bottoms were framed, came two *paisanos*. I wouldn't say wetback nor illegal alien, though you might. I was sure they were from *el otro lado*. What was the big deal? Everyone working around me was from somewhere else—the East Coast, the Midwest, Asia, Europe, Latin America. As they got closer I could tell that one of them was a woman. She carried a small, faded-brown overnight satchel with both hands clutching the leather handle, and she had dark hair tied in a ponytail, which floated around as she walked.

A woman out here was odd. We didn't have them, except for the catering truck drivers. This was Little League in the old days, Pop Warner, topless bars, and the Baja 500 all rolled into one male mindset. Maybe she was labor like the rest of us, I thought, watching them enter our outpost at the base of San Joaquin Mountain.

The man was tall and wore dark slacks with a fleece-lined jacket. He even had black ski gloves. The woman wore faded Levi's and a white blouse covered by a thin red and blue blanket-shawl that crisscrossed her chest and hung almost over her arms. On her feet she wore sandals with thick gray homespun socks. She was short and solid, built to work.

The man would forge ahead, leaving the woman behind, and then he would turn, pulling her up even with him. She resisted his touch subtly and stubbornly, for she continued to slow him down, as if she were either very tired or very willful. I knew there was a trail from the border through the backside of the Murietta Forest, which we were on the west edge of, so I figured maybe the woman had walked the trail. She appeared exhausted.

They marched past me, the man in the lead, the woman following, up to a fire that had old cars around it. Landscapers surrounded the fire, heating coffee. The man and woman had words for a moment, seeming to disagree strongly. After they stopped yelling, the man in the fleece-lined jacket approached the circle of men. He pointed to the woman and said something, which brought laughter from the men. The woman turned away, staring up in the sky. Our gazes locked for just a second, but she quickly looked away, out into the fields.

I looked there too. Tracts were springing up all around us, sort of like a twentieth-century gold rush. Scrapers and earth movers graded quadrants for more houses; shopping centers would follow. Looking back at the landscaper's fire, I saw that the man in the fleece-lined jacket now had a beer. The woman had put her suitcase on the ground and cupped a steaming drink in her hands, sipping from it, yet nodding and then waking with a quick jerk. Someone else, another man, helped her to the fire. Her brown satchel remained outside their circle, looking lost and dingy.

As I scanned the entire tract, I felt a feeling of peace and familiarity. There was a sense of humanity here—the new arrivals were welcome. And we were bonded in work as we gave it our all in fields that would soon become neighborhoods. Yet none of the workers would ever live in these instant affluent communities. But that was okay.

These houses were a huge contradiction. Casterbridge Estates, Phase III. They would start at a quarter million. And that would be for the few single stories. The 3 Plan, the one I was rolling second-story ceiling joist for, would sell for half a million. A lot of the laborers lived in the hills, walking to work, sleeping in the brush, making do with plywood and cardboard lean-tos, or else living in their cars, like Johnny Fasthorse, the guy who built all the kitchen soffits. Lots of guys in the trades were living on the job.

I looked where I'd made my last keel mark. No more snowflake. Mount Joaquin was lost in the mist. Everything was pressed down, the way I felt. So carry on. Don't stop moving. Not when you're in the air, for if you think, then you look down, and if you look down, you fall.

And the incredible thing about the fall is how fast the ground comes up to meet you. Thirty-two feet per second squared. It's one of a few completely fair systems, the same for everyone. You think you'll have time to figure things through, but you won't. It's too fast. So there it is, you and the ground will meet. It's just a matter of time.

No more snowflakes fell, so I started spreading, taking the first boards, which, if the loads were built correctly, would be the ones I needed, to the farthest end of the house. Somehow you walk on top of that three-and-one-half-inch plate, your toes gripping as much as they can through your tennis shoes, with the joist, and eighteen-foot-long-two-by-six, balanced in your arms so that it has equal weight on either side of your body, making you a bit like the tightrope walker, except he has a pole. Not looking down, you walk: one foot over the other, a game of balance, all the way to the edge of the building. On the perpendicular wall you set one end of the joist down while still holding the other end cradled underneath your arm. Then wiggle the board across the wall until it has spanned the room. Lay it on its side and go back for another. Each successive joist gets easier, for you can balance just a second in between the board you've already laid down. After you've spread the room, you have a bunch of sagging joist ready to be rolled.

That was what I did. Mark layout, spread material, roll, block, and cut specials. And since Christmas was almost here, I wasn't working a full day because we were having a party. Efren, one of the stackers, the guys who build roof structures, was across the street stirring *carnitas* in his big copper vat, using a rowboat oar to jostle the meat.

Even from my high vantage point I could hear the crackle of the fire underneath the vat, smell the hot food wafting up toward me. I suppose that *carnitas* from Efren was as close as we'd get to a formal Christmas party, which was okay.

Still, a sense of excitement rode down the streets on small wings of wind, raising everyone's expectations, making us concentrate on anything but the "now," which wasn't all that great.

After I'd rolled the upstairs master bedroom, the second bedroom, and the upstairs den, all I had left were the front two bedrooms. Usually I finish a house while I'm on it rather than setting up again. But I was excited about the party, so I figured if I pushed to finish this house the work would diminish quality-wise. And I hated that, which was why I worked alone, hand-nailing. No compressor and nail gun, no partners, no slave illegal labor. Just my bags and saw and cord. That was it. Light and quick. Agile. Accurate. I took responsibility for my work. I took pride in it, never leaving a house until it was done to *my* satisfaction. The only way to make progress in this world, I knew.

Nobody had taken lunch because we were stopping early, and besides, the catering truck woman wasn't due back until after Christmas. I didn't know how the guys knew the food was done, but more and more men gathered around Efren's fire, drawn to the cooking meat.

The plasterers had stopped, the saws around the tract were falling silent, the job was winding down for the day, even the ubiquitous heavy metal tract music ceased. In spite of the cold, everyone was drinking beer. I blew in my cupped hands, looking for the woman. She was now sitting before the landscapers' fire, her arms folded over her knees, head down, asleep. I pulled up the hood on my sweatshirt.

Before I lowered my saw down, I saw Efren spear a piece of meat from the vat. With his big Bowie knife he placed the steaming pork on a two-by-twelve scrap and then daintily tasted a small chunk. He yelled something I couldn't hear, and his brother came stomping out of a house with a platter.

From the same house I heard yelling and whooping, and I could see color shadows jumping from the hole where the sliding glass doors would eventually go, sometime in the not-too-distant future. Even from high up and across the street I could hear the repetitious moans and pseudo-romantic music accompanying the pornography they were watching. Oh, man. But I had already paid my ten bucks for beer and food, so what the hell? I could get some hot meal and then go home.

Plenty of time to be alone. That was the hardest part of no longer being married. The time alone. And the quiet. All I'd ever wanted was love, yet it seemed I couldn't have it. Maybe it was quite a lot to ask.

"You working all day?" the Cowboy Nazi, who had materialized on the slab below me, shouted. He wore an old Mackinaw hunting jacket and cowboy boots and a black cowboy hat. He carried a pint of Jack Daniels.

"Every fucking day," I answered without looking at him. I didn't like the Cowboy Nazi. His tattoos had color in them, done at a parlor. All the other guys' tattoos were black, prison tattoos.

After he walked off I lowered my saw to the slab. Across the way a buzz of chatter slowly rose. The owner of the framing company had arrived. He would have our money and, if we were lucky, some sort of bonus. I remembered the years they'd given us hams or turkeys, but now they gave us green. Everything was money. What could I do with a turkey anyway?

I climbed down the brace material in the wall, stepping diagonally, as if I were using a ladder. After pulling my cord out of the house, I stretched it tightly from the power pole and began forming big, slack loops.

Maybe the reason I was joisting was because few tools were needed. A saw, a cord, a set of bags, and nails. They supplied the nails. The saw and cord and bags fitted in the front of my car, all I really owned. A '61 Porsche Super Ninety with a sunroof.

When I loaded my *chingaderas* in the trunk, I put on my leather jacket over my sweatshirt and looked up at the sky. It was all gray and silent. That thing that had fallen must not have been snow, I thought.

Approaching Efren and the food, I heard shouting and laughter from the house behind him.

"Get *una plata*," Efren said to me.

"Did you see any snow?" I asked him, taking in a big hit of smell from the simmering vat. I stood close to Efren, almost touching him, warming my hands over the fire.

He stirred in a slow, hypnotic, clockwise motion. The lower part of the oar was all white, the varnish cooked off. He looked at me blankly, as if he were having some sort of mystical communion with the pork in the simmering vat. Efren said, "Al's got a bottle."

At the side of the house, next to the porno room, a group of guys surrounded Al, the foreman. A small paper sack moved among them.

I walked over. "Did you guys see any snow?"

Spot, who had a great red birthmark covering the left half of his face, shook his head.

Little Magua, a laborer, sauntered up and, as if he'd heard my question, said, "Dr. George says snow."

"That weatherman don't know shit from Shinola," Grizzly said. Grizzly was hairy and big. His face was covered with hair, and his hands were as large as bear paws, the tops covered with fur, all the way to his knuckles.

Al handed me the paper sack. He was tall and clean shaven, with a chiseled chin. He wore faded boots with new Dockers and a polo shirt with a red down parka. His hands were clean, though callused.

I took a swig from the sack, letting the brown delicious warmth glide down my throat.

"You ain't got AIDS, Jess?" the younger of the Gold Dust Twins asked. Three thick gold chains flopped on his chest, over his jacket.

I flipped him the bone.

"Dr. George is full of shit up to his ears," Johnny Fasthorse said. He wore his hair long and braided, and was homeless, living in the orange grove in his car. His hands had an orange tint to them from all the oranges he ate.

"I saw snow," I said, passing the sack to Al.

"It's cold enough to snow," Grizzly said.

"More money!" Julio shrieked from the porno room. He'd been decorated in Vietnam.

Al took a nice slow drink from the sack, watching everyone.

Efren carried another full platter into the house as guys from the other trades milled about. Plasterers by the sliding glass opening, wearing their splattered whites with down jackets over them, drinking beer; roofers out by a dually, sharing their own bottle; drywallers, their hands chalky white from handling board all day, in the garage next door, smoking pot; plumbers, their hands permanently flux stained, drinking by one of the coolers filled with beer; and even a bunch of landscapers had returned to the fire out by the grove, but no longer was the woman with them.

"What are all these guys doing here?" Little Magua asked.

"They paid their ten bucks," Spot said. "Who cares?"

"More money for the craps game," the oldest Gold Dust Twin said.

After eating there would be gambling. A lot of cash would be floating around, especially with fifty, sixty guys getting paid green plus Christmas bonuses.

"More money!" Julio yelled again.

The Owner glided effortlessly between plasterers, shaking his head in reaction to the taunt from Julio.

"The baby needs milk," Spot chimed in.

"As long as the eagle shits," Efren yelled in Spanish from across the dirt street.

"I've got your money," the Owner said, reaching into his breast pocket, stretching his camel hair coat tightly so you could see the bulge of his pistol.

I used to run work, even had my own company, employing fifteen guys, and I used to pay in cash too. But packing a gun was one thing I refused to do.

"You guys working tomorrow?" the Owner asked. "You, Jess?" He smelled like Old Spice aftershave.

He knew I always did. I had nothing else. "It's going to snow."

After most everyone had eaten, Big Martian started a fire right on the slab in the garage. Smaller Martians built a backstop for craps. Those Martians were thieves and they loved money and they would get it by any means.

Immediately the garage filled with guys hoping to multiply their fortunes. Only one adjective goes with money: more. And here's the thing, only a few people can ever have a lot of money. Some sort of cosmic law, like gravity or something. One or two guys would win big, most of the others would lose some, and a few would lose big. And those were the ones to avoid, the big losers, because they would, in all likelihood, try to get their money back. They would make the most noise, be the most physical, drink the most. In short, they were the biggest assholes.

The Martian without a shirt was a major ass, but he had a whole baseball team of relatives backing him, so he wasn't such a loser after all. They were all from Florida, brought here in migratory waves by Big Martian, who was a siding pimp and would hire outsiders only as a last resort. They flew Confederate flags in front of all the houses they sided. The Martian without the shirt dropped to his knees on the garage slab and yelled to the afternoon sky, "Come to papa, yeah!" as he rolled the dice. Snake eyes. The loser as bait.

A drywall man stepped up with green in his hand and said, "Let's go, baby."

They rolled. And the clinks of the dice were compounded by the cold, drawing everybody into a tight circle.

Out front Efren was cooking the last batch of *carnitas*, talking to a few latecomers. The porno moaning kept a steady beat, highlighted by sporadic yelling from the garage slab, where the craps game was gathering momentum.

I'd drunk some beers and had numerous hits off whiskey bottles and eaten a hot meal, such as it was. But more important, I was with people.

The clouds had completely deserted the twin humps of Mount Joaquin, making it almost glow from the snow on the very top. A thin streamer cloud blew off the tip as if it were a banner.

While I gawked at the mountaintop, suddenly applause and shouts filled the air. A lot of guys ran toward the garage slab, joining the bulging crowd. Their bodies pushed in and then fell away, like a tidal surge against sea rocks.

At first I thought a fight had started, although in all my years working I'd never actually seen one. But they did occur. This thought quickly disappeared when I heard the gravelly voice of Big Martian yell, "You can buy a WOMAN!"

Upon hearing such a strange idea, I, too, hustled over to the side of the garage, behind which the backboard had been set up, and pushed my way onto the slab. And there, much to my dismay, stood the woman I had seen earlier, for sale.

"Liver," Big Martian said, "Who wants a woman?"

"She ain't even awake," Spot said.

And she wasn't. The man in the fleece-lined jacket propped her up. But in spite of her unconscious state she still clutched her small suitcase.

"You can't buy and sell people," I said.

The Owner said, "I'm history." He split.

"This guy wants to sell her," Big Martian said.

We all looked at the man in the fleece-lined jacket. He stood behind the woman, supporting her, saying something in Spanish that I couldn't quite hear because of all the commotion.

Efren translated and shouted: "He says, 'She's very tired.'"

No shit. But there was something more, there always was.

"I'll give you ten bucks," a drywall man shouted.

"The strippers will be here soon." Al was trying to divert attention.

"They're not coming," Grizzly said.

"I think I'll buy her and fuck her 'til she begs for mercy," Waylon Willie said.

"Easy," Al said.

"Let's all chip in and buy her and then we can have a train," Spot said.

"Shut up," I said to Spot.

"Who knows what diseases it's got," the Cowboy Nazi said.

"Shut the fuck up, you moron," I said to Cowboy Nazi.

The man in the fleece-lined jacket spoke with Efren, who then announced that only one man could buy her.

"What gives him the right to sell her?" I asked.

"He's her husband," Efren said.

That quieted some of the meaner ones in the crowd. Even they knew something serious was happening.

I came back with "So?"

Efren looked at me with squinted eyes, as if he were trying to interpret something beyond his realm of reason.

"I'll get her alone, then," Grizzly said. "Twenty."

"Gash!" someone yelled.

"Is this guy serious?" Al asked Efren.

"I think so."

Al threw up his hands and said, "Forget it." He left the garage slab.

"Twenty-five," Little Magua said.

A roofer chimed in with thirty.

The bidding was serious, everyone wanting see how far it would go. See if things would get out of hand.

"That's too much for a fucking spic," Cowboy Nazi said.

"Hey, white trash," Efren said to Cowboy Nazi.

"Knock it off," Julio said in his deepest voice. He was big, almost as large as Cowboy Nazi. "No fighting on the job."

"Thirty-five," a plasterer said.

"He don't want her no more," Spot said with glee.

Trying to get eye contact with anybody, I said, "You've got to stop this shit."

A yell from Grizzly upped the bid fifty bucks.

"You can stop it with *money*," Big Martian said to me.

I didn't know why, but I thought of my own life and about all the times I'd acted wrongly, or even worse, the times I'd not acted at all. So without realizing the implications of my words, I said, "Two hundred."

A few "whoas" passed through the crowd, followed by laughter. And everything seemed suddenly colder, clearer, and slower.

Big Martian said, "Any other bids?" Nobody responded. To me he said, "You bought yourself a woman."

"I've heard of this in Peru, but never here," Fermin said.

Big Martian grabbed my hundred-dollar bills.

"Enema!" the Cowboy Nazi yelled.

"Helmut, yeah!" Waylon Willie added.

"Hand it over," I said to Big Martian.

Julio snatched my money from Big Martian and said, "Let's finalize this thing."

"Let's shoot some fucking craps," Grizzly said.

The man in the fleece-lined jacket grabbed the woman by her wrist, pulling her forward, waking her. We followed Julio off the garage slab, out front by Efren's now smoldering fire.

Al leaned against his truck. "Now what?"

"I'll get my money back," I said. "Thanks for your help."

Al shrugged.

"It's not done that way," Efren said.

Efren, Efren's brother, Al, and Johnny Fasthorse surrounded Julio and me. The woman was trying to speak with her husband, but he would have nothing to do with her.

"He's right," Julio said. "A deal's a deal."

"I don't want to buy somebody."

"You just did."

"C'mon, Al, help me out here."

"I can't. You had to open your big mouth."

"What? And let Grizzly get her?"

"You're the one that got involved. You're the one that stood up for rights," Julio said.

"She's funky," Efren said.

We all stared at the woman. She looked to be in her early thirties. She was short, her gaze unfocused, and she held her head high. Her hair blew around her face as the wind brushed it. The man in the fleece-lined jacket now held the valise.

A huge roar erupted from the craps game.

"I didn't know you were like that," Efren's brother said to me.

"Like what?" I said.

Efren came up close to me, whispering, "She's got a big toilet." To his brother he said, "Get the copper pot. I want to split before them rednecks really get going."

Oh shit, I thought. "Look, Julio, I just wanted to talk some sense into that asshole," I said, pointing to the man in the fleece-lined jacket. "I didn't want to buy his wife."

"What do you want I should do? This man put her up in good faith." He, too, gestured to the man in the fleece-lined jacket. "Now you want to break the deal? Where would we be without our word?"

I didn't want to hear that sort of bullshit. "You know in your heart that it's wrong for one person to sell another."

"No, it's not."

"We had a war over it. The Civil Fucking War." I looked at Al for verification. He nodded approval.

"These guys aren't Americans."

Julio had me there. "But we are."

"That war don't mean shit to me," Johnny Fasthorse said.

"Maybe we could sell her for a profit," Efren said. "Clean her up, know what I mean?"

"I used to think you were okay, Efren," I said.

"Little Magua will give you twenty-five," Efren's brother said. He closed the back flap on Efren's SUV.

"Why?" I yelled at the husband. *"Por qué?"*

He snickered and said, *"Aquella es malvada."*

"How bad can she be?" I asked.

"She ain't bad," Efren said, starting his rig. He revved the engine. "She's evil," he said, smiling. His rear tires crunched a two-by-four as he pulled away.

"Don't start that shit," I said.

"Why so glum?" Julio said. "You've got a woman." He handed the money to the man in the fleece-lined jacket.

"Don't," I said, making for them. Julio placed himself between me and the man in the fleece-lined jacket.

"Got to," Julio said.

"Have fun," Al said. He started his truck.

"Wait," I said to Al, hoping for a chance to grab the man in the fleece-lined jacket and hoping, too, for some help from my friends.

"What do you want me to do?"

"I don't want to be a part of this."

"You already are. Butch it out."

"Christmas is coming up," I said, as if that, somehow, made any difference.

"You want me to take her home? My wife would just love that."

"Why not?"

Al shook his head. "Have fun," he said again, driving off.

When I looked for the man in the fleece-lined jacket, I caught a glimpse of him entering the orange grove. As I started after him, Julio and Johnny both restrained me.

Fermin walked out to us from the craps game and said, "I've got some poems in my car."

"Shut up, Fermin."

"No, man, she'll like them."

"Get lost." I shook myself free from Julio and Johnny Fasthorse.

Johnny threw up his arms and said, *"Hasta,"* and walked off.

I heard a car start out in the grove, then saw a trail of dust leaving the shelter of trees.

"You shouldn't have got involved," Julio said. He made for his truck, started it, and drove off down the dirt street.

So there we were, the woman and I, standing in the dirt, with the sun almost set, and the air colder and meaner than it had been all day, snowflakes descending all over us, dusting the ground in a white cotton. The yells from the craps game now had an urgency to them that had been lacking previously. I looked at her. Was she a loser? Was I?

"Let's go," I said, gently.

She yawned. *"Soy Luz."*

As the snow now fell for real, I thought, I know, and knew why I'd done what I'd done, knew that everything previous in my life had led to this one moment.

Lost

Building wooden models of sailboats but thinking about Bonita out there putting up signs at the markets and on the corner stop signs and at the elementary school. She's taped one on the window of my car. It says:

LARGE REWARD FOR WILLIE
BRINDLE MALE PIT BULL TERRIER
VERY FRIENDLY TO PEOPLE
KEEP AWAY FROM OTHER MALE DOGS!

We stayed up late last night making those signs on my workbench where I'm now working. My phone number is listed on the sign and so is Bonita's, but she's here most of the time.

The ribbing for the hull is made out of two-by-four scraps that I get across the street. They're building one of those long skinny houses like they do in Corona del Mar, and it reminds me of a boat in some aspects—the cantilevered front deck looks like a prow cutting through almost tropical air. The first step is to cut the scraps into pieces that will act as bottoms and uprights for the siding "planks," which are, in actuality, thin strips of balsa wood. I put the fir strips in a row and then tie them together with a pin through a balsa wood "plank." It's tedious work, and since I don't know shit about boats, it's hit and miss, but it's something to do. Bonita's roommate, Linda, is making batik sails for it and the deck will be teak. But that's a long way off. And I want this one to look good; maybe then I can get in the Sawdust next summer and quit construction for good.

Trimming long pieces of balsa wood to use as siding for the hull when the phone rings. I live in an old house—probably to be removed as soon as the old lady who owns it dies and her asshole son can make it big on the land sale (and then maybe there will be a big boat right here where I'm sitting). After three years living here, I still get disoriented when I stand too fast. The foundation piers are all rotted, so the house leans to the south, or starboard side, and it feels almost like walking in the fun house when you were a kid.

I walk into the kitchen and get the phone. "Hello?"

"What's happening, Juan?"

"Nothing much."

"Wanna come to my party tonight?"

"Who is this?"

"Billy!"

"Oh. Hi, Bill."

"So do you want to come?"

"I don't know. Maybe I'll be by late."

"Well, stop by. It's gonna be big. We got a band."

"Great. Maybe I'll see you later."

Fuck the Fourth of July. There's just a bunch of drunk assholes throwing firecrackers everywhere. Like last year. Ann, my girlfriend last year, got a firecracker to land right on her foot. It didn't bleed or anything; it just turned all black, I suppose, from the powder exploding. The guy who threw it was really drunk, so what are you going to do?

My workbench occupies the entire back wall of the living room and I set it up level, but unfortunately the very far end is unusable because it drops too far below what is a comfortable working height because the floor drops the most at that point. So that's where I have my stereo and store my woodworking tools.

They were my brother's before he dove into the water right at Punta Banda with a big swell running just to see if he could beat the tidal surge that rushes into the rocks and shoots spray at least twenty feet in the air. La Bufadora. The blowhole. The Federales walked the beaches but finally some American scuba diver recovered the body. I went down with my father and never once looked at it, and my father had to pay over a thousand dollars in bribes to get my brother back onto this side, not to mention the cost of the dry ice.

On the way back into the living room I put on *Motown's Greatest Hits* and blast it. The first song is my favorite—"Heat Wave" by Martha and the Vandellas. My brother once took me to Melodyland Theatre, where we saw the Supremes and Martha on this big stage that went in a circle.

I just get back to the chair when there's a tap at the window.

Jim, my neighbor in back, sticks his head inside my living room through the open window and says, "I've got your money, Juan. C'mon back and I'll pay you."

Why doesn't he just give it to me now? I'm always ready to get money, so I walk back to his house. My grass is dead and bristly from the heat of summer. The sun is starting to break up the overcast, the sky looking like a great gray tarpaulin being rolled back. It's going to get hot again.

I open Jim's rusted screen door and step into his living room. His house always smells like someone's dirty hair, so I suppose that's why I don't come back all that often. Jim, who is tall and in perfect shape from surfing all the time and from pouring concrete for a living, stands and offers me a mirror with four tiny white lines stretched out on it. A straw with a jagged edge on one end almost rolls off the small platter. I sniff one of the lines while Jim holds the mirror for me. He then hands it to his friend who's sitting in the beat-up overstuffed pink couch underneath the open window, where red bougainvillea climbs right in the living room.

"Another Fourth down the tube," Jim's friend says.

"There's nothing to celebrate," a new guy says, walking out from the bathroom. "No waves, man."

"I wanted to thank you for loaning me the money," Jim says to me. "You want a beer?"

"It's still a little early."

"I'll get your money," Jim says, leaving for the bedroom. The guy who was in the bathroom sits in Jim's chair and takes the mirror and snorts a line. Then he starts playing with his nose, wiggling it and making snorting horse noises. "Good stuff," he finally says.

"Thanks again, Juan," Jim says, returning from the bedroom. He hands me the hundred.

"My pleasure."

I smile at the surf cats but they can't see me.

Back at the workbench I really don't feel like working anymore because the coke makes me feel like doing something, anything but concentrating, when the front door opens and Bonita walks in with her roommate, Linda, and Linda's boyfriend, Joe.

"Hi," Linda says. "We've been all over the neighborhood but nobody's seen Willie."

Bonita goes and sits on the couch. She has on a big T-shirt over her bare legs. She flops her long hair on her back in a nervous twitch.

"Maybe we should drive around," I say.

Bonita just looks at me.

I let Willie out about four in the morning three days ago when I couldn't sleep. Sometimes I have trouble keeping my eyes closed, so I get up. Willie wanted out, and I let him go. What's the big deal? I'll tell you. He hasn't returned.

"Juan, you remember Joe, don't you?" Linda asks.

"Yeah. How you doing?"

"Hi," Joe says. He pulls out a plastic bag from inside the waist of his cut-off Levi's. His hair is short with a long tail in back. He's slight, looking as if he's never worked. He walks to the couch, sits there next to Bonita, and takes from the glass coffee table a *Fine Woodworking* magazine, which he uses for a plate and starts rolling joints.

I put my tools neatly in the corner of the workbench, folding the chisel set into the chamois pouch that my brother made for them. I go into the kitchen and get some beers. It's a holiday.

Linda is sitting on the floor beside Joe, and she's taken off her tie-dyed beach wraparound. She's in her thirties, in very good shape, and she's vegetarian. It's funny how she and Bonita are roommates because Bonita is only eighteen. Linda and I used to have mutual friends who were married. But they separated and Linda and I stayed friends, and it was Linda who introduced me to Bonita.

"Can I use the phone, Juan?" Linda asks.

"Sure."

Bonita just sits there, her eyes all watery, staring at the wall. She's short, five two, and is really tanned. She's a waitress at Marie Calendar's, so she gets to go to the beach every day, but right now her bottom lip is sticking out. Joe blows out a smoke ring and passes the joint to Bonita.

"Don't you have any other music?" she asks, taking in a big puff. She pauses for a moment and then says, "How about some Wham?"

Smokey Robinson is now singing about shopping around.

"What's Wham?"

"I bought that album for you," she says, standing up and walking over to the rocking chair to pass me the joint.

When she gets right in front of me, I smile and shake my head. She turns to walk it back to Joe but I grab her from behind and pull her on top of me and kiss her neck and squeeze her. Linda comes out of the kitchen and Bonita hands her the joint as she passes us.

"I called my psychic," Linda says, inhaling smoke from the joint, standing in front of Joe.

"What'd she say?" Bonita asks, squirming off my lap.

"She said someone will bring Willie home tonight."

"Couldn't you get an address?"

Bonita shoots me a mean look. That dog is a father-mother-brother-sister all rolled into one for her. He's her best friend and guard dog. He's more dependable than any of her family, and he's certainly been around longer than me, and if he returns he'll be around longer than me.

He's a big tough beast and looks a lot like the dog Petey from *The Little Rascals*. Most of his teeth are missing or broken from fighting and from chewing on rocks. He has the grip that pits have; he won't let go in a fight. I've seen Bonita stick her finger up his ass to get him to let go of another dog before he kills it. In a fight Willie is like a sixty-pound death mouth.

Sometimes after we walked through the little park down on Carnation that overlooks the bay, it would look as if there had been a windstorm because there would be leaves and branches all over the ground from where Willie had hung from limbs, twisting and jerking and pulling and hanging there until the branch fell and he tore it to shreds.

"Wedding Bell Blues" comes on and Linda starts lip-syncing it to Joe. Joe is a lot younger than Linda. Bonita walks to the workbench, to where the turntable is, and starts looking underneath it through the records.

"He's just after pussy," Joe says, exhaling smoke. "I had a dog that was gone for ten days. One morning I opened the front door and he was laying there like nothing had happened." He wets his fingertips and then smashes the fire out of the joint.

"He'll be back tonight," Linda says.

Bonita rejects the record.

Later, as we're driving around in my convertible Karmann Ghia, Bonita says the carob trees lining the streets smell like cum. Then she smiles at me.

We drive down street after street of small, cozy houses with the draperies open to let you see how their decorating scheme looks better than a magazine. The houses are close together; some of the people are mowing lawns or digging in their flower beds, but nobody's seen Willie. I drive up to the stretch behind town where it's still Irvine Ranch land and undeveloped. I get out of the car, walk to the barbed wire fence that is down—pushed over by joggers—and check out the ditch by the side of the road. Nothing.

In the late afternoon we walk to the beach. Bonita and me. I hold her hand. It feels good to have a girlfriend on the Fourth of July.

Big Corona is steaming with people; beach shrieks climb all the way up the bluff and greet us as we begin the descent down to the sparkling water. All of inland southern California is here having barbecues, putting on suntan oil, eating, screaming, kissing, laughing on the beach. There's a traffic jam at the entrance to the parking lot. On the beach below, there's not even any place to spread our towels. In fact, it looks like one of those photos of the French Riviera where the people must all stand because there's no room to do anything else. I go in the water by the low tide rocks so that Bonita will be able to find me. She feels like walking, and in an instant she's lost in the wiggling crowd.

On the way back to my house, we check the park on Carnation. When I get away from Bonita, I check in the bushes because sometimes dogs go off to die.

In the shower Bonita holds me a long time after we've satisfied each other and she cries. I want to tell her that I took off work yesterday and drove to the pound in Huntington, the big one in Orange, and the one out on Canyon Road in Laguna, but instead tell her we'll go on Monday.

Joe and Linda come back from the beach, use my shower, then we all decide to go get something to eat. But first we drive to Costa Mesa to see if Willie has made the long trek back there instead of returning to my house. He hasn't.

So we go to International House of Pancakes. It seems to be the only place open. We all have breakfast, except for Bonita, who won't eat. The service is terrible. The waitress hides every time we want something. And we're the only ones in the huge blue A-frame, and we can't even get our check. Bonita sticks her fingers in her mouth and whistles loud and shrill for the waitress but we all think, hey, that's Willie's whistle.

Outside, Joe says, "He'll turn up."

"He'll be back tonight," Linda says. "We're going to The Annex and have a beer."

Bonita is no way going to get into a bar, even with a phony ID, so we decide to go to the movies. We drive over to Harbor Boulevard. Rates have gone up to six dollars but I refuse to pay that much for a look down a tunnel. Big screens, big sounds, that's something different.

"Let's try the exits," Bonita says. We walk around in back and try the exit doors to see if we can sneak in. Every one is locked.

"Let's go back to your house and see if Willie's there."

"Some psychic," Bonita says on her little couch, sitting next to me, with her new Thompson Twins playing. We're alone in the semidarkness— only the light from the kerosene lamp silhouettes the room. We start kissing. I open her blouse and look at the white part of her breasts, the part always covered by her bathing suit. There's one vein that travels almost to her nipple. Above her breasts she has thousands of tiny sun freckles and when I touch them, for an instant, my fingerprint stays on.

El Milagro and Other Stories

Patricia Preciado Martin

La Tortillera/The Tortilla Maker

Casa donde no hay harina, todo se hace remolina.
In the house where there is no flour, everything will turn to shambles.
(Where there is no discipline, all will be lost.)

There are a few things I must explain about my mother. She has an inborn and natural elegance and grace, a genetic exquisiteness. People turn their heads and stare in admiration when she walks by. I have spent most of my life following a few paces behind her, pretending to carry the train of an imagined magnificent gossamer cape.

She is regal. And there is no place where she reigns more absolutely than in the Kingdom of the Kitchen. There she has decreed irrevocable laws with monarchical absoluteness. There she is the queen and I, alas, the court jester.

These are the Laws of the Kitchen:

Law Number 1: Tamales are not made; they are sculpted.

Law Number 2: Sopa is not soup; it is "the lovely broth."

Law Number 3: One must always wear an apron when embarking on a kitchen mission. The apron must be handmade and embroidered with the days of the week (preferably in cross-stitch), and the correct one must be worn each day.

Law Number 4: A dining table must always have a starched and ironed cloth—never, never placemats.

Law Number 5: Tortillas are the essence of life, the symbol of eternity, the circle that is unbroken, the shortest distance between two points.

Law Number 6: Law Number 5 takes precedence over laws number one through four and the Six Precepts of the Roman Catholic Church.

Law Number 7: The unfortunates who buy their tortillas from the supermarket, wrapped in plastic, might as well move to Los Angeles, for they have already lost their souls.

A day in the kitchen with my mother is an oft-repeated disaster echoing past scenarios:

"Patricia, es lástima that you don't make homemade tortillas more often. Pobres de tus criaturas. Do you want your niños to grow up without culture and underprivileged? How can you expect them to know the meaning of life?"

"You are right, Mamá," I reply. "I just don't ever seem to have the time. And anyway, they never seem to come out right. One time I forgot to put in the baking powder, and they were as hard as soda crackers. The next time I put in too much baking powder, and they puffed up like balloons. They're either too salty or too bland. Sometimes I add too much water, and they have the consistency of glue, or not enough, and they are like rubber. And when I try to roll them out, they're shaped funny."

"That's all right, mijita. You are here today, and you have the time, so let's make them together. I'll go through it with you—for the hundredth time—step by step." She releases an audible sigh.

"Well, Mamacita," I say. "It will be helpful if you give me some measuring spoons and cups. We can measure the ingredients, and then I can write down all the amounts, and then perhaps, when I make them at home, they'll turn out better."

"Measure? Who needs to measure? You can feel it in your alma if the amounts are right. Your heart will tell you. See? I cup my hand like this, and I know it's enough baking powder. The flour—just make a lovely snowy mound of it in the middle of the bowl. And add the salt in the form of La Santa Cruz to bless the bread. Don't worry! La Virgen de Guadalupe will guide you."

I have already broken one of her favorite china cups during our morning coffee session. There is a stain of my scrambled egg glowing fluorescently on her white linen tablecloth with the crocheted hem. She has told me three times to lower my voice and to put on an apron—the one that says "martes." She always keeps a candle burning for me on her bedroom altar with its army of saints, virgins, Santos Niños, and Almighty Poderosos. Her intentions are unspecified, but I think it has something to do with the fact that I cook with frozen food and use paper napkins.

She pours, spoons, sifts, stirs, mixes, and kneads with grace and deliberation. I watch with feigned interest and intensity. I am thinking about the tortillas at the supermarket in the plastic wrappers. The candle on the little altar flares and dies out.

The dough is ready. Now we must make little bolitas of perfectly uniform masa that must "rest" for half an hour under a cross-stitched embroidered cloth that says "Tortillas."

It is now time to roll the tortillas out. We take the cloth off ceremoniously. Mamá's bolitas of masa have expanded into symmetrical mounds of dough. Mine, however, are lumpy and misshapen.

Mamá: "Now we will roll them out. I will let you use the palote that my father made for me when I was a little girl of six. Have I ever told you the story about how I began making tortillas for our family of eight when I was so small that I used to have to stand on a wooden box to reach the counter?"

"Yes, Mamá," I say. This story has been recited so often that it has become part of our family folklore with mythic importance equal to Popocatépetl and Ixtacihuatl.

"You roll them out gently. Now watch," Mamá demonstrates. "Put your right foot forward so that your body will be balanced as you lean forward to roll out the dough. That will ensure that the tortilla will be uniform." (And, incidentally, my life.)

The sweat forms on my upper lip. I take the palote in my right hand, arrange my feet as directed, and try to roll out the dough into the shape of a circle. The masa has a mind of its own. It resists, gathers strength, overpowers and subdues me.

Mamá comments with a patient sigh, "That doesn't look too bad, mijita. It is not quite round, it's true, but let's cook it and see how it comes out."

She places my Rorschach tortilla on the comal. It energizes with the heat. It browns, it puffs, it grows appendages, it hardens. The morning's lesson progresses. My stack of tortillas grows at a precarious tilt, a leaning tower. I am dusted with white flour from head to foot. My fingernails are luminous with dough. I am exhausted.

Mamá announces with pious finality, "There. Now we're done. That was not so hard, now was it? Children! Come and see the tortillas your mother has made!"

From the mouths of little children: "Your tortillas look funny, Mom! How come they don't look like Nani's? That one looks like a rabbit. That one looks like a mushroom. That one looks like Florida! And that one looks like Texas!"

It wouldn't be so bad, I suppose, if one of them had been shaped like the state of Chihuahua. But Texas is unacceptable.

Mamacita relights the candle to St. Jude, the patron saint of hopeless cases.

A la mejor cocinera se le ahuma la olla.
Even the best cook can burn the pot.
(No one is perfect.)

Amor Eterno: Eleven Lessons in Love

Patricia Preciado Martin

Amor Desesperado/Desperate Love

The following note was confiscated by Sister Prudencia in May 1964 from Anna Ortiz as she was passing it to her best friend, Martita López, in English class, Period 4, at Salpointe Catholic High School in Tucson, Arizona. The note remains on file in her records along with a copy of Anna's report card; the following infractions in deportment are highlighted in red pencil: Is Inattentive; Wastes Time; Annoys Others. The end result of this ill-timed discovery causing her to be grounded for a whole month, not that she had been invited to the prom anyway. . . .

Dear Martita,

Wow! What a sexy English composition class this is with Sister Pee Wee droning on and on about dangling participles and ejaculations!!!! Ha. Ha. Geez, I feel hysterical, panicked, depressed, and desperate. The Junior-Senior Prom is only two weeks away and I don't have a date, but my sister does, natch, and my mom made her a taffeta dress that took four yards just for the skirt. Maybe I could go stag—just kidding. Did I tell you about the joke I made up? Do you know why they call them nuns? Because they don't get any. ("Nones"—Get it?) Ha. Ha. Whoops, better sign off. I see Pee Wee is eyeing me. Burn this.

Anna

P.S. Have you voted for my sister for prom queen yet? You better!

Part 1: The Rules

Don't wear your hair too long or you'll look like a pachuca, or too short or you will appear mannish. Keep your ankles crossed, your toes pointed, your knees together, your chin up, your head high, your eyes down (but not shifty), your back erect, your shoulders straight. If you are too quiet, he'll think you are moody; too talkative, frivolous. Too thin, sickly; too plump, lazy. Too studious, haughty; unlearned, dull. Too active, restless; too placid, morose. Too generous, careless; too thrifty, selfish. Too devout, prudish; faithless, loose. If you eat too much, he'll consider you a glutton; not enough, finicky. And try to remember to keep your hands elevated vertically whenever possible so that the veins don't pop out. And never never never go out of the house without a fresh set of underwear that is in good condition because you never know if you'll be in an accident.

Part 2: The Recipes

For the Hair

My abuelita's secret tonic for lustrous hair that will be sure to catch his eye is as follows:

> 6 ounces ethyl rubbing alcohol or strong proof vodka
>
> 1 ounce nettle
>
> 1 ounce rosemary
>
> 12 drops castor oil
>
> 1 ounce salycilic acid
>
> 1 ounce distilled water

Directions: Soak the nettle and the rosemary in the alcohol for a week. Strain into another container and add castor oil and perfumed herbs. Dissolve salicylic acid in distilled water and add to herbal and oil solution and use as a rinse on the hair.

Another tonic for the hair can be made by using gum camphor: Steep 1 ounce of crushed gum camphor and two ounces of powdered borax into two quarts of boiling water for several hours. Massage nightly into the hair and then brush for five hundred strokes. (At times it can be quite helpful to sip the vodka from the first recipe while brushing the hair.)

For the Complexion

A complexion cleansing and circulation mask is made of the following:

> ¼ cake of camphor
>
> 1 egg white

1 peeled cucumber

¼ teaspoon lemon juice

1 teaspoon ethyl alcohol

1 teaspoon witch hazel

3 drops peppermint oil extract

Directions: Crush camphor; add to whipped egg white and cucumber. Blend together. Add lemon juice or cider vinegar, alcohol, witch hazel, and peppermint oil extract. Blend again. Apply as a mask and allow to dry while reclining with feet elevated in a darkened room. Remove in fifteen or twenty minutes. Rinse thoroughly. Close your pores with a strong astringent. (This may sting.)

For Body Odor

An antiperspirant drink that has a valued reputation is made of camphor, lemon, and milk. Soak the peeling of a lemon in warm milk and add three drops of camphor oil to the milk. Before sleeping, drink the milk and chew the rind.

For Fresh Breath

Camphor chalk has two virtues: one in being an inert substance, and the other in being an antiseptic. It is therefore valuable for dental purposes, keeping the teeth white and the breath fresh. Make a paste as follows:

1 teaspoon camphor

1 lump sugar

1 tablespoon crushed almonds

½ pint distilled water

Directions: Powder the camphor and the sugar. Grind the almonds in a molcajete and make a paste by adding distilled water. Brush your teeth six times a day for at least ten minutes. (It is also helpful to brush the tongue.)

For the Hands

Lemon peel rubbed on fingernails strengthens and also cleanses and whitens. A wonderful nail restorer combines equal parts of honey, avocado, egg yolk, and a pinch of sea salt. Rub into nails. Leave for an hour and then rinse off. (This is also useful for whitening the skin, which is a very desirable attribute for getting a summer job.)

For the Feet

Massaging the feet with olive oil will soften the dead tissue and make it easier to rid oneself of impediments. (Physical, not emotional.)

For the Eyes

A tea made of rose hips can reduce puffiness under the eyes. Make a paste of rose hip powder and small additions of parsley, cucumber, lemon peel, and sliced strawberries. Pat on the eyes and allow to dry, preferably with the head at a 45 degree angle. Remove after one hour with warm water.

(In addition, a tea made from the flower of the elderberry tree is an excellent remedy for twitching eyelids, but I can't remember if my abuelita told me to drink it, dab it on my eyelids, or bathe in it. Perhaps all three, if the condition is serious enough.)

For All Disorders of the Body

Garlic has many medicinal uses, including controlling worms, treating scorpion bites, colds, hoarseness, indigestion, and asthma. One old curandera who was a neighbor of my abuelita in Barrio Hollywood describes the use of the center bulblet: Insert into the left ear to relieve symptoms of nervousness.

A cup of tea made from sage, dandelion flowers, and honey will help to bring on a sense of calmness. In addition, hierba buena is an herb that grows wild in the garden. Peppermint tea makes an excellent tonic that strengthens and cleanses the entire body and is soothing to the nerves. For a headache, drink some tea and lie down for a little while.

(The aforementioned ingredients can serve multiple uses should one or more of the tonics or potions fail in their purported usefulness. In various stages of discouragement, I have been known to make smoothies, salads, mixed drinks, appetizers, and salad dressings as a last resort.)

Part 3: The Saints (When All Else Fails)

San Antonio, Evadio, Flavio, Bonifacio, Ubaldo, Venancio, Bernardino, Valente, Epitacio, Donascio, Urbano, Fernando, Marcelino, Norberto, José, Roberto, Gilardo, Feliciano, Cirilo, Bernabé, Nazario, Eliseo,

Modesto, Silverio, Paulino, Juan Bautista, Anselmo, Cornelio, Camilo, Cayetano, Plutarco, Pedro y Pablo, Abundio, Isaias, Nabor, Arnulfo, Vicente, Joaquín, Celestino, Próspero, Justo, Emiliano, Acacio, Eusebio, Librado, Sixto, Filiberto, Jacobo, Bartolomé, Luís Rey, Armando, Agustín, Ramón, Judas, Efren, Carlos, Zacarías, Leonardo, Ernesto, Victorino, Teodoro, Diego, Leopoldo, Fidencio, Ponciano, Gelasio, Erasmo, Crisogno, Conrado, Esteban, Saturnino, Andrés, Francisco, Ambrosio, Damaso, Filogenio, Tomás, Demetrio, Patricio, Silvestre . . . and Santa Imelda, Enedina, Prudencia, Rita, Carolina, Teodosia, Petronilla, Elena, Cleotilde, Emma, Socorro, Filomena, Isabela, Amalia, María Magdalena, Brigida, Cristina, Esperanza, Lidia, Paulina, Susana, Clara, Aurora, Beatríz, Silviana, Aurelia, Cecilia, Natalia, Bárbara, Concepción, Leocadia, Lucía, Victoria, Adelaida, Nuestra Señora de Guadalupe, Nuestra Señora de Perpetuo Socorro, Virgen del Carmen, Virgen de la Soledad, Virgen del Rosario, Virgen de San Juan de Los Lagos, Sagrada Familia, Santo Niño de Atocha, Santo Niño de Praga . . . *please* help me find a husband that will meet my mother's high standards, Amen.

The Truth about Alicia and Other Stories

Ana Consuelo Matiella

The Ring

I'm so glad you could make it today, Comadre. I haven't been to this café in so long. The service is terrible, but all I want is a cup of coffee. How about you? An eclair? That sounds good.

I don't even know where to begin. Rafael has been acting strange in the last few weeks, even more curt than usual. Barking his orders at me in the morning: "More eggs! The coffee is cold." Treating me like I was the servant while Delia was in the room. She finally cowered out of the dining room like a frightened dog.

Delia was with us for ten years, Comadre. She was docile and kind and took good care of us. Ay, Comadre, I feel terrible. I wish I could go back and erase everything. But it's too late . . .

It all started on New Year's Eve, and he hadn't mentioned a thing about going out like we usually do. The casino was having its yearly ball, and you know how I love to dance . . .

I had heard from Arlene that she and Raul were going over to the Robinsons' for a dinner party, and I would have settled for that. It's worth going over there just to listen to Rosita Robinson exaggerate about her children. The daughter who lives in Canada really just lives in North Dakota. Her son, the psychiatrist, is actually a social worker. The one she calls the major is really only a captain. But her fabrications amuse me.

When Rafael finally called, he simply said, "Dress up tonight. We're going out. Be ready when I get there." When I heard his tone of voice, I knew better than to ask where we were going.

I dressed in the black silk taffeta that he bought for me in San Francisco last year. When I tried it on in the boutique, he said I looked like Jane Russell and slapped my behind. I never know what his reaction is going to be, Comadre, you know that. He's like the gringos say, Dr. Jekyll and Mr. Hyde.

I felt good in that dress. Delia had just picked up my black satin pumps from the Gato Negro Shoe Repair. She helped me tease my hair a little bit at the top and sprayed Aqua Net in the back where I can't reach. Pobrecita, poor thing, she stayed later than usual, watching me get ready, paying me compliments, and saying, "No señora, no, señora. You're not fat at all. You just have a full body like that movie star, what's her name, the one with the big bust?"

"Jane Russell," I told her.

That's when I asked her to look for the ring. "Delia, give me the diamond ring the señor gave me for my birthday," I told her. "It's in the little crystal jewelry box, the one shaped like a heart."

She looked in the drawer and said the ring wasn't there. Then I gave her the key to the safe behind the picture of Our Lady of Guadalupe in the hallway, and she looked and said it wasn't there either.

Then I started getting worried, Comadre. And I looked everywhere, and Delia got so nervous she started praying to St. Anthony. Poor thing. I could just die.

We turned the house upside down, and by this time Delia was crying and I knew the ring was gone. I just don't know what happened. I knew something was very wrong . . . I just didn't know what. Delia was acting so nervous. I couldn't believe she would do such a thing, but I panicked, and that's when I told her, "Delia, the last time I saw the ring was on December 22, when I went to Adelita Irastorza's shower. I distinctly remember taking it off and putting it in the heart box."

I guess she sensed my tone of voice. Her back got stiff and her eyes got real black, and she said, "Well, señora, if that's where you put it, that's where it should be."

She went down the hall and said it was late and she needed to go before she missed the last bus.

I followed her and told her, "Delia, the señor, you, and me are the only ones who have been inside this house. There's nothing else missing. If you leave tonight and I haven't found my ring, don't come back."

Ten years, Comadre! How could I do that to her?

She looked at me just once and said, "Sí, señora," then walked out with her paper bag full of leftovers from last night's dinner and some chocolates I had given her for the children.

With my heart in my throat, Comadre, I waited for Rafael. I was in a bad way, really. I was not myself.

When he walked up the stairs about 9:00 p.m., I had already cried myself into a stupor and prayed the novena to St. Anthony several times over. I just wanted to take a Valium and go to bed.

He strutted up the stairs to the bedroom like he does when he's had a few drinks and he's feeling good. He was wearing that beautiful brown gabardine suit that Sosa made for him, and I must admit, Comadre, after all these years, he's still a handsome man.

"Are you ready?" he asked. I don't know what happened, but I felt a tremendous hatred for him at that moment, Comadre. I wished I could push him down the stairs. He can be so cruel. You don't know that side of him. You smell the British Sterling and it's all over for you, but he can be a mean son of a bitch—excuse my language.

Removing the tea bags that had been resting on my eyelids, I said, "Rafael, I am very upset."

Then he said sarcastically, his eyes narrow and mean, "What's the matter, Maria Luisa? Did the vegetable man sell you bad tomatoes again?"

I sat up on the bed and said, "No, the ring is gone."

"What ring?"

"The ring. The diamond ring you gave me for my birthday."

"You mean the one you whined about for years? The one Daniel's charged me way too much money for? That ring?"

"Yes," I said. "That one. And I fired Delia."

"Delia took it?" He looked surprised, Comadre. Then he said, "After ten years she repays all your coddling and pampering by stealing your diamond ring? I told you she was an ingrate, and you didn't believe me. These Indians have no loyalty, you know that. Well, thank god it's insured. So don't worry about it. We'll get you another one."

"No, Rafael," I said. "That's not the point. I designed that ring, and we used one of your mother's diamonds in it. How can we replace that? And then this thing with Delia, it gave me a migraine. . . . I just want to go to bed."

He brushed the whole thing aside as if it didn't matter. And when I told him to go without me, he laughed and said, "You can't stay home, all dressed up and no place to go. I won't have it. That bore Rosita Robinson is dying to tell you more lies about her children, and I promised Nacho we'd stop by the ballroom after dinner. We have some business to take care of."

Just like that, Comadre. That's how he acted. Of course, I thought it was odd that he didn't seem to care that the ring was missing.

He said, "Come on, get your sweet little ass out of that bed and let's go."

Well, like the pendeja that I am, there I go with this beast of a man. Why do I stay, Comadre? Why do I take all these indignities from this overdressed donkey?

I was distracted at the Robinsons'. Rosita has bought one of those golden goddess chandeliers. The plastic goddess twirls round and round, surrounded by a cascading fountain of water. I know it's tacky, but what can I say? It goes well with the rest of Rosita's French Provincial decor. She swears it's imported from France, but what does she think? That we don't go to Casa Marcus? I was there just the other day, and old man Marcus was taking them out of the box. Right there on the bottom of the box, it said Made in Taiwan.

After dinner we left the Robinsons' and went on to the dance at the Casino Ballroom so Rafael could talk to that little pig of a man, Nacho. Nacho with the crotch that hangs to his knees, cigar and scotch breath, and Grecian Formula hair. He and Rafael had business, whatever that means. I just sat there like an idiot while Rafael and Nacho smoked cigars and talked and Raul and Arlene danced the night away. Are those two as happy as they look, Comadre? Arlene's as fat as ever. She wore her tight green chiffon, and Raul held her like she was Gina Lollobrigida.

I couldn't stop thinking about the ring and Delia and the fact that I fired her. I couldn't believe that Delia took my ring, Comadre. It just didn't sit right that after all those years she would steal from me like that. Ten years is a long time, Comadre!

Arlene noticed I was jumpy and kept asking me if there was anything wrong, but I just couldn't tell her what happened. I couldn't bring myself to tell her I got rid of Delia because she stole my ring. After the dance was over and my hair reeked of cigar smoke, Rafael decided we should all go to La Fondita for a late-night bowl of menudo.

Rafael yelled out that it was "the best pinche menudo in the whole damn town!" He was drunk by then. Nacho and Raul had to help him into the car, but I figured the menudo might sober him up and it would be better if I didn't have to take him home drunk.

Well, Comadre, I was not prepared for what happened next. It was the worst night of my life. Rafael walked into the restaurant and yelled out, "Margarita, menudo for everyone!" and Margarita herself comes over and gives us the once-over. Yes, you know the one. She has big sway-ing hips and skinny legs. Yes, I guess if you like that cheap look, you might call her attractive. Well, anyway, listen to this. She looks at me straight in the face and says,

"Buenas noches, Maria Luisa," as if we're all cut out of the same cloth! She's got some nerve.

And then, Comadre, you are not going to believe what happened next because I still can't believe it myself. When she set the basket of bolillo bread on the table, I saw her finger and I was revolted by what I saw. And I thought to myself, as if in a trance, "This finger full of menudo grease has been cutting green onions and cilantro all afternoon."

Then I lost my composure, Comadre. I grabbed her fingers with all my might and crushed her hand in mine. My jaws locked, and I asked her through my teeth, "Where did you get this ring?" And just like that, Comadre, just like that, she said, "Ask your husband."

I must have blacked out. I don't remember what happened next except that later, after Rafael got us all out of the restaurant and into the car, Arlene sat in the backseat with me and said I broke Margarita's finger. She said I got a look in my eyes like a wild animal and dunked her hand in the hot menudo and twisted and twisted and didn't let go.

Did I talk to Rafael, you say? No, I didn't talk to him, Comadre. What good would it do? I slept in the spare bedroom, and the next morning he was gone. Went to Monterey on business. He left a note saying he would be back in a few days and left the brown gabardine suit for me to take to the cleaners.

Oh, Comadre, what should I do? Should I go look for Delia?

El Bebé del Vaquerón

Vaquerón's baby was born in Doña Olga Martin's washroom next to the kitchen. The girl didn't know much about being pregnant, so she didn't know the baby could just come out. Doña Olga delivered the baby right there on the spot, wrapped him in towels, settled the girl in the spare bedroom, and went to Capin's Department Store to buy a package of diapers, some baby undershirts, and one of those little terry-cloth outfits with feet.

When she returned, the girl was still holding her baby tightly. The baby was peacefully asleep. The girl was crying.

To see her, Doña Olga felt betrayed herself. To muster up the courage to ask what was clearly none of her business, she drank tequila straight out of the bottle earlier in the day than usual. She asked the girl, "Who did this to you, little one?"

The girl told her. It was Señor de la Peña. She cleaned their house on Tuesdays. He forced himself on her, she said.

Doña Olga, full of rage and the kind of courage that you get only from drinking tequila in the morning, called the de la Peña household. She groggily told Doña Teresa de la Peña, "The girl just gave birth to a bastard son of your worthless husband." Teresa de la Peña hung up on her.

They call him El Vaquerón because he is a cowboy and he's big. He's strong and dark and good with horses and women. Ranch girls are his specialty, but he's not that particular as long as they are young.

Neli was the girl who came to clean the de la Peña house on Tuesdays while his wife, Teresa, had her hair and nails done at Berta's Salon of Beauty, and that suited him just fine.

After the birth Neli stayed at Doña Olga's for three days. Doña Olga said she was sorry but she couldn't have Neli come to clean anymore. It was too complicated. She had already embarrassed Teresa de la Peña by calling her to give her the news about the baby. She could never go to Berta's Salon of Beauty on Tuesdays again.

On Thursday Doña Olga's chauffeur, Fernando, drove Neli back across the border to the Mexican side of the line. He didn't drive up the cobblestone hill. He dropped her off at the corner in front of Cafeteria Leo's.

Neli couldn't go to the de la Peña's on Tuesdays again and couldn't go to Doña Olga's on Mondays either. She gained a baby and lost two jobs.

Neli's mother didn't know what to say when she saw Neli coming up the steep hill with a baby wrapped up in a white towel. She had been worried for the last three days, wondering why Neli hadn't come home.

Neli usually let her mother know if Doña Olga needed her to stay a few more days.

She had noticed Neli was gaining weight but thought for sure it was all the pumpkin empanadas that Neli ate, pretending to sell them to the neighbors.

When Neli's father, Patricio, came home late that night, the first night she was home with her baby, he asked the same question Doña Olga had asked three days earlier. "Who did this to you, little one?"

With the courage that comes only from drinking tequila in the afternoon, he looked in the bottom drawer of the dresser for the Smith and Wesson.

Just down the hill at the Molino Rojo Bar, El Vaquerón was drinking with his ranch hands and playing pool in the dark, fermented hall. Instantly the coolness of a freshly mopped floor and the smell of years of spilled liquor hit Patricio's hot face as he entered through the double doors of the bar. He felt like the Cisco Kid.

El Vaquerón had known Patricio for years. He never knew he had a daughter. After a long day's work they often played pool together at the Molino Rojo, joking and howling at the women passing on the sidewalk.

El Vaquerón only knew Patricio was a good ranch hand, worked for Don Leopoldo for years at the Tres Hermanas Ranch just outside Nogales.

"I didn't know she was your daughter," he said when Patricio told him why he was pointing the gun at him. But Patricio didn't care. He shot him right there on the spot, almost killed him, but as often happens with tequila in the afternoon, missed his heart.

It's been four months now. Neli named her baby after her father. She helps her mother sew for the neighborhood fat ladies who can't find ready-to-wear dresses at the store. She makes pumpkin empanadas. She packs them in a basket and walks down the hill to the church every day for the seven o'clock mass. She sells some of them.

On Tuesday afternoons she puts her baby boy in her rebozo and goes down the street to the jailhouse to visit her father.

excerpt from

The Peruvian Notebooks

Braulio Muñoz

Chapter 12

"Two O'Clock"

Engulfed in his chaotic memories, sensing his strength giving way to a growing feverish fatigue, at 2:25 p.m., Antonio Alday Gutiérrez is suddenly hit by the realization that he has denied the memory of his old friend for years. He has thought of Alex Sosa now and then, of course. But as the days went by and he settled in his new sitio, first in Philadelphia and now in Delaware County, he came to recall him only in passing. He let time blur the distinctive contours of his long face, the playful light in his dark eyes, the full black beard that covered his pockmarked cheeks. By now he has forgotten the story of his old friend's life.

With no energy left to fend off his accusing memories, Antonio Alday Gutiérrez reaches again for his Peruvian notebooks. He leafs through the brittle pages of red lines and miniscule handwriting, looking for the entry where he had set down Alex Sosa's story. His eyes are now very weak and his hands are trembling uncontrollably again, but he peers at the pages with determination. He peers into his Peruvian notebooks desperately, hoping to recover the anticipation and adventure, the memory of moments of peace and true friendship he shared with Alex Sosa during his early years in America.

Before he can find and attempt to decipher those pages, however, Antonio Alday Gutiérrez is overwhelmed by a bitter realization: he has abandoned and betrayed Alex Sosa in more profound ways than by forgetting him. Wrapped in the soft light of the winter sun, seized by a sudden sadness magnified by fatigue, Antonio Alday Gutiérrez has to acknowledge that over the years, Anthony Allday transformed Alex Sosa into a Portuguese man who was always happy roaming about in New England.

Anthony Allday reconstructed Alex Sosa to populate his own past with agreeable memories. In truth, Alex Sosa was not Portuguese, and he was not always happy.

Chapter 13

Peruvian Notebook No. 2
April 20, 1984

Alex Sosa liked César Romero and Ricardo Montalbán. In fact, he liked all things Hispanic, even though he did not live in a barrio and hardly ever spoke Spanish. I don't speak it because I'm ashamed of my accent, man. You know, when I was a child I used to read everything in Spanish: El Gato Felix, Superman, Linterna Verde, everything. I grew up knowing all that. We lived in Ensenada, a little town on the Mexican Pacific coast, and my father liked to come up north now and again to make some money. Until one day he disappeared. Just like that, man. People said he had died crossing the frontier. Which was probably true. Except that my mother didn't believe it. She refused to believe her Alejo had died like a stray dog in some God-forsaken desert. And so—I only tell you this 'cause I want you to know that I no longer feel cheated by life, man, that I've gone way past it—she took me and my two sisters across the border. She came up to look for him. Can you believe that? We walked and rode and traveled and slept and traveled for God only knows how long. Until we ended up picking melons somewhere in California, or maybe Texas. It must have been around those parts, because there were lots of Chicanos. That's how I ended up in school. Well, I wasn't invited, you know? I was forced to go. One day, some people came and told my mother we three had to go to school. I went because I didn't want my mother to get in trouble. That's when they changed my name from Alejo to Alex.

Alex Sosa paused. He took a swig from the jug of Almaden wine, the only wine we used to buy because, since he had picked grapes at some point in a vineyard called by that name and since we all know wine takes time to mature, he said, perhaps the grapes he had picked with his own hands were now coming back to warm his belly, which would be only fair. Two years, Tony, he said, adjusting himself on a tuft of grass atop the rock promontory overlooking the Atlantic Ocean in Bristol, Rhode Island, by the construction site for the new campus of Roger Williams College, where we had gone to paint. Imagine that! That's how I learned English. I hated it, man. They wouldn't let us speak Spanish. My sisters and I would sneak off and speak it during recess. I think those were the only times when I actually spoke in school. For months, man. People must have thought I was a retard.

I learned all about El Alamo, where Davy Crockett died and we Mexicans were the bad guys. I used to sing songs about the American heroes. You know about El Alamo, right? In any case, I left school less than two years later because my mother decided to take us back home. She told me she had dreamed that my father was in our old house, looking for us. She was convinced it was true because, she said, she had dreamed it just about midnight, which is when the soul opens wide. So we left, and after some weeks I think, we got back to Ensenada. Man! When I got back there, everything was different, Tony. Not only the people, man. I'm talking about the trees, the houses, the sky even. Everything. I didn't like it. I know I should've. But I didn't. Right then and there, I began pestering my mother to come up north. I guess I kind of liked it here. Although if you were to ask me why, I wouldn't know what to tell you. Not then. Not now.

But wait, wait; it gets better. We didn't come back up for another two years. And we came back up north only because one of my mother's cousins told her she had seen my father in San Antonio, in that place where El Alamo is. She said don Alejo Sosa was on his way up to Massachusetts, a place beyond the pampas of Oklahoma, that he had even waved to her from the bus. She swore it was true because she had seen him with her own two eyes.

Another trip. My mother sold everything she had to buy the bus tickets. She didn't like trains. She said her stomach could never settle down. We didn't even have winter clothes. Man! When we got to Boston we were so cold we thought we were going to die. And it was only October. We didn't know what to do or where to go. Can you believe that? My mother just said we had to get to Massachusetts. Of course, we were never going to find my father. He probably died years before. Perhaps crossing the frontier, as they said, on his way back. Because in those days it was more difficult to get back down than to come up here. The coyotes would wait for you at all the crossing places to take your money. My father was probably killed because he refused to give them his money. At least that's what I like to think, man; that he died defending his money.

We ended up in New Bedford because my mother made friends with a fruit vendor at the bus station. After we spent two days there, not knowing what the hell to do or where to go, the lady, who I think was Italian, told her to go to New Bedford because, according to her, there were lots of jobs there. It wasn't true, man. There was nothing there either. Only thing was, we could understand the people there 'cause they spoke Portuguese. Alex Sosa took another swig from the Almaden jug, looked into the blue waters around us, and proceeded to retie his white-and-blue canvas painting shoes. In any case, my mother started working as a domestic in the house of a fireman and my sisters got jobs at a restaurant on La Calle de Saudades. As for myself, I was sent back to school! You see, the fireman gave that to my mother as a condition: You work for me but you send your boy to school. Why did he do that? I have no idea. I guess he wanted what was best for all of us. That's what everybody said to me then: it's best for everyone. And so I was back in school. By this time, I already knew how to speak English. I was quite good at learning, really. I guess that kind of stuff comes easy to me. Thing is, I spent two years in high school. There too, I kinda liked it. Maybe 'cause those kids weren't as mean as the ones in Texas. But, like I said, I didn't graduate from high school either.

See, my mom got sick. Not really sick, like with her liver or anything, only that she missed her family back home. She was losing weight and couldn't sleep at night. She got to wearing only black, like all the old ladies in New Bedford. She looked awful. And so my two sisters—the oldest one, Patricia, was almost twenty years old—decided to take her back home. So they settled the accounts, bought their bus tickets, and took off. I didn't go with them, of course. I liked it here. It wasn't because I hated Mexico or Ensenada. That's what Mr. Rose, the fireman, said: You stayed here because you hated to go back there, Alex. You made the right choice, son. Not at all, man. I just liked it here. What was it that I liked most? I don't know. I guess I mostly liked the idea of finding myself a job and spending my own money. I had already had little jobs here and there, mostly in the summer. I already knew what it meant to earn something. But the deal with Mr. Rose had prevented me from really working. Now that my mother was going back, I thought I would stay, earn some money, and go back to find her whenever I wanted.

Since it was still summer, it was easy to get a job as a painter. I began as a helper. Just like you. Later, I became really good. As I said, things kinda come easy to me. I learned to cut the job, you know? Plass! Plass! Like that! I learned to square the job with the brush. Found a way to make it so that painting was not boring but more like an art. Know what I mean, right? You've got to find that, too. Otherwise, painting is worse than picking melons, man. And Alex Sosa turned around, looking up against the vertical rays of the midday sun. Antonio Allday saw the twinkle in his eyes: I'm an artist, Tony; didn't you know that! I've been painting ever since. It's been my life. Became a foreman only a couple of years ago. Man! I have painted everywhere. I know New England, from Maine to Connecticut, like the back of my hand. I've always liked moving around. Hated to be confined. But now, I don't know. I'm thinking of settling down here, in Providence. It's a good place, Providence. Got lots of friends here. People who had to move out of Fox Point. And Cheryl is here, too. And now so are you.

I just don't want to do anything else, Tony. I like being a painter. Who knows, maybe someday, maybe even soon, I'll have my own little business. Have to, if I'm gonna marry Cheryl and have a family, right? But not for a while. Her family would strangle me now. Especially her brother Bobby. I've got to take care of him. A business would do that. Man! For now, give me another swig. And looking into Antonio Allday's eyes: I like it here, Tony. I like to paint in the full breeze and sun. Don't want to be locked up in some factory somewhere. What the hell. Things will turn out all right. Cheryl will wait. . . . Want to be a painter? I mean, what the hell do you want to be? Don't work in a factory or in the fields, man. That kind of work is only for people who don't really want to stay in America, for people who want to go back. Maybe a mechanic or something. What did you do in Peru?

Antonio Allday told Alex Sosa that he had been an actor, that he had lived in a place called Tacora, in Lima, that he had a brother and a sister and a mother still alive. He told him that he still missed them, now and then, but he was getting used to missing them. Soon it would all be gone. Had to be. It wasn't good to miss people.

Chapter 14

It is strange, Antonio Alday Gutiérrez thinks at 2:30 p.m., Antonio Allday never lied to Alex Sosa. He never told him tall stories. Perhaps it was because Alex Sosa was a man at peace with himself and Antonio Allday wanted to be like him. On the other hand, he never told Alex Sosa all that much about himself, either. He kept his secrets secret. And Alex Sosa never probed. He never expected Antonio to talk about such things. Not even when they had a jug of Almaden and danced to salsa music. Alex Sosa was too American already. He was happy just to have a friend like Antonio with whom to share his food, his drink, his house, his memories. He was not one for hearing confessions. And Antonio Alday Gutiérrez wonders what would have happened if he had shared everything with Alex Sosa. Things might have been different, perhaps. But Alex Sosa never probed.

Alex Sosa must have known Tony was hiding something that gnawed at the blind knots of his being. He knew his friend that well. On Christmas Day 1982, Alex Sosa gave him a set of four notebooks as a present. Maybe you're really a writer, Tony, he said, since you keep bugging Mrs. Rosenberg to lend you all them novels. I think you're wasting your time reading that stuff. Should get a girlfriend or something. But, hey, who knows, man. Sometimes it's good to get things out from the gut. If one's a writer, I mean. So, here. Found them at the five-and-dime on La Calle de Saudades, back in September. I've been saving them for you, man. I bought the whole bunch, though. So make 'em count. It says on the back they were made in Peru. So all the better, right? But if you ask me, they were made in China. Do you remember these kinds of books when you were a kid?

How could he not? The blurry red lines and the smell of dry lemon peels were unmistakable. Everyone used them in school, back in Tacora. Everyone. Including Betti. Only hers were always neat and clean whereas Toño's were dog-eared and covered with blotches of Pelícano black ink. Hers were wrapped in blue kite paper and smelled like Mr. Sato's red roses, and Toño's were doodled all over—except for the ones he first carried in his back pocket and then stashed under his mattress.

Chapter 15

When they were living in Providence, out of the blue Alex Sosa came up with the idea that César Romero was the best Latin lover in the whole world. The man was so fantastic, he said, he was a hundred times better than Clark Gable and even Robert Wagner. If you don't believe me, let's go see *Weekend in Havana*. They say he's great in it, man. Antonio Allday resisted the idea because the movie was supposed to be a comedy, and he had never liked comedies. But Alex Sosa harassed him all week long, until he agreed to go with him to Seekonk. They planned to stop at Guido's, in Federal Hill, and take calzones with them. As Sunday evening approached, Antonio let his guard down and began to expect a good show.

The outing ended in disappointment. César Romero turned out to be a real weakling. He played a character who was always nervous, as if afraid of being caught by La Migra. ¡Carajo! He had a stupid thin mustache, ropy legs, and a shameful accent. Shameful. He was no *galán* at all. Not like Clark Gable. That evening, sitting on the long hood of the hearse with Alex Sosa, feeling the soft breeze blowing from Narraganset Bay, Antonio Allday realized that a man could only be a galán if he was not an outsider. If Antonio were ever to be a proper American, galán or not, he would have to belong. Just as a gringo galán would never fit in Peru because he would be too naïve, too cojudo, a Peruvian galán would never fit in America because he would be too *saltón*, too jumpy. At most he would be like César Romero: an embarrassment. And that evening Antonio Allday decided to become a gringo.

He did not let Alex Sosa know about his decision right away. He let him go on talking about César Romero's virtues instead. He knew Alex Sosa admired Latin actors. Like Ricardo Montalbán, for example, who in those days was starring in *Fantasy Island* as Mr. Roarke. He's so great, Tony. Didn't you see him in *The Conquest* and *Escape from the Planet of the Apes?* Didn't you, man? . . . Alex Sosa was not alone in regarding Ricardo Montalbán as a galán, of course. Everyone in New Bedford, including the old ladies who dressed in black and walked along La Calle de Saudades wearing mantillas, considered Ricardo Montalbán sexy. But to Antonio Allday, the gimpy man was just another disappointment. He used his horrid accent as a little flag: here! here! I am Hispanic. ¡Carajo! All that was good for was that people could say: He's not bad, despite being Mexican. The only thing Antonio Allday conceded to Ricardo

Montalbán was that he knew how to dress well. *Algo es algo*, he would admit, at least it's something.

The best way to become a gringo, thought Antonio Allday in 1977, was by imitating gringo actors. There were so many to choose from, of course. But he preferred Robert Wagner. He liked his worldly ways and his ironic smile, especially when he played Mundy in *The Magnificent Thief*: *I guess there's nothing better than good friends, good books, and good food. What else can a man ask for?* He liked how he dressed: fine black or white jackets, thin black or white ties, long white scarves. He liked the way he put his hands in his pockets, the way he ran, like a feather in the wind, the way he paused to drink his whiskey. But even Robert Wagner could not compare with Clark Gable, especially as Rhett Butler in *Gone with the Wind*. If Antonio Allday wished to learn from Robert Wagner how to project an air of mischievous mystery, he wished to learn from Clark Gable how to be sincere.

I'm not asking you to forgive me. I'll never understand or forgive myself.

Antonio Allday simply had to have that sincerity. And beginning in that summer of 1977, in the little room that Alex Sosa let him have for free in his apartment on Baker Street, Providence, Rhode Island, Antonio Allday spent hours repeating from memory entire scenes from *Gone with the Wind* and practicing Clark Gable poses before the mirror: *If you had it all to do over again, you'd do no differently. You're like the thief who isn't the least bit sorry he stole, but he's terribly, terribly sorry he's going to jail. . . .*

In the cold days of autumn, Antonio Allday spent his weekends walking along the beaches of Matunuck, Jerusalem, and Galilee with his face against the wind, reciting lines from memory and learning to control his blinking. That was something he had not been willing to do in Tacora, despite don Luna's constant harping. A good actor conveys more with his eyes and with his body than with his words, Toño. Don't ever forget that. Even when people can't see your eyes, you must control them. It's the rudder of acting, Toño.

Antonio Allday spent months developing the internal conviction that was to serve as the foundation of his new life. He did not let Alex Sosa see him practicing. He did not want to court his disapproval. Until one day, slowly but as naturally as the waves fell on the sandy beaches of Rhode Island, he began to feel in his innermost self that he could be sincere. By midsummer 1983, he was certain he had finally conquered not only the betraying accent but, more important, the previously constant sense of being an imposter.

It seems we've been at cross-purposes, doesn't it? But it is no use now. . . .

One Friday night, Antonio Allday walked out of his little room feeling like a new man. As he had expected, Alex Sosa was quick to notice the change. The next morning, as they came back from a job, Alex Sosa smiled widely, patted the large steering wheel without taking his eyes off the road, and spoke as if releasing something he had kept in check for a long time: from now on, you're only Tony to me, man! I guess things come as easy to you as they did to me, huh? I know so many who just can't get rid of the accent, Tony. I mean, they can't get rid of the past. Period. 'Cause it's like a curse. You know? My sisters, for example; they never really lost it. They held on to it. Know what I mean? They were afraid of becoming somebody else. I guess you and I have become somebody else. In my heart though, Tony, I'll always be Alejo and a Mexican. It's in my blood. My children will grow up knowing about El Alamo from *my* lips. Know what I mean? But what the hell, a man has to do what a man has to do. And you and I want to stay here.

I overcame all those obstacles, Antonio Alday Gutiérrez defends himself at 2:35 p.m. Completely. I accomplished what most people only dream of doing. Even Alex Sosa. Because, in the end, he was also attached to his past. He could have gone much further in reconstructing himself. He lost heart. Yo sí. Despite the obstacles. The suffering. I became what I wanted to be. Too bad things turned out the way they did. And, just then, the memory of Rhett Butler's words fluttered in his ugly apartment: *You think that by saying I'm sorry all the past can be corrected. . . .* Of course not, Antonio Alday Gutiérrez says. Rhett Butler was right. Nothing changes by being sorry.

The Last Tortilla and Other Stories

Sergio Troncoso

The Snake

The chubby boy slammed the wrought-iron screen door and ran behind the trunk of the weeping willow in one corner of the yard. It was very quiet here. Whenever it rained hard, particularly after those thunderstorms that swept up the dust and drenched the desert in El Paso during April and May, Tuyi could find small frogs slithering through the mud and jumping in his mother's flower beds. At night he could hear the groans of the bullfrogs in the canal behind his house. It had not rained for days now. The ground was clumped into thick, white patches that crumbled into sand if he dug them out and crushed them. But he was not looking for anything now. He just wanted to be alone. A large German shepherd with a luminous black coat and a shield of gray fur on its muscular chest shuffled slowly toward him across the patio pavement and sat down, puffing and apparently smiling at the boy. He grabbed the dog's head and kissed it just above the nose.

"Ay, Princey hermoso. They hate me. I think I was adopted. I'm not going into that house ever again! I hate being here, I hate it." Tuyi put his face into the dog's thick neck. It smelled stale and dusty. The German shepherd twisted its head and licked the back of the boy's neck. Tuyi was crying. The teardrops that fell to the ground, not on the dog's fur nor on Tuyi's Boston Celtics T-shirt, splashed into the dust and rolled up into little balls as if recoiling from their new and unforgiving environment.

"They give everything to my stupid sister and my stupid brothers and I get nothing. They're so stupid! I always work hard, I'm the one who got straight As again, and when I want a bicycle for the summer, they say I have to work for it, midiendo. I don't want to, I already have twenty-two dollars saved up, Oscar got a bicycle last year, a ten-speed, and he didn't even have anything saved up. He didn't have to go midiendo. Diana is going to Canada with the stupid drum corps this summer, they're probably spending hundreds of dollars for that, and they won't give me a bicycle! I don't want to sit there in the car waiting all day while Papá talks to these stupid people who want a new bathroom. I don't want to waste my summer in the hot sun *midiendo*, measuring these stupid empty lots, measuring this and that, climbing over rose bushes to put the tape right against the corner. I hate it. Why don't they make Oscar or Ariel go! Just because Oscar is in high school doesn't mean he can't go *midiendo*. Or Ariel could go too, he's not so small, he's not a baby anymore. And why don't they put Diana to work! Just because she's a girl. I wish I was a girl so I could get everything I wanted to for free. They hate me in this house."

"Tuyi! Tuyi!" his mother yelled from behind the screen door. "¿En dónde estás muchacho? Get over here at once! You're not going outside until you throw out the trash in the kitchen and in every room in this house. Then I want you to wash the trashcans with the hose and sweep around the trash bins outside. I don't want cucarachas crawling into this house from the canal. When I was your age, young man," she said as he silently lifted the plastic trash bag out of the tall kitchen can and yanked it tightly closed with the yellow tie, "I was working twelve hours a day on a ranch in Chihuahua. We didn't have any *summer* vacation." As he lugged it to the backyard, to the corner where the rock wall had two chest-high wooden doors leading to the street and a brick enclosure over which he would attempt to dump the trash bag into metal bins, a horrible, putrid smell of fish—he hated fish, they had had fish last night—wafted up to Tuyi's nose and seemed to hover around his head like a cloud.

"¡Oye, gordito! Do you want to play? We need a fielder," said a muscular boy, about fifteen years old, holding a bat while six or seven other boys ran around the dead end on San Simon Street, which had just finally been paved by the city. When the Martínez family had moved into one of the corner lots on San Simon and San Lorenzo, Tuyi remembered, there had been nothing but dirt roads and scores of empty lots where they would play baseball after school. His older brother, Oscar, was a very good player. He could smack the softball all the way to Carranza Street and easily jog around the bases before somebody finally found it stuck underneath a parked car and threw it back. When it rained, however, the dirt streets got muddy and filthy. Tuyi's mother hated that. The mud wrecked her floors and carpets. No matter how much she yelled at the boys to leave their sneakers outside they would forget and track it all in. But now there was black pavement, and they could play all the time, especially in the morning during the summer. You couldn't slide home, though. You would tear up your knee.

"Déjalo. He's no good, he's too fat," a short boy with unkempt red hair said, Johnny Gutiérrez from across the street.

"Yeah. He's afraid of flies. He drops them all the time in school and el coach yells at him in P.E.," Chuy sneered.

"Shut up, pendejos. We need a fielder," the older boy interrupted again, looking at Tuyi. "Do you want to play, Tuyi?"

"No, I don't want to. But Oscar will be back from washing the car and I think he wants to play," Tuyi said, pointing to their driveway as he began to walk away, down San Lorenzo Street. He knew Oscar would play if they only asked him.

"Ándale pues. Chuy, you and Mundis and Pelón will be on my team, and Maiyello, you have the rest of them. Okay? When Oscar comes we'll make new teams and play over there," he said, pointing to a row of empty lots down the street. "There's more room and we can slide. I'll be the fielder, you pitch, Pelón. And don't throw it so slow!"

Tuyi looked back at them as he walked down the new sidewalk, with its edges still sharp and rough where the two-by-fours had kept the cement squared. Here someone had scrawled "J + L 4/ever" and surrounded it with a slightly askew heart when the cement had been wet. Tuyi (no one called him Rodolfo, not even his parents) was happy to have won a reprieve from midiendo and from cutting the grass. He was not about to waste it playing baseball with those cabrones. He just wanted to be alone. His father had called home and had told his mother to meet him after work today. They were going to Juárez, first to a movie with Cantinflas and then maybe for some tortas on 16 de Septiembre Street, near the plaza where they had met some twenty years before. Tuyi had heard this story so many times he knew it by heart. His father, José Martínez, an agronomy and engineering student at the Hermanos Escobar School, had walked with some of his university buddies to the plaza. There, young people in the 1950s, at least those in Chihuahua, would stroll around the center. The boys, in stiff shirts with small collars and baggy, cuffed slacks, looking at the girls. The girls, in dresses tight at the waist and ruffled out in vertical waves toward the hem, glancing at the boys. If a boy stopped to talk to a girl, her friends would keep walking. Sometimes whole groups would just stop to talk to each other. In any case, this was where Papá had first seen Mamá, in a white cotton dress and black patent leather shoes.

Mamá had been a department store model, Tuyi remembered his father had said, and she was the most beautiful woman Papá had ever seen. It took him, Papá told Tuyi, five years of going steady just to hold her hand. They were novios for a total of eight years before they even got married! Today they were going to the movies just as they had done so many times before. His father had told his mother that he and Tuyi could instead go midiendo tomorrow, for a project in Eastwood, on the east side of El Paso, just north of the freeway from where they lived. Mr. Martínez was a construction engineer at Cooper and Blunt in downtown El Paso. On the side he would take up design projects for home additions, bathrooms, porches, new bedrooms, and the like. The elder Martínez had already added a new carport to his house and was planning to add another bathroom. He would do the construction work himself, on the weekends, and his sons would help. But today he wanted to go to the movies with his wife. They were such a sappy couple.

"Buenos días, Rodolfito. Where are you going, my child?" a woman asked, clipping off the heads of dried roses and wearing thick, black gloves. The house behind her was freshly painted white, with a burnt orange trim. A large Doberman pinscher slept on the threshold of the front door, breathing heavily, its paws stretched out toward nothing in particular.

"Buenos días, Señora Jiménez. I'm just going for a walk," Tuyi answered politely, not knowing whether to keep walking or to stop, so he stopped. His mother had told him not to be rude to the neighbors and to say hello whenever he saw them on his walks.

"Is your mother at home? I want to invite her to my niece's quinceañera this Saturday at the Blue Goose. There's going to be mariachis and lots of food. I think Glenda is going too. You and Glenda will be in 8-I next year, in Mr. Smith's class, isn't that right?"

"Yes, señora, I'll be in 8-I. My mother is at home now, I can tell her about the party."

"You know, you're welcome to come too. It will be lots of fun. Glenda told me the whole class was so proud of you when you won those medals in math for South Loop School. I'm glad you showed those snotty Eastwood types that a Mexicano can beat them with his mind."

"I'll tell my mother about the party. Hasta luego, señora," Tuyi muttered as he walked away quickly, embarrassed, his face flushed and nervously smiling. As he rounded the corner onto Southside Street, his stomach churned and gurgled. He thought he was going to throw up, yet he only felt a surge of gases build somewhere inside his body. He farted only when he was sure no one else was nearby. He had never figured out how he had won three first places in the citywide Number Sense competition. He had never even wanted to be in the stupid competition, but Mr. Smith and some other teachers had asked him to join the math club at school, pressured him in fact. Tuyi finally stopped avoiding them with his stoic politeness and relented when he found out that Laura Downing was in Number Sense already. He had a crush on her; she was so beautiful. Anyway, they would get to leave school early on Fridays when a meet was in town. Tuyi hated the competition, however. His stomach always got upset. Time would be running out and he hadn't finished every single problem, or he hadn't checked to see if his answers were absolutely right. His bladder would be exploding, and he had to tighten his legs together to keep from bursting. Or Laura would be there, and he would be embarrassed. He couldn't talk to her; he was too fat and ugly. Or he wanted to fart again, five minutes to go in the math test. After he won his first gold medal, all hell broke loose at South Loop. The school had never won before. The principal, Mr. Jácquez, announced it over the intercom after the pledge of allegiance and the club and pep rally announcements. Rodolfo Martínez won? The kids in Tuyi's class, in 7-I, stared at Tuyi, the fat boy everybody ignored, the one who was always last running laps in P.E. Then, led by Mrs. Sherman, they began to applaud. He wanted to vomit. After he won the third gold medal in the last competition of the year at Parkland High School, he didn't want to go to school the next day. He begged his parents to let him stay at home. He pleaded with them, but they said no. The day before the principal had called to tell them about what Tuyi had done. He should be proud of himself, his mother and father said, it was good that he had worked so hard and won for Ysleta. The neighborhood was proud of him. His parents didn't tell him this, but Mr. Jácquez had told them that there would be a special presentation for Tuyi at the last pep rally of the year. He *had* to go to school that day. When Mr. Jácquez called him up to the stage in the school's auditorium, in front of the entire school, Tuyi wanted to die. A rush of adrenaline seemed to blind him into a stupor. He didn't want to move. He wasn't going to move. But two boys sitting behind him nearly lifted him up. Others yelled at him to go up to the stage. As he walked down the aisle toward the stage, he didn't notice the wild clapping or the cheering by hundreds of kids. He didn't see Laura Downing staring dreamily at him in the third row as she clutched her spiral notebook. Everything seemed supernaturally still. He couldn't breathe. Tuyi didn't remember what the principal had said on the stage. Tuyi just stared blankly at the space in front of him and wished and prayed that he could sit down again. He felt a trickle of water down his left leg which he forced to stop as his face exploded with hotness. Thank God he was wearing his new jeans! They were dark blue; nobody could notice anything. Afterward, instead of going back to his seat, he left the stage through the side exit and cleaned himself in the boy's bathroom in front of the counselor's office. The next day, on the last day of school, when the final bell rang at 3:30, as he walked home on San Lorenzo Street with everything from his locker clutched in his arms, he was the happiest person alive in Ysleta. He was free.

Tuyi walked toward the old, twisted tree just before Americas Avenue, where diesel trucks full of propane gas rumbled toward the Zaragoza International Bridge. He did not notice the Franklin Mountains to the west. The huge and jagged wall in the horizon would explode with brilliant orange streaks at dusk, but now, at mid-morning, was just gray rock against the pale blue of the big sky. His shoulders were slumped forward. He stared at the powdery dirt atop the bank of the canal, stopping every once in a while to pick up a rock and hurl it into the rows of cotton around him. He threw a rock against the 30 mph sign on the road. A horribly unpeaceful clang shattered the quiet and startled him. A huge dog—he was terrified of every dog but his own—lunged at him from behind the chainlink fence of the last house on the block. The black mutt bared its teeth at him and scratched its paws into the dust like a bull wanting so much to charge and annihilate its target. At the end of the cotton field and in front of Americas Avenue, Tuyi waited until a red Corvette zoomed by going north, and then ran across the black pavement and down the hill onto a perpendicular dirt road that hugged the canal on the other side of Americas. There would be no one here now. But maybe during the early evening some cars would pull up alongside the trees that lined this old road. Trees that grew so huge toward the heavens only because they could suck up the moisture of the irrigation canal. The cars would stop under the giant shade, and groups of men, and occasionally a few women, would sit and laugh, drink some beers, throw and smash the bottles onto rocks, just wasting time until dark, when the mosquitoes would swarm and it was just better to be inside. Walking by these trees, Tuyi had often seen used condoms lying like flattened centipedes that had dried under the sun. He knew what they were. Some stupid kids had brought condoms to school for show and whipped them around their heads at lunchtime, or hurled them at each other like giant rubber-band bombs. Tuyi had also found a ring once, made of shiny silver and with the initials "SAT" inside. He didn't know anyone with these initials. And even if he had, he probably wouldn't have returned the ring anyway: he had found it, it was his. Tuyi imagined names that might fit such initials: Sarah Archuleta Treviño, Sócrates Arturo Téllez, Sigifredo Antonio Torres, Sulema Anita Terrazas, or maybe Sam Alex Thompson, Steve Andrew Tillman, Sue Aretha Troy. After he brought the ring back home and hid it behind the books on the shelves his father had built for him, he decided that "SAT" didn't stand for a name at all but for "Such Amazing Toinkers," where toinkers originally referred to Laura Downing's breasts, then later to any amazing breasts, and then finally to anything that was breathtaking and memorable. The sun sinking behind the Franklin Mountains and leaving behind a spray of lights and shadows was a "toinker sun." The cold reddish middle of a watermelon "toinked" in his mouth whenever he first bit into its wonderful juices.

About a half mile up the dirt road, Tuyi stopped. He was at his favorite spot. He shuffled around the trunk of the oak tree and found a broken branch, which he then trimmed by snapping off its smaller branches. In the canal, he pushed his stick into mud—the water was only a couple of inches deep—and flung out globs of mud. He was looking for tadpoles. The last time he had found one, he had brought it up to a rock near the tree. Its tail was slimy and slick. He found a styrofoam cup, which he filled up with water. Under the tree, he watched it slither around the cup, with tiny black dots on its tail and a dark army green on its bulletlike body. After a few minutes, he flicked open his Swiss army knife and slit the tadpole open from head to tail. The creature's body quivered for a second or two and then just lay flat like green jelly smeared on a sandwich. Tuyi noticed a little tube running from the top of the tadpole's head to the bottom, and a series of smaller veins branching off into the clear green gelatinous inside. He found what he took to be one of the eyes and sliced it off with the blade. It was just a black mass of more gushy stuff, which was easily mashed with the slightest pressure. He cut the entire body of the tadpole in thin slices from head to tail and tried to see what he could see, what might explain how this thing ate, whether it had any recognizable organs, if its color inside was different from the color of its skin.

But today he didn't find anything in the mud except an old Pepsi bottlecap and more black mud. He walked toward the edge of the cotton field abutting the canal. Here he found something fascinating indeed. An

army of large black ants scurried in and out of a massive anthole, those
going inside carrying something on their backs, leaves or twigs or white
bits that looked like pieces of bread, and those marching out of the hole
following, in the opposite direction, the paths of the incoming. The ants
would constantly bump into each other, go around, and then follow the
trail back toward whatever it was that kept them busy. How could ants
follow such a trail and be so organized? Did they see their way there? But
then they wouldn't be bumping into each other all the time. Or did they
smell their way up the trail and back home? Maybe they smelled each
other to say hello, such as one might whose world was the nothingness of
darkness. Tuyi wondered if these black ants were somehow communicat-
ing with each other as they scurried up and down blades of grass and
sand and rocks, never wavering very far from their trails. Was this talking
audible to them? Was there an ant language? There had to be some sort of
communication going on among these ants. There were too organized in
their little marching rows for this to be random. Maybe they recognized
each other by smell. He thought this might be the answer because he
remembered what a stink a small red ant had left on his finger after he had
crushed it between his fingertips. This might be its way of saying, "Don't
crush any more red ants or you'll be smeared with this sickly sweet smell,"
although this admonition could be of no help to one already pulverized.
This warning might have been to help the red ants of the future. Maybe,
ultimately, red ants didn't care if any one of them died as long as red ants
in general survived and thrived without being crushed by giant fingers.
Anyway, this would make red ants quite different from humans, who
were individualistic and often didn't really care about anyone else except
themselves. For the most part, humans were a stupid, egotistical mob.
Tuyi decided to find out if black ants could somehow talk to each other.

Finding one ant astray from the rest, Tuyi pinned it down with his
stick. This ant, wriggling underneath the wooden tip, was a good two feet
from one of the trails near the anthole. Its legs flailed wildly against the
stick, tried to grab on to it and push it off, while its head bobbed up and
down against the ground. After a few seconds of this maniacal despera-
tion—maybe this ant was screaming for help, Tuyi thought—six or seven
black ants broke off from a nearby trail and rushed around the pinned
ant, coming right to its head and body and onto the stick. They climbed up
the stick, and just before they reached Tuyi's fingers, he let it drop to the
ground. It worked. They had freed their friend from the giant stick. Tuyi
looked up, satisfied that he had an answer to whether ants communicated

with each other. Just about halfway up from his crouch he froze: about three feet away, a rattlesnake slithered over the chunks of earth churned up by the rows of cotton and onto the caked desert floor. He still couldn't hear the rattle, although the snake's tail shook violently a few inches from the ground. Tuyi was a little hard of hearing, probably just too much wax in his head. The snake stopped. It had been crawling toward him, and now it just stopped. Its long, thick body twisted tightly behind it while its raised tail still shook in the hot air. He didn't move; he was terrified. Should he run, or would it spring toward him and bite him? He stared at its head, which swayed slowly from left to right. It was going to bite him. He had to get out of there. But if he moved, it would certainly bite him, and he couldn't move fast enough to get out of its way when it lunged. He was about to jump back and run when he heard a loud crack to his right. The snake's head exploded. Orange fluid was splattered over the ground. The headless body wiggled in convulsions over the sand.

"God-damn! Git outta' there boy! Whatcha doin' playin' w'th a rattler? Ain't ye got no *sense*? Git over here!" yelled a burly, redheaded Anglo man with a pistol in his hand. There was a great, dissipating cloud of dust behind him; his truck's door was flung open. It was an INS truck, pale green with a red siren and search lights on top of the cabin.

"Is that damn thing dead? It coulda' killed you, son. ¿Hablas español? Damn it," he muttered as he looked at his gun and pushed it back into the holster strapped to his waist, "I'm gonna haf'ta make a report on firin' this weapon."

"I wasn't playing with it. I was looking at ants. I didn't see the snake."

"Well, whatcha doin' lookin' at ants? Seems you should be playin' somewhere else anyways. Do you live 'round here boy? What's yer name?"

"Rodolfo Martínez. I live over there," Tuyi said, pointing at the cluster of houses beyond the cotton fields. "You work for the Immigration, right? Can you shoot mojados with your gun, or do you just hit them with something? How do you stop them if they're running away?"

"I don't. I corner the bastards and they usually giv' up pretty easy. I'm takin' you home, boy. Git in the truck."

"Mister, can I take the snake with me? I've never seen a snake up close before and I'd like to look at it."

"Whatha hell you want w'th a dead snake? It's gonna stink up your momma's house and I know she won't be happy 'bout that. Shit, if you wanna take it, take it. But don't git the thang all over my truck. Are you some kinda' scientist, or what?"

"I just want to see what's inside. Maybe I could take the skin off and save it. Don't they make boots out of snake skin?"

"They sure as hell do! Nice ones too. They also make 'em outta elephant and shark, but ye don't see *mae* cutting up those an'mals in my backyard. Here, put the damn thang in here." The border patrolman handed him a plastic Safeway bag. Tuyi shoved the headless carcass of the snake into the bag with his stick. The snake was much heavier than he thought, and stiff like a thick tube of solid rubber. He looked around for the head and finally found it, what was left of it, underneath the first row of cotton in the vast cotton field behind him. As the INS truck stopped in front of the Martínez home on San Lorenzo Street, and Tuyi and the border patrolman walked up the driveway, the baseball game on San Simon stopped. A couple of kids ran up to look inside the truck and see what they could see.

"They finally got him. I told ya' he was weird! He's probably a mojado, from Canada. They arrested him, el pinchi gordito."

"Shut up, you idiot. Let's finish the game. We're leading 12 to 8. Maybe la migra just gave him a ride. Why the hell would they bring 'em back home if he was arrested?"

"Maybe they don't arrest kids. He's in trouble, wait till his father gets home. He's gonna be pissed off. They're gonna smack him up, I know it."

"Come on! Let's finish the game or I'm going home. *Look* it, there's blood on the seat, or something."

"I told ya, he's in trouble. Maybe he threw a rock at the guy and he came to tell his parents. Maybe he hit 'em on the head with a rock. I tell ya, that Tuyi is always doin' something weird by himself. I saw him in the canal last week, digging up dirt and throwing rocks. He's loco."

"Let's go, I'm going back. Who cares about the stupid migra anyway?"

"Ay, este niño, I can't believe what he does sometimes. And what did the migra guy tell you, was he friendly?" asked Mr. Martínez, glancing back at the metal clanging in the back of the pickup as he and his wife pulled up into the driveway. The moon was bright tonight. Stars twinkled in the clear desert sky like millions of jewels in a giant cavern of space.

"Oh, Mr. Jenkins was muy gente. I wish I could've given him lunch or something, but he said he had to go. He told me Tuyi wanted to keep the snake. Can you believe that? I can't even stand the thought of those things. I told Tuyi to keep it in the backyard, in the shed. The bag was dripping all over the kitchen and it smelled horrible. I hope the dog doesn't get it and eat it."

"It looks like everyone's asleep. All the lights are out. Let me get this thing out of the truck while you open the door. Do you have your keys? Here, take mine."

"I'm gonna put it in the living room, está bien? That way we can surprise him tomorrow. Pobrecito. He must've been scared. Can you imagine being attacked by a snake? This was a good idea. I know he'll be happy. He did so well in school too.

"Well, if it keeps him out of trouble, I'll be happy. I hope he doesn't get run over by a car, though," said Mrs. Martínez while pouring milk into a pan on the stove. Only the small light over the stove was on, and that was nearly covered up as she stood waiting for the milk to bubble. "¿Quieres leche? I'm going to drink a cup and watch the news. I'm tired, but I'm not really sleepy yet."

The house was quiet except for the German shepherd in the backyard who scratched at the shed door, smelling something powerful and new just beyond it. Princey looked around, sniffed the floor around the door, licked it, and after trotting over to the metal gate to the backyard lay down with a thump against the gate, panting quietly into the dry night air. Inside the house, every room was dark except for the one in the back corner from which glimmered the bluish light of a television set, splashing against the white walls in sharp, spasmodic bursts. In the living room, a new ten-speed bicycle, blue with white stripes and black tape over the handlebars, reclined against its metal stop. Some tags were still dangling from its gears. The tires needed to be pressurized correctly because it had just been the demonstration model at the Walmart on McCrae Boulevard. It was the last ten-speed they had.

Punching Chickens

I remember the chickens. I also remember how scared I was. At about five in the morning, on a Saturday too, my mother woke me up. She had told me the day before that I would have a job this summer, one way or another. I remember how she said it too. Her large brown eyes glared at me, as if she knew a secret I didn't, and then she smiled. This was after I told her I needed money to go to the movies with my friends. I already had a ride to Cielo Vista. I just needed the three dollars to get in. But I should've kept my mouth shut. I should've asked Jaime for the money. I should've stolen it. "No," she said quietly, "that's not how we're going to do it from now on. Vas a trabajar. Como cualquier otro. A trabajar y ahorrar." She told me she had already spoken to Pepe's mother about it. All of *those* boys did it every summer. One way or another. If I didn't want to help my father load bricks in our truck, then she would find something for me to do before I started high school. "Be ready tomorrow morning, en la madrugada. I'll pack you lunch," she said with her slight smile.

Pepe and his cousin Carlos were already waiting for the truck at the corner. They just sat on the curb of San Lorenzo and San Simon and smiled at me as I sat next to them. I noticed they had bad teeth. Chipped and yellowish. I had played football with them a few times, but I didn't really know them. They lived in front of our house, and in a poor neighborhood they were the poorest of the lot. They were much tougher than I was, however. I had once seen Pepe in a fight with a cholo who shouted "¡Chinga tu madre!" about something or other, and Pepe immediately stiffened like a statue. I thought I saw the short black hair on the back of his neck stand up, like black bristles. He jumped on the cholo, slammed his head against the rock wall behind our house, and choked him until the guy turned blue. I tell you, Pepe and his whole family were tougher than me. Real trabajadores. Me? My brother said I looked like a real ugly girl.

Strange as it may seem, I think Pepe and Carlos were a little shy around me. I mean, we didn't hang around the same group at South Loop school. I was with the brainy group, more or less. But I didn't kiss any teacher's ass. I didn't get my grades the way Nancy Montes did. I just liked to read, and I liked to get things right. Sometimes I did do things that were sort of stupid too. During track season in P.E., I had hurled the shot put right onto Mauricio Pacheco's fat foot. It wasn't my fault, really. I told him to move. He just laughed at me and dared me to come close, like the pendejo that he is. You should've heard his awful scream when that iron ball caught his big toe. The coach was all excited and angry and made *me* run ten laps after school. I tell you, they talked about it at South Loop for days. Suddenly even the potheads were smiling at me. So I got good grades, but in a way I didn't really belong with the brains. I knew what my brother meant too. It was my face and my hair. I couldn't do much about my face, but I should've shaved my head years ago. Maybe that would've helped.

Pepe, and sometimes Carlos, hung out by the fence on Gonzalez Street. I never saw them in school much. But when I did, it was there, just outside school property, maybe one of them leaning against a low rider, not theirs, a friend's maybe, never smoking pot but with a cigarette. I would always say hello and Pepe would push his chin out with an "ese vato" nod, and sometimes smile a little, cool yet definitely friendly. Doña María and my mother were best friends, so in a way we were connected. But really, we were from two different worlds. My older brother Jaime was more like them, and I usually just stayed away from him.

The farm truck stopped at the corner at exactly 6:15 a.m. We had barely jumped on the back bumper when it lurched forward into the darkness again. I just made it over the high wooden slats around the truck bed. A few hands helped me over, pulling on my T-shirt and even my pants. Maybe it had been Pepe and Carlos. But I didn't really know. I couldn't see anybody's face in this dark and sweaty pit I was now in, this pit that was rattling wildly toward the cotton fields beyond my house, deep into Ysleta or Socorro or God-knows-where. I think there were nine or ten of us in there, bouncing around like loose haystacks every time the truck hit a bump. We were on a dirt road for a while, that I do remember. I think animals had been transported on this truck, because I thought I smelled animal shit, and I did smell hay. I mean, it could've been human shit I was smelling, but I just didn't want to think about that possibility then. I'm sure it was animal. Don't ask me how I know. My chest was scratched and bleeding. I had caught a pencil-like splinter on one of the slats when I had been pulled into the truck. I was looking at the streak of the Milky Way high above the desert sky. I started praying for a quick sundown.

After a while—it seemed like forever to me then—I began to see their faces. The bright orange rays of the sun punched through the horizon like a gigantic crown of thorns on fire. It was already hot, and some of them were sweating, their skin almost maroon, leathery, and old looking, even if they weren't very old. In fact, I think I was the youngest one there. There was one other "kid" who was not as fat as I was, about the same height, with dusty black hair, and baby fat on his cheeks. He could've been younger than me. But even then I could tell from the start that Rueben could've eaten me alive if he wanted to. His arms rippled with blotchy little biceps. His legs were always in a boxer's stand, ready for a fight. He usually scowled when he was by himself, yet later, much later, I did see him smile once. I still remember those big perfect teeth, like a hyena's.

No one smiled now. A few brief conversations came and went, all in Spanish. But no one smiled, much less laughed, on the way to the farm. El rancho del señor Young, I heard someone say. There were a few old men who looked like my abuelito, maybe slightly younger, but just as crappy-looking. Most of the men were in their thirties or forties, my father's age. But they were different from him. Their jeans were frayed and ripped. Their skin stony and lean. They were, for the most part, thin. Only their hands looked like my father's hands: calloused, thick, and strong. Sure, my father had never been rich. In fact, I remember when we had an outhouse in the backyard, and awful kerosene lamps that released a quivery jet of the blackest, most acrid smoke. But now my father had men like these working for him, even if only a handful. My father's construction business even turned down a few jobs once in a while. Now, my father really smiled when he ate breakfast with my mother.

Just about the time I was thinking we'd be in this shitty truck all day, we turned off the dirt road. We drove toward a faraway complex of huge buildings in the middle of a flat plain of perfectly straight, planted rows. I really didn't know exactly where we were, but I did know we were miles from home. Somehow I immediately felt like a prisoner here. There was not another building for miles. No stores. No cars. Not even a highway. Just a few farm trucks now and then. Already two more trucks like ours had arrived, and their men milled around impatiently near the machines that had brought them here, anxious like hungry cats. We jumped out of our truck as soon as it stopped and waited too.

"What now?" I asked Pepe, who had sat down against one of the truck's wheels. These were my first words to him since we had left San Lorenzo and San Simon. Pepe was as big as my brother, and probably stronger. He had beefy arms, a kind round face, and huge feet. He'd always been a power hitter in our softball games, an enforcer in football. Yet I had never seen him get angry. I remember now that we hadn't played together for a while, ever since he had gone to Ysleta High School. Was he even in high school anymore? Jaime had never mentioned him as one of his buddies there. I really didn't know Pepe at all. It occurred to me that it was strange to live so close to someone for years, see him grow up—from trips to the canal to look for cangrejos, to driving around in a Chevy Impala with a smiling girl—and not really know him at all. Carlos I knew even less. He apparently only stayed with the Quinteros during the summer. He was a good football receiver, furtive and quick like a weasel. That day he just seemed like a gangly mute.

"Ahorita viene el patrón," Pepe said quietly, in an Indian squat, just staring at the dirt. For a second, he looked like a big kid again. "There's probably nothing ready yet, para pizcar. But they'll have something for us. They always do. They'll need us later in the summer for all sorts of things. He'll come out and tell us what we're going to do and what we're going to make."

"How much is it usually?"

"Well, I don't know. It depends what they have. If it's cotton or chile, then they do it by the twenty-pound bag. The more you pick, the more you earn. But I don't think anything's ready, ése. One summer I shook pecans off the trees. The machines were broken. So it could be anything, Manny. Sometimes they do it by the day."

"By the day?"

"Sí, by the day. You work until it's dark."

"All day?"

"All day."

"¡Ay, cabrón! I thought we'd be home early, *before* it was dark."

"Este güey," Carlos sneered. "No seas huevón, Padilla! What do you think this is, Disneyland?" I ignored him. He was just an idiot. Pepe didn't even look up from staring at his hands. He didn't seem to give a shit what his cousin said either. Carlos scowled at both of us and stomped away to the other side of the truck.

"Don't worry. You'll get home. One way or another."

"Ése, Pepe. What if it's not enough, what they pay?"

"Not enough?"

"I mean, what if you want more money?"

Pepe looked at me and with his beady brown eyes basically said, "What the fuck are you talking about? I thought you were the *smart* one in that family." He was exasperated with me, but something kept him from dumping me in that heap piled high with all the idiots of the world. Maybe my mother had said something to his mother, and his mother had said something to him. Maybe I was being babysat. *Right.* What did they know anyway? I didn't need anyone. I just wanted to be left alone. Pepe finally shifted his big body, stood up, brushed off his butt, and stretched his arms skyward in a big yawn. His muscles were definitely bigger than my brother's. Suddenly Pepe reminded me of Lennie in Steinbeck's *Of Mice and Men*, except, of course, Pepe wasn't retarded. "That's just not the way it is," he finally said. "They pay you what they pay you."

"And you have no choice at all?"

"Pues, you don't have to work. Nobody does." There was a brief silence between us. I must've looked alarmed. Either that, or maybe I looked like I was capable of anything. Capable of embarrassing the shit out of him in front of these men who didn't talk to each other, who didn't know each other, who just seemed *there*, like the trees. Because he immediately added, "But the pay's not bad. Not bad at all," although I knew, from his forced little smile, that he had never given much thought to the pay being good, or bad, or shit. It was *there*. That was enough for him.

A large güero walked from one of the smaller buildings, the only one with windows. He was wearing a cowboy hat and looked chunky, and overweight Marlboro Man. He talked to the three drivers of the trucks, who were sitting apart from us, and apparently waiting for further instructions. El güero walked back into the building. Each driver talked to a group of us, told us what the job was, how much they would pay. I heard something about chickens but didn't really pay attention after I heard what I wanted to hear: $1.50 an hour, about eight to ten hours of work more or less, in any case, most of the day.

Fifteen dollars for the day! My mind reeled with images. I could go to the movies for almost an entire week with this money! I could go three times a week and buy as much popcorn as I wanted! I had never actually *seen* fifteen dollars in my hand. My mother gave me only a dollar or two at a time. Three if I begged her and agree to scrub the trash bins, wash Elmo with the black disinfectant soap from Juárez, clean out her flower beds, and pull out the weeds from the front and back yards. It usually took me most of the day, and she inspected everything I did. If I complained, she'd tell me that at her father's ranch in Babonoyaba they had suffered and worked, and suffered and worked, from dawn until midnight. She'd tell me about milking the cows and feeding the pigs and cleaning the barn and cooking and cleaning and not having shoes in grade school and walking five miles to school every day . . . and . . . and . . . ¡YA! I should feel *lucky*, she'd say, to have only these little chores to do. I should feel lucky. Well, with fifteen dollars in my hand every once in a while, I'd definitely feel lucky from now on.

I remember that I never figured out who got to unload and who got to carry. I'm not sure it would've mattered anyway; I got to carry and at least saw the light of the sun for a few seconds at a time. The other thing about carrying was that you could take your time, especially when your hands and arms and shoulders started to twitch and then simply disobeyed your brain's commands. When I wanted to faint, just about an hour before we finished, these few seconds of daylight, precious seconds when I suddenly remembered that I was hungry or out of breath or so god-awful sore I almost cried, these seconds were my only life. My real life.

There were three eighteen-wheelers backed up against a huge warehouse. Three metal ramps dropped from the back of these trucks more or less in the direction of the warehouse. The warehouse itself was like a cavern: dark, eerily quiet, and spooky. The air was thick inside, as if the shadows were somewhere between being nothing and becoming black gelatin. The cages and the smell. That's what I noticed first. Hundreds and hundreds of small cages. All in neat rows. Planks on the floor separating each row of cages. And a horrible smell of feathers and chicken shit and dust everywhere, this impossibly *thick* air! A stench that made me gag at first. Yet, after the first hour, I didn't smell it anymore. I also remember that, before we started, when the warehouse was quiet, the feathers and pieces of feathers dangling from the wire mesh seemed even delicate.

We were to unload the semis and carry the chickens to the warehouse and put them into cages, two in each cage. We were to unload and carry chickens. A few men climbed into the truck; I stood with Pepe and Carlos and a few others outside. Then we started to work. The warehouse was gloomy and quiet, but the inside of the truck, this long and suffocating tunnel, was a riotous chaos of flying feathers. The chickens were inside wire-mesh racks. Those unloading flung open a door, grabbed whatever chicken legs were nearby, and yanked the shrieking animals out, a pair at a time, and handed them to us, upside down. We took a pair with one hand, waited in this wretched din and half-light, grabbed another pair with the other hand, and carried them out.

It was a damn good thing that Pepe was in front of me. At least I could see what to do a few seconds before I descended into this madness. The claws! My God, I saw them! These ugly, yellow, scaly claws and legs! You had to grab them, keep them from tearing at your hands. Why didn't we have gloves? Why? Some of these guys were wearing gloves! When you were carrying them, the first time I carried them, you focused on these powerful claws and legs, how they kicked away from you, how they'd scratch and rip your flesh if you didn't carry them just right. It was all a matter of half inches, of keeping these little evil, manic claws from reaching a finger or the fleshy part between your thumb and your index finger. I got careless only once, when I was so tired I didn't care anymore. This yellow claw from the depths of hell curled itself around my thumb and squeezed it until I thought it would snap off. After that, the shock of this awful pain flushed out just enough energy and will to carry me through the final hour.

Down the ramp we went, two dangerous, screeching chickens in each hand, their heads, these quavery masses of eyes and red flesh and beaks, pecking away at our knees and thighs whenever we dared to drop our outstretched arms. I think it might've been easier to carry snakes for a living. I hated seeing their spasmodic upside-down chicken heads stretching to puncture my flesh. I imagined once that they reached my groin and pecked out my penis and my huevos and kept pecking until they got to my gut and my eyes and my brain, until I was just a pecked-out piece of human meat surrounded by thousands of nervous, dirty white chickens. I think that was about the time I fucked up a pair of chicken heads against a warehouse wall when no one was looking. Well, almost no one. Rueben was right behind me, and that's when he grinned his stupid grin. Maybe he hated the chickens as much as I did. Maybe he just knew que ya me iba también a la chingada. Maybe I was going on my first joyride to hell and back, and it was fun to watch.

My first four chickens in hand, I followed Pepe to the cages. The birds squawked and tried to yank free. Their heads swiveled wildly. Their bodies, grayish and yellowy underneath their legs, lurched up in spasms, like the bad end of shredded electric wire. I could see their butts. I realized I'd be looking at chicken butts the whole day. Some of these fucking chickens were shitting in midair. Maybe I'd lose a little control too if some giant bastard grabbed me by my ankles and hoisted me upside down to God-knows-where. Maybe I'd smell the barbecue sauce too. A drop of chicken shit had already smeared one of my sneakers.

¡Ay chingada! I couldn't get the damn chickens into these cages! They squawked even louder as I lifted them up to the open mesh door and contorted their feathery bodies, swiping at my stomach in a crazed fury. It was awful. That first time, when I felt I was gripping my way up one cliff of shit after another, was the most awful. How was I going to do this for hour after hour? I almost dropped my four chickens right there. I almost dropped them and walked home. Fortunately, Pepe was right next to me and probably noticed the terror and anger in my eyes. Without saying a word, he took the two chickens from my right hand, found an open cage door next to him, and *punched* the fuckers home. Their little bodies twisted horribly, unbelievably, through the door. Yet, like old tires, they popped back up and ran circles inside the cage. My first "punch" almost made me feel good again. Pepe winked at me, and I almost smiled back.

It took me about a half dozen trips to the semi before I started to look around again, before I started to ignore what the chickens did in their panic. They became simply pieces of dangerous meat I had to deal with, for a few long minutes at a time. I didn't give a damn about the chickens, and I'm sure they weren't in love with me either. My arms were already becoming sore. My hands were turning yellow! The scaly skin on these chicken feet was rubbing itself into my own flesh. This yellow slime mixed with dirt. ¡Híjola! My hands stunk! It was horrible, like the smell of a rusty open can of tuna abandoned in the refrigerator for years. A tide of vomit surged up my throat but splashed back into my stomach. I kept my hands away from my mouth and my nose. I would never eat chicken again.

I remember that, after three hours, my arms suddenly started dropping immediately to my sides whenever I punched in another two pairs of chickens. My arms and my shoulders. I couldn't control them completely anymore. For a few minutes right before lunch, my right shoulder became numb, and I had the sensation that it glowed brightly, as if some madman had jabbed a blowtorch into my muscles and revved up the heat for good measure. I shook it back to life. Time after time my arms and shoulders would drop listlessly next to me, exhausted and inert. Yet, just as I left the sun behind and entered this loud cramped tunnel of flying feathers, I forced my hands and arms to reach up again, to grab on to these animals as if they were saving me from a fall into a bed of razors. I fought back a blinding pain.

Why did I do it? Why did I keep doing it? The whole thing seems crazy to me now. I wasn't thinking then. I *couldn't* think. I remember that I felt ashamed of my weakness. I remember that I stared at these old men, these viejitos, and they were going back and forth, up the ramp, into the truck, and back to the cages. Like machines. Four chickens at a time. Their faces were stoic and hard. Their pace was sometimes even faster than mine. Their muscles—old, decrepit, sinewy muscles—seemed oiled with sweat, stronger at each turn, packed with a deep reservoir of power that I didn't have. Work begat power, which begat more work. Four fucking chickens at a time. I wasn't about to quit. Not now. Just one more time, dear God. Just one more time! But I would not quit *now*.

As soon as someone said it was lunchtime, as soon as this chain of chickens and men stopped just as suddenly as it had started, I deflated like a punctured inner tube. I could barely move my arms, and even squeezing my hands into fists seemed painful. I wanted simply to chop my arms off. When I carried my bag lunch to the trees where some of us were sitting, my fingers quivered and would not close tightly around the paper bag. I was afraid I would drop it. I was afraid they would know I couldn't do it. More than anything else, I was ashamed of this weakness inside of me that screamed to burst into the empty cotton fields. But I did not do anything. I did not show them any pain. When they smiled and asked where I was from, only then did my heart begin to break away from the agony of my body.

It was strange, but they were very friendly to me, friendlier than they were to Pepe or Carlos. My two friends seemed to slip into the background. The older men, especially the ones that looked like my grandfather, they wanted to know about my father and mother, whether I had ever worked on a farm before, what school I was at, and so on. One of them had a grandchild who went to South Loop School too, but only a third-grader. Another said he thought he had met my father at a boda last year. These viejitos, with their dirty jokes and banter, made me forget my pain. I remember their smiles too. Really nice smiles. Wide open, toothy, and mischievous. Secret smiles only for those who belonged underneath the trees. Wonderful smiles for me. I also remember how they laughed and how much they made me laugh. I think that's the first time I laughed from my gut. I couldn't move my arms, but I could still laugh from my gut.

One of them mentioned something about the pace of our work. It was much too fast, he said. We were already done with over half the semi. He motioned to two of the "younger" men leaning against a tree, and they seemed to agree. Much too fast, they also said, these two who were my father's age. So it was settled. Just like that. After lunch, we'd each carry only two chickens at a time, one in each hand. Slow the pace down. If we needed to, some of us could pick up the pace toward the end of the day to make sure we finished our work. There was no need to cut short our own time, someone else said. "Shit yeah," one of the "younger" ones said. "I heard one of the drivers say they'd be back around six or so, after they finished some errands for el güero." We just needed to look busy and keep an eye out for the big guy, in case he came around to see how we were doing. The other two semis would do the same. Get the work done, but slow the pace down. That's what we would do after lunch. Shit yeah, I said too, without uttering a sound.

I remember that the first hour after we ate our lunch, that first hour back to work, was brutal. My muscles would not work. I could not move my arms. I felt that God himself had severed the connection between my brain and my arms. We were walking back to the semi, and I was panicking. My God! Just one chicken in each hand! That's all I had to do! Just one horrible little chicken! What's wrong with me? My arms! I needed new arms! There was also, all too suddenly, this piercing pain across my lower back. I had just been sitting down, eating my lunch. I should've felt better now. I should've been ready. But my body! Now, as I walked back, I couldn't even stand straight, or so I thought. My spine seemed about to snap. One wrong step and this delicate balance between my back and my hips and my legs would implode like a termite-eaten shack collapsing onto itself.

I remember that when I grabbed my first two chickens after lunch, the guy unloading handed them to me around my thighs. I simply could not lift my arms. He said nothing, quickly grabbed another pair for the next guy, and I walked down the ramp, the chicken heads going to town on my knees. I didn't care. I just didn't want to collapse. I just wanted to get it done. I remember that each step of my sneakers, each step into the soft chicken shit on the floor, seemed a glorious victory. I was a tank trampling through chicken mud. I would not quit now. I found an open cage and swung my arms over, in a clumsy arc, it seemed, and smashed the chickens through the hole. After every trip, for a while at least, my arms felt better and returned to me. For a while at least, until the end.

I did finish, and I did not faint. In many ways, the claw that nearly tore my thumb in half, that greedy yellow claw, saved me. I woke up. I went back. And again. Until the semi was empty, and they were turning us away. The sun had already set. At first I couldn't believe there were no more chickens. I had this wild desire to rush into the truck and see for myself that it was absolutely quiet. But I didn't. As soon as my mind realized that we had stopped, as soon as I knew it was over, I needed to focus on standing up. I think my legs were shaking, but I'm not sure. I tried to be calm, and I waited quietly next to the truck, unsure about what my body would do next. I imagined that I suddenly found myself in this dark haunted house which threatened, among other things, simply to disappear in the cold empty space. But nobody paid any attention to me, and I was grateful for that. Pepe sat next to me, leaned against the truck tire just as he had when we first arrived, and closed his eyes. He seemed peacefully asleep. I didn't see Carlos again until we were inside the truck, on our way home.

One of the last things I remember about that day, my first day of work, was that when el güero handed me my fifteen dollars, I didn't even look at it. I stuffed the crisp new bills into my jeans and walked away and tried not to fall flat on my face. The crisp green paper crinkled in my hands for a moment, like the wax paper around candy bars, and I really did not want to touch it. I didn't know why. My hands were smeared with chicken slime, my sneakers were caked with chicken shit, and I wanted desperately to go to the restroom. I had only one thought in my head: how was I going to climb into the truck again if I couldn't lift my legs or move my arms? I still don't know how I did it. I guess I did lift myself to the bumper, I guess I did lift my arms over the wooden slats, and I guess someone did push me from behind and someone else pulled me in. But I don't remember any of that. I remember only that the money in my pocket crinkled again as I went over the slats and that I was relieved to be in this dark pit again, alone with my pain.

At San Lorenzo and San Simon, I walked up our driveway and around to the back door. I pushed off my sneakers before I stepped into the house. Elmo immediately took an interest in them but then just as quickly walked away into the darkness. My mother, who hears everything, heard the screen door slam shut and said, "Manny, is that you? Dinner's ready." From the hallway, without ever seeing her big brown eyes, I said that I was taking a shower, that I was really tired, and closed the bathroom door behind me. I could hear her walk up to the bathroom door and stop in the hallway, waiting, before she asked, "So, how was it? What did you do?" I had already taken my T-shirt off, and I was sitting on the toilet slowly removing my dusty, shit-splattered jeans from my legs, which were dotted with welts around my thighs and knees. Finally, I was naked, and my entire body throbbed with pain. "Nada. No hicimos nada. Cargamos gallinas." There was a silence on the other side of the door, at least I think there was a silence, because I don't remember that I said anything else to her. I don't remember that I responded to anything else anymore. I stared at my swollen thumb; I couldn't move it. Finally, after a while, the hot water seemed to wash the crap away. But really, it didn't. I could smell the chicken shit for days.

✳ Nonfiction ✳

I follow the lines of memory, but don't want to see them as memory any longer. They have become images I keep focusing on, people rising and moving and coming toward me as if they have never left and have always known me. I wait in those thoughts as if I have never moved from that past moment that is the present and will always be the future.

—*Ray Gonzalez*

Of Earth and Sea: A Chilean Memoir

Marjorie Agosín

Words

I don't know how or when a love of words was born in me. Was it the sounds, the elongation of the letters, the furrows in a thick piece of paper? I loved the Hebrew letters; they had forms and textures that seemed to be awakening from an ancient dream. My grandmother, before starting her day, when dawn appeared like a golden canvas that barely peeked over the surfaces, would read in Hebrew, silently and aloud. At that moment it was impossible to approach her. She belonged to a distant sovereignty, to a site of prayers that was hers alone; that is what I imagine this memory to be.

Hebrew seemed to me a secret and peaceful language. We lived with it always, but it was the language of prayer, of sacred zones where God and man exchanged the audacity of the secret writings. I also grew up with Yiddish, a mischievous and substantial language, a language capable of cursing and loving with equal fervor, and with the same passion for madness that made us burst into laughter. Mama would tell me sometimes that she needed other people's problems like a hole in the head. Once I heard her say she would like to go far, far away, to the place where black pepper grows, but I do not know where black pepper grows.

Papa—my grandfather—speaks German with Grandmother. Sometimes I think this language is like Yiddish, but it is harsh and has strange intonations. It is rough, like the shouts I hear at times when the girls see me passing by. Nothing about this language appeals to me, but Papa says it is good to know German. I want to learn other languages because it seems to me that they are secret passages to other voices and other things. There is a family here in Santiago from Czechoslovakia. They understand German but they speak Czech.

I like Spanish because languages above all must make us happy, and I play in Spanish. I play blind man's bluff and hopscotch, imagining that with a single leap I can conquer the sky or the earth.

I like to write. Papa gave me a notebook without lines. I think I will be a poet. They talk here about a very strange woman named Gabriela Mistral.* They say she has no husband, no children, and that she does not have a desk, that she writes on her knees while staring at the sky. That is what I want to do, write on my knees that are always trembling.

Violeta Parra

Yesterday Violeta Parra[†] committed suicide in her tent in La Reina, where heaven and earth are hidden and the rain never ceased. All the newspapers talk about her life, and I think perhaps they are telling the truth, that she killed herself for love. I respect not only her suicide, but her life also. It is the winter of 1967; I am an impressionable adolescent. The wooden houses of my country sob, and the rafters of the high roofs seem to thrash about from grief. I remember the days in Osorno that seemed like night, when the rain was our only guest and the wind seemed to moan like a lost bird.

Now in Santiago, this winter marks the suicide of Violeta. She was childhood and innocence, a challenging presence. Her voice belonged to this world and the other. The divine and the human were intertwined in a sound of gratitude in time with time. While all the radios of the country announce her death, and on the hill where she lived torches appear, I gaze at the rain and the sky with my eyes open, and I make certain that Violeta Parra has died and that she has not gone to the promised land, since her paradise was this land. Today I hear her echoes and her footsteps, and only her soul illuminates this night that is as long and solitary as this land.

*Pseudonym of Lucila Godoy Alcayaga, Chilean poet, educator, and diplomat, winner of the 1945 Nobel Prize for Literature.

[†]The well-known singer and composer of countless Chilean folk songs—the most famous of them "Gracias a la vida" (Thanks to life)—and sister of the poet Nicanor Parra.

November 1, The Day of the Dead

Suddenly a deep silence overcomes me, a silence that lasts one night, or perhaps it is a night that lasts for years. The country and I have become dark. Fear dominates us; from the earliest hours of the morning we become obedient creatures. At night we return home, carrying out the functions that assure our ephemeral survival. At night I go out on the balcony of my city that is now only the city of my dead grandparents. I recognize the stars but my face does not accept any gaze. The roses are drying up, the hyacinths do not bloom, and the forsythia does not display the same shade of yellow. Around me, the air itself is strange.

Since childhood I have loved to play with flour, letting it slip through my hands, realizing that later it will become bread, sustenance of our days. Sometimes I liked to make mountains out of it, beat an egg and pretend it was a sublime volcano. I did not learn any wonderful recipes, but I did learn to feel humility and passion for bread, for the braided crown that covered the table. My grandmother would make challa on Fridays and Sundays; the women of the town seemed like queens selling their kneaded bread. In the smell of these beloved things, I found happiness.

Those memories become more remote when I hear they are arresting people, carrying them off in the middle of the night. Sometimes my friends tell me they sleep with their clothes on, ready to be taken away. Still, I continue to wear silk at night. I tell myself the stories of a thousand and one nights that I heard beside a brazier at the end of the world.

Nights of Exile

Sometimes I imagined night in my country on those days when absence seemed to gnaw away at my days. I imagined night arriving like a lark, night falling in every season, especially in summer when you could recognize the rhythm of objects by their fragrances. From the balcony of my grandmother's house, I would stare at the drooping honeysuckle, the jasmine. I would stare at the benches in the plazas where lovers played with fireflies and desire. I loved the night that seemed to be at times a panting heart and, other times, a heart in love.

I liked the night in order to sit with my arms naked and a light shawl covering my shoulders. I felt protected by the delicacy of this light fabric that made me understand the impermanence of objects, the fragility of the passing of time. But at the same time, night seemed to be a queen to me, a pathway of routes, a fountain in the midst of darkness.

Sometimes I loved the winter nights when I would go out on the balcony to make certain of the darkness beating inside me, a darkness that also imagined the light coming after night. I went out to savor the smell of burning logs, roasted chestnuts, of lovers woven together, one hand over the other, like the beginning of trees planted nearby that recognize each other.

I loved the night because the women in our house told me this was the moment to invent fables, and they would sit in the garden in the light of white candles to conjure up the story of the disappeared, nocturnal witches perpetually navigating through southern seas.

In exile I fled from the night. And exile was not only a word bound to nostalgia, it was a profound grief, like an iceberg sailing through our souls and freezing our bodies. I returned to closed rooms, silenced hotels, the silence of strangers in rooms without a balcony, without memory. Then in order to sleep I would conjure up the arrival of night and dream about the stars of the Southern Hemisphere or simply devote myself to holding a conversation with God.

Exile marks us like a talisman or tattoo. It teaches us how to endure long nights and short days.

And Finally, Returning

I return without haste, do not fear the call for a truce. I simply return and it is the sea that grants me the gift of recognition. I am a sympathetic traveler. In my feet I preserve the secret of darkness and its alchemy, pathways of light. I return, I have been returning home forever, recognizing the wind that stirs the trees of the dead, and rush to the call of those who still wait in the generous land. I return by night, the sea dwells in the nape of my neck, hair swaying as if it were the wave where the algae rest. And in that desolate distance, in lands where no one called my name, I imagined the roaring of the sea, the vertiginous and husky sound, that sound that traps me to bury itself in its plentitude.

I have returned home, and on every balcony, I am the only one who can see the sea, the little bonfires of summer lovers, and more than anything else, those I love, Maria waiting in a rocking chair, Grandmother Josefina covered in her shawl, and all my friends, living and dead, singing the same melody. Happiness is a kiss from the waters that swirl around my feet.

The Illusion of a Firefly

Perhaps we did not know the revolving rhythm of time, the obligations that only promote rituals. Perhaps we thought the future was too uncertain, and our plans were reduced just to the transparency of the moment. We did not pursue great trophies. Nor did we pray in enormous concrete cathedrals. We pursued only the illusion of a firefly circling like a mischievous bride over the forests. We simply decided that life was worthwhile only according to the dimension of one's dreams and justice at every table.

They called us the disenchanted generation; we demonstrated political activism with poems under our arms and anointed ourselves with branches of dry leaves. We disappeared and even after death we learned it was possible to reconcile our dreams, freedom like a word with a voice made of water.

From my country I learned so much, above all to experience life, the air on my body, the rain on my cheeks, the paradise of the present.

The Desert Remembers My Name: On Family and Writing

Kathleen J. Alcalá

My Week as a Mexican

My parents always told me I was Mexican. I was Mexican because they were Mexican. This was sometimes modified to "Mexican American," since I was born in California, and thus automatically a U.S. citizen. But, my parents said, this, too, was once part of Mexico. My father would say this with a sweeping gesture, taking in the smog, the beautiful mountains, the cars and houses and fast-food franchises. When he made that gesture, all was cleared away in my mind's eye to leave the hazy impression of a better place. We were here when the white people came, the Spaniards, then the Americans. And we will be here when they go away, he would say, and it will be part of Mexico again.

Although he was originally from the town of San Julian in Jalisco, Mexico, my father put down deep roots in East Highlands, California, around 1918. This was an unincorporated community of orange pickers and railroad workers outside of Redlands, in Southern California. Having lived there since the age of seven, he felt completely at home, and despite the deep poverty in which he was raised and his experiences with the racism of that time and place, my father seemed to think that it was all temporary, that all would be made right in the end. This optimism has allowed him to live into his nineties.

Each summer we piled into our station wagon—my parents, my two older sisters, and I—and drove two-and-a-half days to Chihuahua, Mexico, to stay with my mother's sister and her family. We all looked forward to it, I think, as an escape from our carefully measured lives in San Bernardino. In Chihuahua, anything could happen, and it was usually beautiful, delicious, delightful. Much to my father's satisfaction, it was also usually paid for by my uncle. It was like living your life in black and white most of the year, then spending two weeks living it in full color. There were several band concerts in the park, fireworks available all year round, and delicious meals both at my aunt and uncle's house and in restaurants. It meant mango *paletas* and a piñata for my birthday, which was celebrated jointly with one of my cousins, and trips to the Santa Helena river.

As we got older, I could see that my five cousins were very different from us. While they loved American popular music—my cousin did a pretty good Elvis imitation—and comic books, I could tell that they lived by rules and regulations, social nuances, that did not coincide with ours. By the time we were teenagers, it was clear that our lives where on very different trajectories, directions determined, in large part, by which side of the border we lived on. I struggled to understand the political discussions between my father and my uncle, and my cousin Danny's profound anger and frustration with the government after the massacre of student demonstrators in 1968. There was unrest in the United States as well, but I could not believe that the Mexican government could do such things to its own people in a modern age. Danny died shortly after that of scarlet fever that was incorrectly diagnosed, a tragedy so great for the family that even today I cannot describe it.

I had a "twin" cousin named Ruth, born a week before me. Once a year, all through our growing up, our heights, our coloring, our coordination, charm, and precociousness were compared. Ruth always took the honors—taller, lighter skinned, more graceful, possessed of an innate dignity and charm that earned her the nickname La Princesa from her four siblings.

One of my earliest memories is visiting Mexico City with my cousins. Each family had a blue-and-white Ford station wagon. We went to the zoo and saw giraffes. We were about two years old, approaching three, for we have late-August birthdays. I remember that Ruth was already toilet trained, and so able to wear frilly panties. Whether she was drawing attention to this or not, I don't know. I only remember that I was acutely conscious of my inferiority in this matter.

That was also the trip on which we were in a major earthquake in Mexico City. I was sleeping on the floor of a hotel room when the sound of the closet door swinging open and shut, open and shut, woke me. My mother and her sister were sitting on the edge of the bed, their arms around each other. My father was not around. I asked what was going on.

"Oh, it's just an earthquake," said my aunt. "Go back to sleep."

So I did. Since we lived on the San Andreas fault in California, I was used to earthquakes. Only later would I learn the extent of the damage, and that my father was considered a hero because he had kept people from running out into the street, where others were killed by the stonework that fell from the exteriors of buildings.

By the time we were twelve, I had caught up to my cousin Ruth in height, but she had begun to develop the womanly curves that would attract the eye of her future husband, Felipe. Ruth's best friend, Gloria, was married on her fifteenth birthday. Ruth married on her eighteenth, and I was one of six bridesmaids in the all-white wedding—white dresses, white bunting, the entire inside of the church blanketed in white gardenias. The sickly-sweet smell was overpowering. I think Felipe's aunt designed the wedding, and the lack of color emphasized Felipe's dark good looks and maturity—several years older than we were. I kept the bridesmaid dress for a few years, but the only occasion for which I think it would have been suited was a coronation. With the end of the sixties, the formal dress had become passé.

The idea of marriage, much less married sex, was too much for me to even contemplate, and I remember thinking how glad I was it wasn't me.

It was a fairy-tale wedding for La Princesa, followed by a honeymoon on which she became pregnant. Her mother, my aunt, had told her that Norforms, a vaginal suppository, were a form of birth control. At eighteen, Ruth delivered a little girl in Piedras Negras, Mexico, close to the Texas border, where her husband worked for an American mining company. It was a difficult birth, with the assistance of a midwife. Due to oxygen deprivation, Carla was born with cerebral palsy and will require twenty-four-hour care for the rest of her life. Until recently, Ruth and her family lived in "The American Compound"—housing owned by the mining company outside of Chihuahua. Over thirty years later, Ruth continues to care for a strong and vibrant Carla, her other children grown and gone.

This has been my experience with Mexico, both a fairy tale and a stern taskmaster that, while gracious, has no patience for the romanticism or idealism it is so easy to bring to such a beautiful country.

My visit to Mexico City, forty years later, while researching my novel, *Treasures in Heaven*, brought back both of these views. It was the first time I had traveled to Mexico by myself as an adult. Naturally, my father forbade me to go, since I would probably be kidnapped by drug dealers.

I have since joked that none of my research trips are official until my father forbids me to go.

A few years earlier, when my son was five months old, I had traveled to Chihuahua with him and my Anglo-American husband. This had resulted in the interesting charade of people outside of the family addressing my husband in Spanish, my translating, and then answering in Spanish, and the next line being addressed again to my husband, in Spanish. It was like the *Saturday Night Live* skit of closed-captioning for the hearing impaired, where someone in a little circle in the corner yelled out the news.

Since I was by myself this time, people had to address me directly. They were unfailingly polite and kind, even when they really wanted me to go away. As a woman in my forties, I was the age of most of their mothers, so they could not help but be polite to me. In my persistence, I was American. Told that a certain book or document was missing, inaccessible, or at a different location, I simply went on to the next thing on my list. Eventually, the librarians and archivists and receptionists would surrender and give me something to work with.

They also, in some cases, gave me their own stories, and asked me for mine as well. After all the trouble of getting through security into the Jewish archives, the receptionist told me that no one was in that day who could help me. After I inquired about some photos on her desk, and she proudly described her family's historic relationship to the Jewish community in Mexico City, the receptionist showed me some unpublished academic papers that provided invaluable information. In this way, I was Mexican, for this was the way I had been brought up—to do business with someone, you had to know who they were, who their people were. I was prepared for this with pictures of my family, stories about my extended family and ancestors, and copies of my own books in Spanish.

One day, after a visit to the Cólegio de México, a policeman secured a little green taxi ("Don't take the little green taxis!") for me after the car from the hotel where I was staying refused to come back for me. I insisted that he write down the license of the taxi in case I was never seen again. As I climbed into the back seat, the driver said, "Are you a Christian?" I looked up to see that, where the front right seat of the Volkswagen had been removed, as is the custom, he had set up a tiny shrine to the Virgin of Guadalupe. It was a sequined image in full color, with a cloth rose laid at her feet. I proceeded to tell him the story of my mother's family, Jews become Catholics become Protestants, as a way of gently telling him that

I was not Catholic. He seemed calm about that, something I'm not sure would have been true even twenty years earlier. I was expecting him to proselytize, maybe hand me a brochure and ask for a donation. Now I think he may have asked because I did not cross myself upon entering the car, something most of his fares probably do if only out of sheer terror of the Mexico City traffic.

As in my early visit to Chihuahua, I felt set apart by my duality, yet invisible. During my travels as an adult—both in Mexico and in Europe—people always assume I am a native. Maybe it has something to do with my one travel rule—no white shorts. I felt, in some way, protected during this visit, perhaps in the same way that we were spared years earlier during the earthquake. Although I received a distinct, unspoken message that my visit to the pyramid at Tepotzlán needed to be brief, I never felt unsafe or unwanted. Powers were in effect that said, "Observe, but don't touch." And so, I did.

Found in Translation

I was born the youngest in a Spanish-speaking household. My parents and aunts and uncles spoke Spanish, and we, the children, listened. As my two older sisters went to school and brought home English, I heard more English than the others, and gradually, less Spanish. It was said that my early language had a Basque accent, because my uncle, a runaway Basque Jesuit priest who married my aunt, talked a lot. No one said whether my accent was in English or in Spanish. It didn't matter, and we didn't remember, because the languages were interchangeable.

As I grew older and tried to analyze my relationship with language, I realized that I had spent most of my life translating. I processed the Spanish in which I was addressed into the images in my head, and answered in English, because that was the language in which I was educated, starting at the age of five. Before entering school, I don't think I was expected to answer, only listen. At the same time, I was trying to understand what was expected of me at school and translate that into what I had been taught at home. I was considered shy, at first, because I would not look an adult in the eye. In college, I was horrified to find that I was expected to address my professors by their first names, and mostly didn't address them by name at all. I don't think I even knew my parents had first names until I was a teenager.

I survived the traumas of young adulthood, but just barely. Add to the usual mix the differences in dating expectations, humor, and the self-image of a young woman—and this is in the seventies—and you get the idea. I was not only miserable, but I made those around me miserable. I tried, I really did try, but I had been raised to be a proper young woman comfortably ensconced in Northern Mexico in, say, 1895. That is why it was easy for me to write about nineteenth-century Mexico. I didn't just read about it, I lived it. My mother's father's family—before the Revolution, before my grandfather's conversion and expulsion from the family home—was our point of cultural reference. The intervening years and change in economic and social status, from upper-class landowners to the people near the tracks in Southern California, were incidental.

Much has been lost in translation. In our case, we will always be a subgroup of a subculture—Jews who don't know Hebrew, Indians who don't pray to the morning star. Those of you who have tried to return to the past know that things are irrevocably altered by the passage of time and history. You can go back, but not to what your ancestors, or even a younger self, left behind.

We are misinformed, misunderstood, misled, and mistaken for something else.

"Are you Hawaiian?" people ask me. "Filipina? Finnish?"

No, I answer, my parents are from Mexico. My uncle used to tell people he was an Abyssinian Jew, a concept obscure enough at the time to throw his questioners off long enough for him to make an escape. But behind the questions is a search for connections. We each seek to retrace those steps that led us from where we once were, to where we are now. A familiar-sounding name, the slant of an eye, can evoke the memory of that path in a passing observer.

But I had a special gift. One of my first jobs was in the press office of the Democratic National Committee in Washington, D.C. They used to send me the crank callers, the ones who wanted to talk about the conspiracy in the media between the national parties and the major networks, how it was all a trick to promote consumerism.

"You're right," I would tell them. "We take big money from special interests and buy advertising with it. What are you going to do about it? Do you vote? Are you registered to vote?" Most of them were incredulous that anyone would bother to engage them in dialogue. Some of them even thanked me for being honest.

Later I moved to western Colorado and worked for three counties and a small city—Ouray—to bring in public television from Denver. I had to write the grants, order the equipment, and supervise the construction of an elaborate translator and microwave system. I had no idea what I was doing, but the county commissioners—mostly small-business owners and ranchers—trusted me to explain this stuff to them. Terms like *line of sight* and *height above average terrain* and *footprint* rolled off my tongue as I justified this $300,000 project.

In Seattle, I went to work for the Catholic archdiocese, helping ethnic minority communities to organize and raise funding for their specific projects, often youth related. I would go to a party, or a dinner, or a funeral, where the elders—a tribal chairman, a grandma with knitting in hand—would graciously welcome me as an observer while they discussed the issues at hand. By some miracle of talk, they would resolve differences and reach a consensus without any one person seeming to take the lead. I then returned to the archdiocese to explain how these decisions had been made to a deeply, *steeply*, hierarchical system of men in black.

About six months before my son was born, in 1989, I turned full-time to writing. I had written and published a few short stories, and set out to finish my first book-length collection of work.

I do a lot of research for my writing, and much of it is in Spanish. Over the years, I have learned to read Spanish, and I don't even use a dictionary very much. Usually, it is not the words that trip me up, but the intent: why did the author write this? For example, a few years ago I found an article on the Opata written by a Mexican economist.[1] He kept referring to the indigenous problem. What problem? I could not figure this out. I finally realized that the problem, fifty years after the Mexican Revolution, was that the indigenous people of Sonora don't produce exportable capital. They live a self-sufficient lifestyle in which they grow the food that they eat. Because this does not contribute to a national or international economy, it is considered a problem. The attitude echoed exactly that of *los científicos*, Porfirío Díaz's group of advisors who, in the late 1800s, helped him convert Mexico to a modern economy at the expense of its working people. This was one of the major causes of the Mexican Revolution.

Another example of this sort of decoding of text came in newspaper accounts of that time. I came across an article decrying the large number of women who worked as prostitutes in Paris, and what a shame it was that they could not be educated to do something else for a living. Why should people in Mexico City care about this, I wondered. Then I realized that the article was really about Mexico City, in a roundabout way. Prostitution was a huge problem in Mexico City at the time, many women having been displaced from the countryside and winding up living on the streets. In those days, you could hire a woman to work in a factory for half the daily wage of a man, and a child for one-third the wages of a man. People were desperate, and there were calls almost daily in the paper to include women in the educational system. But Mexico City looked to Paris as the example of what it wanted to be when it grew up—not New York, not London, but Paris. So by discussing the problem in Paris, the writer was really calling attention to the situation in Mexico.

A reverse example of this is time I spent in the town of Tepotzlán, located near Cuernavaca. After spending five days in Mexico City researching, I escaped to Tepotzlán for the Day of the Dead. Here is an excerpt from my journal, about an event in which ancient symbols had been translated for a modern celebration:

> Several of the artists had made an ofrenda, a offering in the shape of an altar, for the Day of the Dead. It was quite beautiful. There were several tiers with candles, and cut-out designs in blue and yellow. On the ground were flat sculptures in sand, of the sort Lázaro Fulgencio, an artist in Seattle, knows how to make. In front of that was the large shape of a valentine made of whole marigold flowers. At first I thought that part of the bottom had been displaced, since it trailed downward in a straight line, and almost moved it back with my foot. Then I realized that it was a stylized bleeding heart. From the rafters over the whole hung tissue paper cut-outs in many colors. In this case, modern artistic representations had been re-imagined to serve an ancient purpose.

* * *

I am a person born not only of translations, but of transitions—my very existence marks that conjunction between one culture and another. By claiming this borderland as my own, by acknowledging that I am neither one nor the other, but both, I have been able to reach out and find the parts of each culture that pertain to me. I will never really understand Mexican politics, or be able to tell a joke in English; but I appreciate the beauty and magic inherent in both languages.

I have come to realize, finally, that my life's work, whatever it has been called, is the act of translation. Not necessarily from one language to another, but between world views. I am a translator between worlds, between cultures, between jargons and contexts. And in trying to explain these many worlds to others and to myself, I have become a writer.

With the translation of my work into Spanish, as well as other languages, I feel that my writing is on its way to coming full circle. For that is how my stories started—told to me in Spanish, and written down to be found in translation.

Note

1. Ignacio Zuñiga, "Opatas," *Rápida ojeada al Estado de Sonora, Territorios de California, y Arizona, año de 1835* (Mexico: Vargas Rea, 1948): 115–33.

The Woman Who Loved Water

Once there was a woman who loved water. On dry land, she could merely walk. But in the water, she could fly. She spent as much time as possible in the water, and that is where her husband first saw her—floating on her back in a swimming pool, completely at ease. He vowed to meet her, and eventually, they were married.

The two of them were very happy, and they wanted to have many children. The woman continued to swim until her first child was born. For a time after that, the water seemed to whisper unfamiliar things to her, strange things, but she did not listen. After their second child was born, the water began to whisper again, more strongly this time, but the woman stopped her ears and said "No, no, no!" until the whispers receded. The woman loved her children very much.

Her husband proposed that they free themselves of earthly possessions, that they live simply and concentrate on their family. They sold their home and most of their possessions and moved to a small trailer. But they were near the water, and so the woman was happy.

After the birth of her third child, the waters in her head came back more strongly. She had to concentrate to block out what the voices were saying. It was exhausting, scary. She confessed to her husband that it was hard to be with three children in such a small space, to care for them by herself while he was gone all day, to teach them and cook for them and clean.

And so, the family moved closer to his parents. They bought a house. The waters in her mind receded, and the woman was happy again. A fourth child was born. The waters surged forward, as though waiting, waiting for her. In order to hold back the whispers, to keep their meaning from becoming obvious, the woman had to concentrate all her energy on the breaking waves in her head. She could no longer eat. She could no longer sleep. She could no longer care for her children. The man took her to a doctor, who gave her medicine. The doctor told the husband that the woman would be all right, that the water in her head was only temporary, but that it was strongest when she had just had a child. The doctor suggested that they have no more children.

But they did. And with the fifth child, the dam that the woman had so carefully constructed between her mind and the black, surging waters finally broke. She could no longer hold them back, nor could she ignore what the whispers had been trying to tell her all along. She finally listened to the voices, and did as they told her. The woman filled the bathtub and drowned her five children.

* * *

This is a terrible story, based on an account of Andrea Yates's murder of her children in *Time* magazine. "She was a person who was more graceful in the water than out of it," said her husband, Russell (Rusty) Yates.[1] I read about the case and heard about it and flinched with each additional detail. I scrutinized her photograph in the paper to see what I could discern about her state of mind from her appearance. The whole thing seemed unbelievable.

But there was something disturbingly familiar about this tale, as well.

One day, I realized why. I have been hearing this story, in one form or another, all my life.

One version goes like this: Once there was a woman who fell in love with a man. He was very handsome, and all the women desired him. Eventually, she attracted his notice and they were married. They were very happy, or so she thought, and had many children. One day, the woman went to the river to get water and saw her husband with another woman. In a fit of rage and jealousy, she drowned all of her children. She was put to death for her crime, but continues to haunt the river, looking for her lost children. She can be heard late at night, weeping.

This is, of course, the most famous of Mexican folktales, the story of La Llorona, the weeping woman. There have been songs written about her, and there are many versions of the stories and the songs, with echoes of her undying love for both the children and the absent father.

"How does a person survive who cannot speak up to explain what she wants," asks Rosemarie Coste in "La Llorona y El Grito/The Ghost and The Scream: Noisy Women in Borderlands and Beyond," her exploration of the Llorona myths and their interpretations, "who cannot argue when she is pushed in a direction she does not want to go, who cannot insist that she be consulted when decisions are made about her future?"[2]

This seems to describe Andrea Yates, a woman wracked by mental illness, in a marriage based on the fundamentalist teachings of Michael Woroniecki, a preacher unaffiliated with any established religious group who traveled around the country in a camper with his wife, Rachael, and six children, often speaking at college campuses, and homeschooling his children.

Russell Yates admired this lifestyle. "Man is the breadwinner and woman is the homemaker," he told prosecutor Joe Owmby under cross-examination at Andrea Yates's trial. "It's the way it's been for years." Social worker Earline Wilcott, who counseled Andrea Yates for years, testified that she met Russell Yates once and learned that his beliefs included that a wife should submit to her husband.[3] This belief is based on Ephesians 5:22–24: "Wives, be subject to your own husbands, as to the Lord. For the husband is the head of the wife, as Christ is also the head of the church. . . . But as the church is subject to Christ, so also the wives ought to be to their husbands in everything."[4] These few verses have been the subject of much discussion over the years, as women have struggled to reach religious parity with men. Both sides usually ignore the instructions to men that follow.

A more sinister view of women, however, shows up in Woroniecki's teachings: "Woroniecki preached a stern and patriarchal doctrine. In letters and taped messages to the [Yates] family, he claimed 'all women are descendants of Eve and Eve was a witch. The women, particularly women who worked outside the home, are wicked.'"[5] The Yateses purchased Woroniecki's old motor home, with 350 square feet of living space in which to live, in 1998. Only after Andrea attempted suicide twice, and at her parents' insistence, did they move back into a house in Houston.[6]

Andrea Yates had worked as a post-op nurse at M. D. Anderson Cancer Center before she met Russell and until the birth of her first child, and continued to act as a caregiver for her father, who had Alzheimer's and had never fully recovered from a heart attack. Her father, Andrew Kennedy, died a few months after the birth of Andrea's last child, Mary, and shortly before her last breakdown.[7]

La Llorona weeps wordlessly, "unspeakably," Coste continues, "expressing her longing for the precious things she has lost and cannot find: her home, her family, her body, her life. The many versions of her story differ as to what her losses were and how they occurred, but they unite in judging her to be certainly miserable and probably dangerous, jealous of those who still have the treasures she long ago lost."[8]

When Yates was hospitalized with postpartum depression, her friend Debbie Holmes testified, Russell could not understand why his wife couldn't keep up with taking care of the children and homeschooling them. He admired another woman in the neighborhood: "She's got nine kids, teaches her kids tee ball, and she does just fine. I don't know why Andrea's having so much trouble," said Russell Yates, according to Holmes.[9]

"A woman who will not suffer silently, who makes her displeasure heard and expects it to be dealt with, is an exceptional and amazing creature in a culture like the one that created La Llorona's legend, a culture that values patient endurance above many other virtues."[10]

In *Borderlands/La Frontera*, Gloria Anzaldúa writes extensively about attempts to silence the Chicana, the mixed-blood Latinas of the border between Mexico and the United States.

> *En boca cerrada no entran moscas.* "Flies don't enter a closed mouth" is a saying I kept hearing when I was a child. *Ser habladora* was to be a gossip and a liar, to talk too much. *Muchachitas bien criadas*, well-bred girls don't answer back. *Es una falta de respeto* to talk back to one's mother or father . . . *hablar pa' trás, repelar, hocicona, repelona, chismosa*, having a big mouth, questioning, carrying tales are all signs of being *mal criada*. In my culture they are all words that are derogatory if applied to women—I've never heard them applied to men.[11]

Anzaldúa is one of the few people who has attempted to rewrite the Llorona myth, in her children's book *Prietita and the Ghost Woman/ Prietita y la llorona*,[12] which features a benevolent Llorona guiding a lost girl, first to a medicinal herb for her mother, then to rescue. Interestingly, this ghost woman is completely silent.

While there are many differences between Andrea Yates's situation and those of Latina women, the fundamental Christian belief system to which she adheres values the wife who submits to her husband, and there is some indication that this was true of the Yates family.

Frank Ochberg, MD, a psychiatrist and the author of *Post-Traumatic Therapy and Victims of Violence*,[13] said in a talk in Seattle that the first sign of trauma is speechlessness. Most violence is in the home, he says, and so is especially difficult to treat. "If the language of the victim or advocate is too strong," he says, "ears close. If it is too soft, it is not heard."[14]

Sandra Cisneros also retells the Llorona myth in her story "Woman Hollering Creek." In it, Cleofílas finds the voice to tell a health worker of her abusive situation, and is rescued by a woman who, "when they drove across the *arroyo* . . . opened her mouth and let out a yell as loud as any mariachi."

"'I like the name of that *arroyo*,'" she tells her startled passenger. "'Makes you want to holler like Tarzan, right?'"[15] In this case, Cisneros shows that the silence of abuse can be escaped, and the legend reimagined to show a woman who stands up for herself.

There is no indication that Andrea Yates ever complained about her situation, or even saw herself in that light. The worst that was put in writing was that "the patient's husband might be a little bit controlling."[16] Rather, according to Sergeant Eric Mehl, the officer who responded to her 911 call and took her confession, "She would sit in 15 seconds of stone-cold silence if he asked too much. She could give only short answers to simple questions in their 17-minute conversation as she twice recounted the order in which her children were born and died."[17]

✻　✻　✻

Another version of La Llorona goes like this: a man and a woman fell in love and married. They were very happy, but very poor. They did not have enough food or money to feed their children, and so the man left their village to look for work. The woman was left alone with the children, and, after the man had been gone a long time, they began to starve to death. Finally, the woman drowned her children in the river rather than watch them starve. To this day, she grieves, and can be heard calling for them along the riverbank, looking for her lost children. You can hear her there, calling late at night, and if she mistakes you for one of her children, she might take you, too. I was told this version in the 1970s by a college classmate, the daughter of farmworkers, who went on to become a lawyer for the Mexican American Legal Defense Fund.

On June 20, 2001, Andrea Yates, 37, told Officer Eric Mehl that she drowned her five children—Noah, 7, John, 5, Paul, 3, Luke, 2, and 6-month-old Mary.

Three weeks later, she told psychiatrist Phillip Resnick that she was failing as a mother and believed she had to kill the children to keep them from going to hell. "These were their innocent years," she told him. "God would take them up."[18]

Yates drowned her children to save them from eternal damnation. Because she had been a bad mother, she reasoned, her children were also turning out to be bad. Only by drowning them while they were still young and innocent, by sacrificing herself to the laws of secular man, could she assure their eternal salvation. She, in turn, would be executed by the state and Satan would be eliminated from the world.

"I realized it was time to be punished," Yates told Sgt. Eric Mehl.

"And what do you need to be punished for?"

"For not being a good mother."[19]

After her imprisonment, Yates told doctors that the death of her children was *her* punishment, not theirs. It was, she explained, a mother's final act of mercy. According to the Bible, it was better to be flung into the sea with a stone tied to one's neck than cause little ones to stumble.[20] And she had failed them.

This is an important point in Yates's system of belief. It had been her job to instruct her children, both in secular studies and religious studies, since the Yateses did not attend church. Rather, they held Bible studies three evenings a week. Yates had "earmarked pages in her Bible about a mother's obligation to raise her children or face the consequences. . . . She came to believe that she had failed so badly to measure up to her own extreme ideals of motherhood (she thought the kids should say their ABC's by age 2) that, as she told the psychiatrist, the kids were destined to perish in the fires of hell."[21]

Hamida Bosmajian, a professor of English at Seattle University, has made a study of the use of language in the indoctrination of children by the Nazi regime. During the Third Reich, power was achieved primarily by the use of language. First, it was used to divide people from each other, then to unite those who were left. "Children in particular were reshaped as warriors," said Bosmajian. They were told that individual identity counted for nothing. Finally, the general population was encouraged to "become like children" and let the people in power maintain the material conditions of life.[22]

Only by making sure that her young children were well-versed in the beliefs of their elders could they become warriors for Christ. If they could not read the Bible, this would not be possible. "They did a lot of silly stuff and didn't obey," Yates said. "They did things God didn't like."[23]

Because Andrea Yates was unable to do all that was expected of her, she was a bad mother. Because she was a bad mother, her children were bad. Only her execution would rescue them from the evil inside her—a state-sanctioned exorcism in which George W. Bush, the former governor and now president, would come to save her from the clutches of Satan.[24]

In the last days before the drownings, Yates had also wanted to have her head shaved so that she could see the mark of the beast as described in the Book of Revelation,[25] the number 666, that she was sure was emblazoned on her scalp.

After Yates's arrest, Michael Woroniecki tried to downplay the influence he had on the family through personal correspondence and through his publication, *The Perilous Times*, a copy of which was put into evidence by Yates's attorney.[26] In it, a poem laments the disobedient children of the "Modern Mother Worldly," ending with the question, "What becomes of the children of such a Jezebel?" Woroniecki wrote a letter to *Newsweek* magazine denying responsibility for Yates's actions. But his views of women were shared by Russell Yates, who saw his wife's mental illness as an indication that her resistance to evil had been lowered.

At one point when court-appointed psychiatrist Phillip Resnick was interviewing Yates, he asked her how she felt about her children.

"I didn't hate my children," she responded.

"Did you love your children?" Resnick asked.

"Yeah," she responded after a long pause. "Some. Not in the right way, though."[27]

According to Coste, folklorists claim to see, in the hundreds of variants of the La Llorona tale, "Mexican-American cultural attitudes toward mothering activities and . . . the conflicts and stresses that Mexican-American women experience in relation to the mother role," as well as "insight into the interpretation of the infanticide motif as a psychological device related to the frustrations of child care," showing that "contemplation of infanticide provides a momentary 'escape' from the problems of child rearing."[28]

Like all living mythology, there are newer versions of La Llorona. Coste has found "the first signs of a merging of the traditional La Llorona legend and the contemporary stories of babies found abandoned in trash dumpsters, a more modern method for disposing of children than drowning."[29]

Coste also found research showing that La Llorona is known to the female inmates of juvenile hall, even by those who do not know her by name. Of thirty-one ghost stories collected by researcher Bess Lomax Hawes, twenty-eight were about adult women, most of whom were threats to the living. This is in contrast to ghost lore in general, in which most ghosts are males who are indifferent to the living. The girls' stories varied in many details, but all featured ghosts that were female, vicious, and very much inclined to attack. The most frequent themes were infanticide and other aggressive crimes committed by women, punishment or aggressive crimes against women, inconsolable grief or loss, and mutilation, another kind of loss.[30]

Of the two versions of La Llorona I have recounted here, I suspect that men are more likely to tell the first version—of the woman who drowns her children for spite—and women the second—the woman who drowns her children to spare them suffering. One is a story of jealousy, and the second, a story of desperation. One could argue that, if La Llorona killed her children out of spite and jealousy, she did it for the wrong reasons. If she killed her children out of pity and mercy, then she did it for the right reasons—still wrong, but motivated by compassion.

"Even though she knew it was against the law," said psychiatrist Phillip Resnick, "she did what she thought was right in the world she perceived through her psychotic eyes at the time."[31]

Which version is closer to the truth? And which model did the jury have in mind when they convicted Andrea Yates of murder on March 12, 2002? Under Texas law Yates "could have been found not guilty only if jurors believed she suffered from a mental defect that prevented her from distinguishing right from wrong."[32] The jury took less than four hours to reach a verdict. During the deliberations, the jury requested an audiotape player and may have listened again to the 911 recording of Andrea Yates's call to the police and her taped confession. This suggests that they concentrated on her actions the morning of the killings, rather than the extensive testimony describing her history of mental illness.

"The way she did it and the way she acted afterwards was inconsistent with somebody who didn't know what she was doing," said Rusty Hardin, a former local prosecutor who watched closing arguments.[33]

In the Llorona tales, the townspeople feel the same way. In some versions, she is stoned or hung by the other villagers when it is discovered what she has done. In others, she stays by the river and wastes away on her own, until only the wail is left.

"The loving act of a mother was to leave [Noah's] body floating in the bathtub," said prosecuting attorney Raylynn Williford, sarcastically, in closing arguments. "She made the choice to fill the tub. She made the choice to kill these children. She knew it was wrong. . . .

"At one point during Ms. Williford's arguments, Mrs. Yates cried silently at the defense table."[34]

Sadly, Noah was named after the biblical patriarch to whom God made the promise that the world would never again be destroyed by water.[35]

✳   ✳   ✳

What is La Llorona trying to tell us? And why is the Andrea Yates case so eerily similar?

Tales of the supernatural persist because they portray a situation that we continue to understand over the passage of time and place. They carry some universal meaning that allows them to be adapted to current circumstances, always timely, always applicable. The specific characters may change, but as editor Rob Johnson says in the introduction to *Fantasmas: Supernatural Stories by Mexican American Writers*, these stories "never forget there is a spiritual side of life, but even more importantly, don't ignore social reality."[36]

La Llorona is, in part, a story about power—power over our own circumstances. What control do we have over what happens to us, over what happens to the closest thing that we have to an extension of ourselves, our children? The song versions of La Llorona, in particular, tell us that she was dark: "*Todos me dicen el negro, llorona/Negro pero cariñoso.*"

And so most likely, lower class and powerless. Some versions of the Llorona story, those that fall into the jealous-woman category, also say that she is lower class, and her husband/lover is of the upper class. But she is also reminiscent of the beautiful lover in the Song of Songs:

I am dark, but comely . . .
Don't stare at me because I am swarthy,
Because the sun has gazed upon me.[37]

What does a middle-class Anglo woman, supposedly living in comfortable circumstances, have in common with a poor, dark woman from Mexico? These questions continued to haunt me as I traveled to Texas and Mexico in April 2002, closer to the origin of the Llorona stories.

✳   ✳   ✳

In Saltillo, Mexico, I took the opportunity to ask a couple of people their version of La Llorona. It turned out to be quite different from that recounted in the United States.

My cousin, Amalia Moreira Narro de Heede, who is in her seventies, told me a version she had heard from her great-grandmother on her mother's side. This is a pre-Hispanic version, she said. In it, a woman had a premonition that the Spaniards were coming to Mexico and would slaughter her children. She began to cry, "*¡Ay, mis hijos! Ay, mis hijos!*" She appeared in a long white dress, with long hair to the ground.

On the plane to Houston, I asked a man, who appeared to be in his late thirties, if he had heard the Llorona story. He was reading an American murder mystery in Spanish. He said that he was originally from Reynosa, Mexico, but worked in McAllen. The man put down his book and thought a minute. He said that his grandmother used to read a lot, and liked to tell them stories. Yes, he said, he had heard about a woman in a white dress calling *"Ay, mis hijos, ay, mis hijos,"* because her children had died. He could not remember why they had died, or how.

As I thought about it, the long white dress gave me a clue: the priests and holy people in the court of Moctezuma wore long white gowns, and were not allowed to cut their hair. It was caked from dried blood due to their almost daily ritual of bloodletting. The image of the woman was a warning to others, like the warnings of the dreamers disregarded by Moctezuma until it was too late. This Llorona starts to sound a lot like the dreamers in Ana Castillo's *Massacre of the Dreamers: Essays on Xicanisma:*

> Moteuczoma [*sic*] called upon the thousands of dreamers who were sharing the same premonition: the prophesied arrival of Cortés and the subsequent annihilation of the Empire. Moteuczoma's order to have the dreamers murdered en masse did not stop the landing of those alien ships that were already on their way. . . .
>
> Moteuczoma, who relied heavily on mysticism and having received various ominous omens about the fall of his empire, also consulted with his greatest wizards and magicians. These, unable to advise Moteuczoma as to how to prevent what had already been divinely decreed were imprisoned. But being magicians they mysteriously escaped. Moteuczoma avenged them by having their wives and children hung and their houses destroyed.[38]

Nearly the entire time that I was in Texas and Mexico, it rained. They told me it had not rained for months, and my relatives began to call me Tlaloc, the rain god, because I had brought rain from the Northwest. Like columnist Patricia Gonzales, in her essay of March 8, 2002, "I carry a pot of tears on my head. . . . La Llorona tells us there is something wrong with society, that there are many forms of madness."[39] It occurred to me, as I jumped across puddles in my sandals, that the drownings of these children, in Andrea Yates's universe, might have been a sort of baptism. Romans 6:4 encourages us to be "buried with Him through baptism into death, in order that as Christ was raised from the dead through the glory of the Father, so we too might walk in newness of life."[40] In her attempt to save her children from her own madness and powerlessness, Yates may have taken the only tangible step that promised salvation at the time.

After a spectacular lightning storm the night before, my last morning in Saltillo dawned calm and sunny. I turned on the shower to warm up the water before getting in. When it still seemed cool, I gave it a few more seconds. That's when I heard a noise near the ceiling and instinctively ducked away from the open shower door. An enormous crash followed. When I looked around, the shower was filled with the wet, sparkling shards of a huge light fixture that had detached from the ceiling and broken to bits on the concrete shower floor.

"We have, at this point, some hope and expectation that Ms. Yates will receive the same or better care than she received before she was arrested," said Joe Lovelace, a public policy consultant for the National Alliance for the Mentally Ill of Texas. "That's not saying a lot."[41]

I may never fully comprehend why a woman who loved water drowned her own children, but I will take it as a warning that "it is not [La Llorona] who will 'get' us if we are not careful, but our own ordinary and dangerous lives."[42] I suspect that Andrea Yates's story will be added to the La Llorona lore of Texas. The old stories persist because the old ills persist. And the old ills persist because, in the end, human nature does not change.

(A Texas appeals court in early 2005 reversed the capital murder convictions of Andrea Yates. She now resides in a state-run, maximum-security mental hospital.)

Notes

1. June 20, 2001, quoted in Timothy Roche, "The Yates Odyssey," *Time*, January 28, 2002.

2. Rosemarie Coste, "La Llorona y El Grito/The Ghost and The Scream: Noisy Women in Borderlands and Beyond," Dec. 15, 2000, www.womenwriters.net.

3. Associated Press, Houston, "Mental Decline of Yates Documented," CourtTV. com, *Texas v. Andrea Yates*, February 27, 2002.

4. *New American Standard Bible* (La Habra, California: Foundation Press Publications, 1972).

5. Ellen Makkai, www.ezboard.com, March 23, 2002.

6. "Yates Odyssey," *Time*, 10.

7. "Yates Odyssey," *Time*, 6.

8. Coste, "La Llorona."

9. AP, Houston, "Mental Decline."

10. Coste, "La Llorona."

11. Gloria Anzaldúa, *Borderlands/La Frontera* (San Francisco: Aunt Lute Books, 1999): 76.

12. Anzaldúa, *Prietita and the Ghost Woman/Prietita y la llorona* (San Francisco: Children's Book Press, 1995).

13. Frank Ochberg, *Post-Traumatic Therapy and Victims of Violence* (New York: Brunner/Mazel, 1988).

14. Ochberg, "The Languages of Emotional Injury" (symposium, Seattle University, April 26, 2002).

15. Sandra Cisneros, "Woman Hollering Creek," in *Woman Hollering Creek and Other Stories* (New York: Random House, 1991).

16. Social worker Norma Tauriac, "Yates Odyssey," *Time*, 8.

17. "Yates Odyssey," *Time*, 16.

18. AP, Houston, "Yates Claimed She Killed Kids to Keep Them from Going to Hell," March 1, 2002.

19. *Houston Chronicle*, February 21, 2002.

20. *Standard Bible*, Matthew 18:6.

21. Timothy Roche, "The Devil and Andrea Yates," *Time*, March 11, 2002.

22. Hamida Bosmajian, *Sparing the Child: Children's Literature about Nazism and the Holocaust* (New York: Routledge, 2001).

23. CourtTV.com, March 4, 2002.

24. "Yates Odyssey," *Time*, 16.

25. *Standard Bible*, Revelation 13:6.

26. *Newsweek*, "Michael Woroniecki's Influence over Convicted Murderer Andrea Yates," March 18, 2002.

27. AP, Houston, March 4, 2002.

28. Coste, "La Llorona."

29. Ibid.

30. Ibid.

31. AP, Houston, March 4, 2002.

32. Jim Yardley, "Texas Jury Convicts Mother Who Drowned Her Children," *New York Times*, March 13, 2002.

33. Ibid.

34. Ibid.

35. *Standard Bible*, Genesis 9:15.

36. Rob Johnson, introduction to *Fantasmas*.

37. "The Song of Songs, I:5,6," *Tanakh*, translated by the Jewish Publication Society, 1985.

38. Ana Castillo, *Massacre of the Dreamers: Essays on Xicanisma* (New York: Plume/Penguin, 1995): 16.

39. Patricia Gonzales, XColumn, Universal Press Syndicate, 2002, www.azteca.net/aztec/literal/xcolumn.html.

40. *Standard Bible*, Romans 6:4.

41. Ed Timms and Diane Jennings, "Guilty Verdict No Surprise Given Texas Laws, Legal Experts Say," *Dallas Morning News*, March 13, 2002.

42. Coste, "La Llorona."

The Underground Heart:
A Return to a Hidden Landscape

Ray Gonzalez

The Border Is Open

Home is where our individual memories are rooted and never disappear, the place where our inner being begins and ends, a haven for birth and death. Home is the place where we return when we need to adjust to new energies the world presses upon our daily lives. Home is comfort and uneasiness. Despite the age-old cliché of not being able to go home again, we carry home wherever we dwell. If we never leave our hometown to live elsewhere, which is true for a large percentage of the American population, we create our territory of existence in the place where we were born—home. The character of that home is vastly different from the one created elsewhere by people who left their hometown ages ago. Home as territory—fortress or open house.

As a native of the Southwest, I know my home will always be the desert surrounding El Paso and the southern New Mexico area. I left in 1979 but have never been able to create a natural sense of home in other cities where I have lived. The memory of the desert creates an invisible nest of roots that allows a native to wander far before finding a way back. The memory of the Rio Grande passing its vein of mud south is one I sleep with, then wake to see if the level of the current has gone down. The stark peaks of the Franklin Mountains dominate the city that grows in a horseshoe shape around them. El Paso spreads for miles into the desert east of the mountains. Housing developments tear high into the Franklins themselves. The horseshoe is now bent and twisted, its boundaries of my childhood gone. I gaze up at the bare face of the Franklins and conclude that the crown of my home has eroded over the forty-nine years of my life. Each time I come home, the mountains are closer to the ground.

Memories of wandering the desert alone as a boy and teaching myself about the rocks, the fossils stuck inside them, and the tarantulas scuttling across my dirt path pull me back home. Childhood memories that made me leave rise when I visit my home—the silent father, the boys who chased me off the football team, the grandmother who always wanted me by her side. The happy experiences—the climb up muddy arroyos after a desert rain, riding tiny paddleboats at the amusement park on the other side of town—have me wishing I could go back in time. Home is the generator of longing. It is the yearning for a united family, happy Christmas days, innocent adventures with the kids next door. It is also the place where the person we wanted to be when we grew up never appeared, because we became someone else. The great Catholic fear during Sunday mass and the racism in high school stand out in my mind. Later, it was my divorced parents and my dreams of being successful in careers that never material- ized, until I accomplished many things I never thought I would. Home created a different individual because El Paso educated my heart and mind, placing its limits upon me. Such limits often match the city limits of our hometown as we grow up, so we are forced to go live elsewhere.

I visualize rattlesnakes, lizards, bats, turtles, scorpions, hawks, and coyotes. I recall the onion, chile, lettuce, and cotton fields of La Mesilla Valley. When I think of home, these creatures and food sources as a major part of my memories. When I visit, I know where to go if I want to explore the natural world of the borderlands. This inner pull is similar to my rattlesnake dreams, drawing me to walk along the river where I mark the changing course of the Rio Grande and learn where the bridges of home span the muddy stretches. This magnetism helps me to identify where the adobe ruins stand in La Mesilla Valley, thirty years after I first found the row of migrant worker huts as a boy.

I do not believe in the loss of home. An earthquake or other natural disaster can wipe out the town of our origins and it will still be there. Our private sounds and memories tell us where home lies eternally. Navajo people believe sacred ground must be earned. You are not born into a fam- ily and automatically given a place in the world. You must earn it. As you pay for it, the joys and sorrows that grow on sacred ground are identified for you as the citizens of your place on earth. You can celebrate or mourn the area where you grew up, with its stage of autobiographical failures and triumphs, but you have earned them and can't abandon them completely. The Navajos say it comes down to belief. The things you believe in are the factors that will protect or diminish your origins and your home.

October 14, 1934: The most damaging dust storm to hit El Paso shifted tons of sand from the barren desert onto city streets. The area was covered for several hours and everything came to a stop. Several cars were involved in accidents as the thick waves of sand kept drivers from seeing where they were going. Major streets downtown were closed due to drifts of sand, averaging two feet in thickness. Power lines came down and the Rio Grande turned a soft brown, its busy waters churning the mud on its way south. Huge piles of tumbleweeds appeared against buildings, and clusters of them were removed by city workers, private citizens, anyone who could grab a rake or shovel; some even used their bare hands and risked being cut by the dry weeds. Dust hung in the air for two days, immersing the city in a brown fog that made thousands sick, increased the crime rate for forty-eight hours (the dust a perfect shield for robbery and theft), and allowed an extra thousand or two illegal workers from Juárez to cross the river under its protection. Four people drowned in the Rio Grande, south of downtown, during those two days of dust, and eighteen murders were reported by the El Paso police. Ten of the victims were found covered in sand at various crime scenes around the city. Three building fires were reported, but two of them were extinguished by heavy rolls of dust that prevented the flames from breathing. The third fire resisted the brown particles and wiped out an old pickle factory in east El Paso.

I have been gone from the desert Southwest for twenty-five years, yet I continue to write about it. As the years go by, it is easier to acknowledge this landscape that "covers the past and hangs as the ember of thought/ wisdom molded out of the falling world," as I wrote in one of my poems. I cannot let go of the Chihuahuan Desert, the Rio Grande, the Franklin and Organ mountains, El Paso, and La Mesilla Valley—the falling world of my childhood and teenage years when I became a writer through the sheer immersion in an isolated yet vibrant place. I have lived elsewhere since 1979 and have written more poems about my home than I did when I lived in El Paso; biological time leads me to a new sense of home as a new century begins. The fact is, I have produced a large body of work that could not have been written if I had stayed in west Texas. This is hard to admit, but does not require sadness or romantic longings for home. It does call for occasional visits to see how Mexico, with its exciting cultural and monumental problems, has transformed El Paso into an American version of itself. I had to leave my home two decades ago to be a writer who could face family issues, religious and spiritual conflicts, and the overwhelming presence of the desert from a safe distance—with a more objective view of how a childhood of isolation influenced the way I respond to the world and to re-create the border in my poems and stories. What this means is contained in what I have not created yet, though it can be found in what I have already written. It includes journeys home to witness the great transformations and conflicts taking place from San Diego, California, to Brownsville, Texas—political, economic, and environmental forces that point to the border where I grew up as a stage for the unfolding of the future of the United States and Mexico.

I walk along the Rio Grande at the millennium and it is not the same river, flowing steadily, then drying up before the next surge of water retraces its course. The Great River, to borrow Paul Horgan's phrase, is a line of water that traces and surrounds every conceivable problem and some of the solutions that New Mexico, Texas, and Mexico face—illegal immigration, water rights, radioactive waste, and the struggle to find new ways to attract outside investment and tourism to an area that traditionally has been one of the poorest in North America. The cottonwoods in La Mesilla Valley stand taller and thinner than when I last saw them as a young man. Much of the desert where I wandered as a boy is gone, replaced by strip malls and new housing that cover the trails I used to explore alone. In the middle of this growth, the tragedy of Mexico expands across the invisible border to reinforce a social and cultural poverty—a timeless erosion that eats away at the metropolitan region of El Paso and Juárez. Both legal and illegal workers from Mexico continue to cross, and I find more houses in El Paso with iron bars on the windows. Even the neighborhood where I grew up, with the exception of my mother's house, is saturated with the protective bars. Why has my mother not barred hers yet? Nostalgia for a time when there was less crime? More men, women, and children are coming across the border to take jobs U.S. citizens don't want. The average salary of working people in the area remains one of the lowest in the country. Poverty, crime, and the disappearing desert result in distrust and segregated neighborhoods. These stark but complex images are the first I see each time I visit.

A 1999 national survey found that Texas and New Mexico were the forty-eighth and forty-ninth worst places to live in this country. This conclusion was based on the quality of education, jobs, and the crime rate, but a May 2001 survey found El Paso to be the twelfth safest city in the United States—one of the best towns in one of the worst states, George W. Bush's legacy in Texas, long established before he became president.

El Paso is the state's most isolated city, lying six hundred miles west of Austin and San Antonio, and to have it declared a safe place in a notoriously backward state says a great deal about the insulation the Chihuahuan desert offers from the rest of the Lone Star state. These two surveys also represent the contradictions on the border: Low wages, a low cost of living, and an illegal, underground economy characterize a city that prefers to keep things that way, although one look across the international bridges on Stanton and Santa Fe streets reveals a different story, that of Mexico's rapid, unstoppable expansion north of the Rio Grande, and the source of a militarized border.

The June 11, 2001, issue of *Time* magazine features a major section on my home. "Welcome to Amexica" is the large headline, its letters painted in red, white, and blue, plus the red and green of Mexico. Two Mexican American children playing with colorful toys smile from the cover. I shake my head in the Minneapolis airport, where I first spot the new issue, because I've seen this media dance over the border many times before. The subtitle declares, "The border is vanishing before our eyes, creating a new world for all of us." Major news organizations like *Time*, ABC News, and several Internet media centers proclaim a week-long focus on illegal immigration, the drug wars, NAFTA, and the blending of everything American with everything Mexican. One *Time* reporter proclaims, "Salsa is more popular than ketchup; Salma Hayek is bigger than Madonna—and the border is everywhere!" The national media act as if life on the border is a brand-new phenomenon—or the latest Ricky Martin tune you can dance to.

To draw the reader into the long articles about life in Nogales, Laredo, Matamoros, and Juárez, *Time*'s editors highlight what they consider to be flabbergasting facts about the region in the post-NAFTA madness: The Wal-Mart in Laredo, population 193,000, is the highest grossing one per square foot in the United States; the border population is growing at almost twice the national rate; 31 percent of all tuberculosis cases are found in the four border states; apprehension of illegal aliens through March 2001 dropped 24 percent from the year before. Maps and charts of the New Frontier, or La Nueva Frontera, show key cities like San Diego and El Paso and are dotted with those well-known *Time* magazine polls on whether Canada is more important to the well-being of the United States than Mexico, which country has more of an impact on Americans, and, the one that stands out for me, "Do you think it should be easier or harder for people to cross the border into the United States?" Fifty-three percent of the people polled decided the already highly militarized and dangerous border should be made harder to cross from the Mexican side. Wal-Mart can make millions of dollars each month in Laredo and keeps its doors open to Mexican shoppers every night of the week, but the 53 percent who want to make it harder to come across illegally represent a growing attitude in a region torn by differences that a treaty like NAFTA will never change. Let's take those Mexican dollars but only if the cashiers can see some green cards? I don't know how many extra copies of the June 11 issue of *Time* sold as a result of ABC's nightly news stories on the border, but by June 18, Amexica is forgotten by the national media, as stories on President Bush's misbehaving daughters take the spotlight away from those late-night Wal-Mart shoppers in Nuevo Laredo.

My parents, sisters, and nephews live in the midst of great chaos and change. They don't have to read about it in the national media, as I often do. These days my family can't even use the border Spanish we were raised to speak. When my sisters, who are all teachers in public schools, use words like *palomitas, carro, tenny shoes*, and other bilingual mutations, their fellow teachers scold them and try to correct their Spanish. These defenders of traditional Spanish, often young men and women born in Mexico but educated in the United States and now working here, refuse to acknowledge calo—the border speech Chicanos love and identify as a part of their culture—because this language represents the union of people who share their lives on the border.

A perfect example appeared when I overheard a Mexican American woman cashier in a busy cafeteria in El Paso tell her coworker to answer the phone by the cash register because she was too busy waiting on customers and the lights on the receiver "estan blinkiando." It was an old telephone with blinking lights for the different phone lines. I was paying for my food and saw the lights, then heard her say "estan blinkiando," so I knew I was home again. Blinkiando is the invisible border that crosses into the backyard of every member of my family, blinking from English to Spanish, then back again. It would have fit on the cover of *Time*—Amexica Blinkiando!—political and cultural conflicts perhaps too overwhelming for most writers of the desert to address in their poems, stories, and essays as they leave it to the national media to analyze why the border constantly flashes signals that it is okay to live in a prosperous region that really doesn't want its thriving citizens there.

After reading the border feature in *Time*, I grieve for what is gone, but this is nothing new for a writer. Growing older is the companion to the universal cycle of watching the past become dust, grasping this pollen by writing about a place where I no longer fit. Since 1979 I have written from Denver, San Antonio, Chicago, and now Minneapolis, needing these cities to be able to yearn for the desert from afar. When I admit "there is no limit to returning," I go back to search for what I have not seen before, what I overlooked in fleeing. I want solid trails cut through an arroyo I used to explore as a boy. I want to touch the cracked bark of the cottonwoods along the Rio Grande because "tomorrow I will see another kind of growth." What the invisible border gives, it takes away with the turbulent blending of the blinking populations of El Paso and Juárez, the brown and white faces becoming one profile. They now populate one city, one metropolitan region that is more Mexican than anything else. New elements of border life blend with the old and writers will be there to find them, despite the reality that the past century has changed their home forever.

One of the most common questions I am asked when I give talks on autobiographical writing is, "Where are you from?" When I answer "El Paso, Texas," I always get a handful of people raising their eyebrows as if to say, "Oh, that's out in the middle of nowhere," or "Oh, yeah, I drove through there once. Those brown mountains are amazing, but I didn't really like the place. There is nothing to do there." For most of my adult life, I agreed with these reactions; I wanted them to be the answers I gave from the city in which I resided at the time. It has taken twenty-two years of living elsewhere, almost as many years as I lived in El Paso, to conclude that I grew up in an isolated place that had a great deal to offer me with its abundant human and animal life, a place where great, historic events of exploration and conquest took place, only to have them return as contrived notions from tourist bureaus searching for more dollars. Welcome to Amexica, land of rewritten history, where the Spaniard and the conquered Indian are noble, and where the enormous illegal immigrant population is supposed to remain invisible. The bureaus don't want that working force to block entrances to popular museums, only to sweep their floors at midnight when all the tourists are gone.

My home contains an environmental, historical, and cultural richness I could not appreciate as a withdrawn boy who loved to collect fossils and dig under tumbleweeds during his lonely hikes through the desert. For two decades after I moved away, I told friends I left El Paso because there was nothing there for me. The more I believed this, the deeper I buried its cultural forces under the desert. It was easy to write about the landscape itself and how I explored it as a boy, but it was harder to write about my

Catholic upbringing, the racism in the public schools, and how a Chicano should relate to Mexican nationals who, for the most part, saw my border upbringing and its contradictions of trying to be Mexican and a U.S. citizen at the same time as ridiculous. What the hell was I doing north of the international bridge when my family and I, and millions of other Chicanos who identified with sixties protest movements, were calling for a rebirth of our Aztec-Mexican roots?

Now I want to dig up the hidden landscapes of family and race, while I feel the tightening tensions of an invisible, international border that the U.S. media finds so captivating, as if spotlighting the border will help to find solutions to centuries-old problems. I had to go away and grow older to finally admit that my home has always been a life-giving, spiritually sustaining place. Too many people dismiss it as the land of the illiterate, the frontier of desperate people, or the breeding ground for the next generation of drug lords. They make these conclusions because they know nothing about the area. Or they play the tourist game of romanticizing life in the Southwest. This has resulted in the rise of heritage tourism, the ability of southwestern states to rewrite history for economic rewards. In cities like Albuquerque, El Paso, and Tucson, this means millions of tourist dollars are made by misinterpreting and romanticizing the exploration, conquest and settling of the West—not the newest or most profound revelation when it comes to the story of this country, but in the Southwest, heritage tourism takes on new meaning when museums are built to glorify nuclear war, to salute the art of capturing illegal immigrants, and to show how American might defeated "deranged" revolutionary heroes who never needed U.S. help to stage their own downfalls in the first place. The results are strange tourist centers that draw outsiders to give them a distorted view of southwestern life as they leave their dollars in museum gift shops and go home weighed down with pounds of Indian jewelry around their necks.

I studied heritage tourism on the border during several trips I took to the Southwest in 1999 through 2001. What I found in museums and art galleries differs greatly from what *Time* magazine featured. After returning to my home as a native, and playing tourist from the point of view of someone who grew up in the desert of Juan de Oñate, Robert Oppenheimer, and Pancho Villa, I conclude that beautiful Indian ruins, the horrors of Trinity and Los Alamos, and racist stereotypes from south of the border could take place only along the timeless current of the Rio Grande because New Mexico and west Texas have magnetized their bloody past and present with the forces of once powerful civilizations, weapons of mass destruction, and revolutionary movements that tore international boundaries open. These tumultuous events have been calling to people to gather and cross at the border—dead Spanish conquistadores lying alongside vanished tribes and the buried secrets of government knowledge.

Many of the people I meet in El Paso today didn't grow up there, though they control Chamber of Commerce and Tourist Bureau offices. Their generalizations about Mexican food, the "beauty" of the desert, and their ways of shrugging off racial and class separations were shaped by their lives elsewhere and their acceptance of heritage tourism as an attractive, monetary truth to add to border liquor, Mexican food, stripper bars, and beautiful vistas with a turquoise coyote howling at the moon on t-shirts, cups, necklaces, and expensive pendants.

Each time I go home, the boy who isolated himself by wandering the desert reemerges to give me something new. The more I visit, the more that mute boy shifts from mourning what can never be relived to one who celebrates the place that made him who he is, despite the dynamics of an external manipulation and its realignment of life in El Paso and other southwestern cities. Tucking away parts of my past helped me find the courage to leave the area, though it took years to get rid of the anger over a life I didn't understand there. Now I wander a place undergoing enormous changes, while parts of it hang onto a decaying environment influenced by poverty, illegal immigration, and dying cultural traditions. Amid these shattering dramas, I return with love and compassion as I try to understand what has happened to my beloved Chihuahuan Desert and Rio Grande.

December 14, 1947: The hardest dust storm to hit El Paso in several years uncovered fourteen headstones at Concordia cemetery. As the oldest graveyard in El Paso, in constant use since 1851, Concordia has layer upon layer of ancient graves, tombs, and headstones. Besides sweeping tons of sand across the old grave markers, the storm lifted tons more to reveal the previously unknown markers near the southeast corner of the huge cemetery. Most of the markings on the headstones eroded long ago, but three sites were identified as belonging to Rosario Vargas, 1872–1890; Pedro Ochoa, 1879–1890; and Maria Lopez, 1872–1890. City and cemetery records were found for Ochoa and Lopez, the documents stating the two deceased were drowning victims of a previously unknown Rio Grande flood of 1890. No details could be found on Vargas or the eleven other unidentified graves.

During my first trip to El Paso after the turn of the century, its familiar and strange characteristics bring back memories of becoming a writer. This recollection comes from the routine I had as a boy during hot summers. One July night as I lay in my bedroom, I went through my nightly habit of opening the window to let the cool desert breeze blow in through the screen. I turned on the tiny radio I kept on the nightstand near the bed, its volume low as Wolfman Jack played the latest Top 40 hits. I lay in the dark and stared at the blackness of the room, waiting for the distant sound of trains. The railroad tracks were three miles south of the neighborhood, and the whistle and faraway rumble of the engines came around midnight. By then, my parents and sisters were asleep in other parts of the house. It was soothing to lie in the quiet room and wait for the familiar sounds. I wondered where the trains went, wanting to know where the tracks ended—what state, what city? As any eleven-year-old might fantasize, I wondered how old I would be before I could jump onto one of those trains and be taken to a new place. I had fun during the summers away from school, but the feeling of wanting to go somewhere else intensified when I listened to the trains.

This night took a different turn. As soon as the distant whistle died away and the tracks stopped their metallic rhythm, I heard the cry of a coyote. Startled, I sat up, turned off the radio, and listened. The second wail came through the window and sounded like the animal was in the front yard. I was scared because I had never heard a coyote so close to the house, and it was rare to hear coyotes in the desert surrounding the neighborhood. I went to the window and peered across the street. No homes had been built there, our house being on the edge of a new housing development. Fifty yards from out front door, the empty lots turned into the desert hills I explored alone during the hot days.

When my eyes adjusted to the dark, I thought I saw something moving at the top of the hill. It was a clear night with stars glittering across the desert sky. The coyote howled again and sent shivers down my back. I did not go outside to get a better look, even though my room had a door to the front porch. Two more cries were followed by a stark silence, and I went back to bed. The following day, I wrote what I clearly remember to be my first poem. I wrote about the railroad and the coyote—the train pulling me away from El Paso and the chilling cries of the coyote keeping me in the desert.

Renaming the Earth: Personal Essays

Ray Gonzalez

excerpts from

A Different Border

I want to stand on a different U.S.–Mexican border that accepts the fusion of English and Spanish that dominates El Paso. You can say it is bilingual or *caló* or Spanglish, whatever. On a different border, the language would be taught, made official, and accepted outside of the Southwest with its blend of Mexican and American cultures. This speech with its origins in two countries is spoken here all the time. Who cares if it is official or not? You don't have to teach it. Growing up in a border town like El Paso includes naturally picking up the bi-tongue and expressing it. I like that combination—bi-tongue. Two roots, two mouths, two ways of expressing how we live and how we survive in a region that has redefined what it means to live in the United States. Most El Pasoans don't realize that by living on the border they have created a unique America.

A different border would also mean a lower poverty rate, less crime, and the taming of a highly visible and dramatic racism—a separation to be tested further by the intrusion of National Guard troops and the plans to build a longer wall between the United States and Mexico. It would end the erosion of cultural traditions from native Mexico and reinforce traditions created by earlier generations of Mexican Americans, who had to change their way of life and adapt to living in the United States. Whenever I visit El Paso, I drive around the area and gaze at the slow destruction of the city's infrastructure, its monuments, its heritage, and watch as the new El Paso rises out of the desert, unable to decide if it is a version of twenty-first-century Mexico or an island of bilingual Americans with their own habits, beliefs, and ways of doing things. As I drive up and down Interstate 10, I can see the Rio Grande and the shacks of the *colonias* east of Juárez that dot the dusty hills by the river. I make my way through central El Paso, and those shacks reappear on city streets, on either side of alleys, and around empty lots that are the latest image of a place tearing down the old to keep up with the new. *The El Paso Times* runs regular stories on the plight of the economy and celebrates the fact that seven thousand more army troops are being sent to Fort Bliss in the next few years. The newspaper quotes businessmen who are pleased that more young people in uniform are arriving because they will spend more money in El Paso.

What does this have to do with a different border? Mexico's illegal immigration problem and the tightening of security along the border after September 11, 2001, will affect things, but they will never create an invulnerable border. Such a thing doesn't exist; it never has, and, despite the current mania against immigrants, it never will. El Paso is located in an isolated region of West Texas, and the area is known as one of the top drug-smuggling regions in the country. Younger generations of Mexican American kids on El Paso streets can't speak Spanish and don't know what the word *Chicano* means. El Paso means the loss of jobs, but also cheap labor where you can find it and where employers have to use that labor to survive and maybe profit. Cheap labor and profits go hand in hand, and new anti-immigration legislations in these repressive times will not change anything. Another problem is a weak tourist trade because city officials have lagged behind other cities in creating attractive museums or places where people can go when they don't want to cross the international bridge and wind up in Juárez. The fear of going to Juárez because of the hundreds of young women who have been mysteriously murdered there permeates the area. El Paso is a city that has always had a confidence problem, an image problem, a passive-aggressive resistance to both change and finding ways to integrate its beauty and history into that change. I can make this grand conclusion because I am a native El Pasoan and can never forget its history in the midst of political forces that constantly tear at the city's ancient foundations.

The military has come back to life with the war in Iraq and the patriotic fever of thousands of families in El Paso. I go to malls and movie theaters here and spot young men and woman in fatigues everywhere. One of the latest to be wounded in Iraq is shown on local television. A nineteen-year-old soldier named Ben Gonzalez is carried off a hospital plane as his family waits for him. He is nineteen years old, and his future as a normal person is in doubt as he faces a long recovery period and rehabilitation. Ben Gonzalez. No relation, though the television pictures also remind me of the fact that Iraq has already hit home on my mother's side of the family. Tony Mena, my nineteen-year-old nephew and the youngest of three sons, is beginning his second tour of duty in that war-torn country. The different border in 2006 is one where the military is dominant in the news, in the economy, and in the daily life of El Paso.

Does a different border mean that the violent history of the conquest of the Americas, the settling of the West, the genocide of native people, and the racism arising from a dual way of life along an international boundary line have come full circle because the region is proud to highlight its contribution to American imperialism—a strong military presence that is extending the long history of Fort Bliss's impact on El Paso? The area can't solve its illegal immigration problem, its lack of jobs, and its high poverty rate, but it can certainly support the troops and depend on them to show people there is one aspect of living on the border that the entire nation can accept.

The border is becoming different when El Paso looks like an armed camp, not in the traditional sense of many Texans owning guns or being able to carry them because of laws allowing concealed handguns, and not even in the almost stereotyped sense of drug dealers, cheap pot, and drug cartels fighting it out across the river in Juárez. Because of George W. Bush, El Paso resembles an armed camp because there are military personnel all over the city, spilling over from Fort Bliss and dumping millions of dollars on the local, desperate economy. I have stated this before, but repeat again because I have not seen such an intense patriotic fever as the one I find in El Paso in the summer of 2004. American flags everywhere, along with bumper stickers and signs supporting the war in Iraq. Young people love the patriotism, and I don't mean the nineteen- and twenty-year-olds who appear all over town in their fatigues. I mean local citizens and members of military families whose time under the Southwest sun includes waving the flag, supporting George Bush, and proclaiming that their sons, husbands, wives, and daughters are doing their duty so "America can be safer." El Paso has always been a conservative town, and, again, Fort Bliss has a long tradition in the area, but this latest rallying around the war is stunning. Sure, a large military population is going to reflect its beliefs, but, as a native of the area, I feel the militaristic drama is somehow out of place here. Many natives and experts on El Paso will laugh at me and ask, "What did you expect? This is Texas, and this is surely a military town." The answer is not that simple, though, because El Paso, situated on the tip of West Texas, had developed its own version of a New Mexico Native American posture that kept the city years behind the national times and reinforced the notion that El Pasoans were sleepy, passive, politically naïve people. In other words, El Paso had the reputation of being one of the conquered, not the one doing the conquering. Today's different border has changed that. The Stars and Stripes have woken El Paso and put a pair of cojones on it. One question to explore is, What eventually will become one of the key factors in the new border dynamics—the eternal clash between Mexicans, Anglos, and Mexican Americans, or the rise of the new military metropolis that, to me, is a major contradiction of the old El Paso and its vanished way of life?

I fly into El Paso on the hottest day the region has had—107 degrees—and enter the furnace of the desert as if I had never lived here. I sit next to a couple of young people returning to Fort Bliss—a young woman in the military, twenty-three years old, who tells the man sitting next to her that she would rather be stationed in Kuwait and Iraq, from which she is returning, than cross the border into Juárez. The forty-year-old black man agrees and says that Juárez is more dangerous than the Middle East. I am stunned to hear this and can't believe two people in the army would rather face the dangers of the war than life on the U.S.–Mexican border. The girl, a mechanic whose unit came under attack during the first stages of the invasion of Baghdad a few years ago, laughs and says, "Yeah, give me the terrorists over there any day. That's not as hard to take as all the dead girls they keep finding in Juárez." They continue talking about their military lives throughout the flight from Houston to El Paso. She had started the conversation by asking the stranger where he was stationed. When he told her he worked for the government and didn't reveal the line of work, she said, "I thought only military fly into El Paso these days." I try not to listen to their conversation after that, but the crowded flight has us sitting side by side. I keep reading my book, but pay attention to one final statement the girl makes before we glide in for a rough landing in El Paso. "Yeah, we train harder and we fight harder because our commander in chief made a mistake." We arrive.

✳ ✳ ✳

I saw a different border when I realized I no longer had to search for home. Home was El Paso. It always had been, and the years of wanting it to be something else were gone. The border town has changed with its larger population, its destruction of old buildings, and the rooting of a twenty-first-century Latino culture that is a hybrid nation of Mexican nationals who want a life in the United States and Mexican Americans who want to be accepted as the majority and see themselves as "Americans," without the word *Mexican* in front of the label. Growing up in El Paso made it difficult for me to see this kind of culture develop over the decades. Border life has transformed the segregated little town of my childhood into a metropolis of fast Latino zip codes. I will say it again—fast Latino zip codes. In other words—fast cars, low- to medium-paying jobs, strip malls, fancy restaurants, endless rows of new apartment complexes all looking the same, a macho and rather conservative lifestyle, the bilingual tongue of "*carros*, tenees, TV, popcorn," and other mutations of English and Spanish. The Latino zip code means El Paso is populated by a younger, well-educated generation of Latinos, many of them born and raised in other parts of the country. They have somehow wound up in El Paso for high-tech jobs and industry, the civilian sector supporting Fort Bliss and its large military population. Many of them are also here for unknown reasons, both legal and illegal. The evolving border allows the Latino zip code occupant to play out a daily routine of cell phone calls inside new Hondas and Toyotas screaming down Interstate 10 on the way to work or to happy hour or for a quick lunch with friends at the latest trendy Mexican restaurant. This scene sounds cynical and very American, but it is far removed from the border that shaped the ancient, quiet, small town of the old El Paso I used to know.

The different border has done away with Chicano pride from the 1960s and 1970s, has torn down old Catholic churches from a pre–World War II landscape, and has stretched the city limits beyond the horizon. El Paso cannot be tied down to old border ways any longer because generations of illegal immigration, drug dealing, cheap labor, segregation, only half-successful integration, the rise and fall of thousands of small businesses, and a poor public-education system jockey for position with the Latino zip code—again, a world where the cell phone, the quick beer, the rented apartment, and the low-paying job (compared to the rest of the United States, that is, though great for El Paso) say you can be young and happy on the border. You can play and work and sleep and fuck and do drugs or drink and go to the latest movie in the new stadium-seating theater or marvel at the very first Best Buy electronics store to open in town. The Latino zip code dweller could care less about "illegal aliens," U.S. Border Patrol abuses, the destruction of the environment at the hands of North American Free Trade Agreement (NAFTA) overlords, and the fact that Texas ranks next to last in every quality-of-life survey (New Mexico is fiftieth). Believe it or not, the Latino zip code dweller often votes Republican and has no sense of history when it comes to the desert Southwest. It is a different border because the need to assimilate, or become "American," has called for the extermination of the old boundaries that kept El Paso on its desert island.

* * *

Wandering through Sunland Park Mall near my mother's house, I got into a Suncoast media store, a national chain that sells DVDs. I never know what I will find in one and have come across hard-to-find old movies and rock music concert discs in Suncoasts from the Twin Cities area. I don't expect much from the Sunland Park one, but am surprised and delighted to come across a copy of John Carpenter's *Dark Star*, an obscure 1974 science-fiction film whose little known re-release on DVD is making some fanatics of Carpenter's weird films start to claim that *Dark Star* will become a cult classic. I have never seen it, but have read several reviews of the disc version. It is about a spaceship that has been hurtling through space for twenty years. Its crew is made up of hippie astronauts whose long hair and beards, rock music, drugs, and wacko antics are necessary to survive the trip. It is a "dark" comedy, Carpenter's take on 1960s culture and the U.S. obsession with outer space following the NASA moon walks late in that decade. The first DVD I ever bought for my strange film collection was Carpenter's remake of the old 1950s classic *The Thing*, and I have been interested in some of his other work, though I have passed on several of his mediocre vampire films. I had searched in the Twin Cities for a copy of *Dark Star*, had pondered ordering it through Amazon.com, but here it is in El Paso—one copy originally priced at $25 on sale for only $9.99. I grab it, and in my glee at the counter I tell the clerk that the DVD is hard to find. He looks at me suspiciously when the cash register drops the full price down to the great sales price and stares at the disc.

I put the disc into the media program on the laptop I travel with and can see right away why Carpenter fanatics might be giddy over this hilarious film. Of course, the underlying and serious hit on our culture of the 1960s is the fact that the spaceship, the *Dark Star*, carries nuclear bombs that can destroy "unstable" planets. Each bomb has a number and its own voice, and each talks back to the astronauts. A rogue bomb eventually disobeys computer orders from the ship, disengages from the bomb bay, and hangs below *Dark Star*, ready to blow its unstable crew into darkness. Funny, but I can't follow the story or laugh yet because the opening scene and credits startle me when one of the hippie astronauts presses a button and a song called "Benson, Arizona" starts to play. It is an odd country-western tune I have never heard before.

I can't believe it because Benson, Arizona, is my mother's birthplace! The old railroad town lies east of Tucson and will probably soon be swallowed up by that city's spreading population, but my grandfather's family lived there in the 1920s and 1930s when he was a crew foreman on the railroad. Benson, Arizona. What was John Carpenter doing putting a song called "Benson, Arizona" into a crazy film about spaced-out astronauts? My mother's hometown is being sung about in this bizarre sci-fi joke. Is this the reason I have been searching for a copy? The singer, whoever he is, does a cheap imitation of Johnny Cash and sings, "How I miss the desert skies. My body flies the galaxies. Benson, Arizona, blows the wind through your hair. My heart longs to be there. Benson, Arizona, the same stars in the sky. They seem kinder when we watch them, you and I."

I have wanted to write about the heat in El Paso and its powerful furnace atmosphere during the summer. Living in Minnesota with its cool, though often humid, summers, I miss the hot intensity of the desert in July. The border would be different if it truly had four seasons, but it doesn't. Climate is one of the reasons many people retire in this area. Despite the scorching temperatures during the summer, the attraction to this area could be an extension of the Southwest's reputation as the place where perfect weather (and to many people the heat is perfect) can keep you going, can keep you awake and alive. In the 1870s and 1880s, thousands of people from all over the country were sent by their doctors to New Mexico for "climate therapy." They came to the desert to cure their tuberculosis. In the late nineteenth century, doctors claimed that pulmonary tuberculosis was the number one health problem of an industrial society. By 1920, there were forty sanatoriums, or "sans," in New Mexico. One of the largest and most popular was the Holy Ghost Sanatorium in Deming, though you could check into one in Las Cruces and Santa Fe or in more remote towns like Lincoln and Carlsbad. Treatments used previously, such as bleeding the ill person two or three times a week, did not work, so doctors decided good air would do the trick. Climate therapy involved spending a long amount of time breathing in

New Mexico. Doctors assured their seriously ill patients that the high altitude of the desert had purer air and lower air pressure that would heal their sick lungs. Plus, the heat and the strong sun were there to back up the purity of the New Mexico environment. New Mexico became a health seeker's haven and attracted hundreds of doctors. Some historians claim the care and treatment of tuberculosis was an essential factor in the economic development of New Mexico in the late nineteenth century. The Great Depression of the 1930s brought it all to an end, however. No more sans were opened, and many closed after World War II. The evolution of medical science led to other treatments for tuberculosis, and doctors concluded that rest, good food, high altitude, and the pure air of New Mexico did not contribute to curing TB.

The regenerated border keeps bringing me back to the dominant role of Mexican food. Mexican culinary delights have an immense power that continues to influence and shape border culture. By "shape," I do not mean making it overweight, though Mexican food goes heavy in that direction. Mexican food can be used to measure how racist stereotypes (bean and tortilla eaters, Frito Bandidos) have becomes rooted among its consumers. The commercialization and creation of Mex-slop (Taco Bell) and the fact that Mexican food is found in every state in the United States say that its staples are everywhere, cooked in a thousand different ways that are far removed from its authentic, delicious origins. If you grew up in El Paso, you can rightly claim it makes the best Mexican food in the United States. If you are new to the border, your taste buds can be numbed by new heights of jalapeño strength or by the soft delicacy of homemade tortillas. If you live in other parts of the United States and have known real Mexican food, you can pretend that the Mexican restaurant in St. Paul, Minnesota, comes close. In the end, the new border is the fresh-smelling border where its people put an incredible energy into the cooking, selling, and eating of Mexican food. The result is that this food has a power unique in the area and is a magnetic force beyond the mouth and stomach, a force that most El Pasoans depend on daily to get by.

Yet the fluid border and its food face great challenges. Promoters of Mexico's traditional fast foods are fighting McDonald's, Burger King, Pizza Hut, KFC, and other foreign chains that are competing with sales of tortillas, tacos, and *tortas*. The Associated Press reports on Mexico's first Torta Festival in Mexico City. They hope to promote the overstuffed sandwich of bread, beans, and cheese and to offset the fact that Mexicans are eating more American hamburgers, fried chicken, and pizza these days instead of their traditional on-the-run staples of tacos and quesadillas. The news report quotes Francisco Juárez, head of the Mexican National Restaurant Chamber's Mexico City chapter, as saying, "The torta is not in danger of extinction, but its sales have declined by 50 percent over the last decade because of the competition from pizza and hamburgers." Between 1998 and 2004, tortilla consumption fell by 25 percent, from an average 308 pounds per person per year to 228 pounds, according to the National Corn Processors Chamber. After reading these numbers, I wonder how anyone could measure how many tortillas or pounds of tortilla a person ate in one year? Did they do a survey or ask? Who monitored this study? The point is not to question the data, but to give way to the magnitude of tortilla consumption and the reality that Mexican food's once invincible hold on people is weakening. This trend fits right into a new border landscape where perhaps too many false and awful mutations of authentic Mexican food have destroyed people's tastes and sent them elsewhere. The survey was conducted in interior Mexico, but tastes and trends immigrate, legally or illegally, toward the north, where larger and fatter consumers of Mexican food wipe their lips with their napkins and serve themselves a second or third helping.

It may not be very nice to criticize people's food habits considering that I love Mexican food and gorge on it whenever I visit El Paso, but my time in the great restaurants that I try for the first time is ruined a bit when I read the incredible headline in *The El Paso Times*, "Agents Strive to Keep Immigrants Nourished." In a region with a long history of abuse of illegal immigrants, it is hard to believe that Border Patrol agents are actually feeding good Mexican food to individuals they capture every day. The U.S. government usually issues turkey sandwiches with potato chips and apple juice to hungry illegal immigrants caught by the Border Patrol. The policy is that if an immigrant has not eaten in more than four hours, he or she must be fed. Most of them get granola bars, boxed juices, and microwaved frozen burritos kept at the Paso del Norte Bridge facility. The supplies also include baby bottles, formula, and diapers. The annual budget for these items is $50,000 in El Paso. Remote Border Patrol stations make their own arrangements. In changing times, agents are making runs to many restaurants and fast-food joints to feed men, women, and children in detention cells because the chains are best equipped to handle large orders. In Fabens, Texas, the "illegals" love McDonalds. In Deming, New Mexico, they order frozen meals from Amigos Mexican Food. In

Carlsbad, they go to Wendy's and Taco Bell, but a large number of agents there order at Lucy's Mexican Restaurant, a local landmark. OK. More business is pumped into the economy by Border Patrol agents' walking up and down rows of jail cells taking orders. Forty orders per week at Lucy's may influence the way the owner, Lucy Yañez, might feel about immigration laws and tighter borders. Anti-immigration activists, mostly racist and right-wing, constantly scream for a harder crackdown. Do that, and Lucy is out forty orders per week.

My brother-in-law Willie Mena used to work in an immigration detention center when he was in his early twenties. Thirty years ago undocumented immigrants who were caught and incarcerated rarely got fed. One night during his shift, a Willie who was very green at his new job found himself being asked for food by a crowd of young Mexican boys. "Algo pa' comer, Meester," they kept shouting at him from behind bars. In the first few days of working at the center, Willie noticed an old Mexican woman with long white hair who was the cook in the center. He wasn't sure if she cooked for the Border Patrol agents or if she did feed some of the captured Mexicans. He noticed that she did not like the illegal immigrants and was hostile to them. The night of the mass begging for food was too much for Willie, and he gave in, stormed into the center's kitchen, dug through several refrigerators, and found a huge baloney sausage. With echoes of "Dame de comer, Meester" at his back, Willie quickly sliced the baloney and made sandwiches. This was a major mistake because the next day when the old woman found out what he had done, she threw a fit, tore into him, and kept repeating, "Son de halla! Son de halla!" She kept screaming at him that they were from "over there, over there"—Mexico. Thirty years ago you didn't feed illegal Mexican immigrants unless you had to.

Now this act has become another major contradiction on the changing border—catch, incarcerate, and keep "illegals" out of the country. As you do this, though, you should feed them because they are hungry. Let the food money trickle into local outlets, which stay happy and open. It is logical to conclude that restaurants will want those illegal immigrants to keep crossing. Louie Gilot, the reporter, quotes Lucy as claiming that "The agents buy burritos. We have big, jumbo burritos with meat, potatoes, and chile. Sometimes, they get hamburgers and chips and salsa. They really love our salsa. The immigrants must like it because the agents keep coming back."

In George W. Bush's America, more people have been violent against illegal immigrants, and a harsher reality has made it harder to cross, though thousands keep coming. As for Lucy's Mexican Restaurant, the salsa will keep pouring because on the different border of the new century we want to feed everybody, no matter where they come from. Tortillas, beans, salsa, and government dollars are being spent on futilely keeping people out while they pour hot, delicious salsa on burritos from thriving border restaurants.

❋ ❋ ❋

Armed vigilante Minutemen patrol the border to make sure no one crosses into the United States illegally. Then the Department of Homeland Security decides that by 2008 passports will be required by those who wish to cross between the United States, Canada, and Mexico. A few months later, this outrage is shot down in Congress, although in the current anti-immigrant atmosphere I believe such a law will be enacted. It would be further proof that the monumental changes this country has experienced since September 11, 2001, are still having an impact on people's lives. For residents along international borders, the possible future requirement of having to get a passport means they would be taxed for living in a region with economic and cultural dynamics created by a vibrant union between countries. Despite the negative aspects of a changing border I have described here, these perpetual political conflicts can't remove the fact that the El Paso border region is a unique part of the country because it is here that two worlds have come together.

The bilingual character of the border with Mexico would be further separated because people would have to wait months to have their passports approved. The ninety-seven-dollar fee to get a passport processed would be a new border tax that would bring millions of dollars to a government who would collect it in the name of tighter security. It would force people to get their pictures taken because the immigration policies of this administration have failed. It is easier to demand personal identification of its citizens and to mask failed policies with a call for passports than to guard nuclear power plants, vulnerable seaports, and railroad lines. It is easier to get a U.S. Customs officer to stare at you to verify your face is actually on your passport than to increase security funding for cities like New York. What about the millions of people who will not be able to afford to get a passport? Where should they line up? Like many things in the Bush era, even the crossing of international boundary lines is a case of have and have not. It hasn't happened because the threatened requirement was cancelled, but in light of the fresh plans to build the border wall it will happen, and so the different border is dark.

This growing void between classes of Americans is not a price that has to be paid for September 11. It is an excuse to impose tighter control over a region that quite often is not in line with the Bush conservative curtain, even if the region can be found on an election night map as lying in several "red states." The dangerous Minutemen are a visually dramatic example of citizens who claim they are doing their part to safeguard the country against terrorists, as they play out their dreams of taking the law into their own hands when it comes to illegal immigration. Armed vigilantes fit into the game plan for the border. If you want to cross illegally, guns will be waiting. If you want to cross the right way, make sure your passport is stamped and your check for ninety-seven dollars is good at the bank.

These barriers do not take into account daily jobs, cross-border commerce, or economic interaction between two countries. How many lawmakers in Washington know how family and business relationships between El Pasoans and people in Juárez work? Who is going to identify how many terrorists were kept out of the United States because they didn't have a passport? When will the U.S. Border patrol admit that testosterone-healthy men with rifles in Arizona are making government agents' job more difficult as the risk of a major border incident grows? By claiming tighter security as a reason for its actions, the current administration is accelerating the failure of more businesses, restaurants, and retailers. It is turning its back on the fact that cities on both sides of the border depend on each other.

On a recent visit to El Paso, I see that news stories continue to appear about the growing tensions on the border. The Minutemen and their opponents have rallied their forces across the border region several times in 2005, squaring off on the immigration issue and refocusing attention on border policy questions and decisions that need to be made on a national level. I drive around El Paso as these forces gather for conflict and quietly watch my hometown; it looks exactly like that—my quiet hometown. The mobilizations of the Minutemen have come on the heels of figures that reported an all-time high of more than 400 deaths of migrants attempting to cross the U.S. border from Mexico during the U.S. government's fiscal year, which ended on September 30. Border tension also intensified after the U.S. Congress's approval of the Homeland Security bill to increase U.S. Border Patrol personnel by 1,500 agents. Chief among the hotspots for border mobilizations is the El Paso–Juárez–southern New Mexico border corridor, a big region where the number of individuals detained by the U.S. Border Patrol has increased from 104,399 people in fiscal year 2004 to more than 120,000 in fiscal year 2005.

Texas Minutemen, tracked by observers from the American Civil Liberties Union, deployed in early October 2005 on public and privately owned land southeast of El Paso–Juárez and in the Fabens–Fort Hancock region, a popular Texas border-crossing zone for undocumented workers. I drive to Mesilla, New Mexico, one of my favorite getaways in the southern part of the state, only to hear a radio report that a Minuteman group, New Mexico Border Watch, was reported patrolling the southern New Mexico border. As I turn into the ancient town square of Mesilla, I gaze out of my car window, expecting to spot one of them on horseback at any second. Of course, questions come up about how closely the Minutemen work with the U.S. Border Patrol.

In 2005, UTEP, my alma mater, debated free speech by forming a faculty committee to study it. At the same time that it was dealing with internal problems with student organizations on campus, a Chicano activist and legendary figure passed away in Denver, Colorado on April 12. Rodolfo "Corky" Gonzalez died at the age of seventy-six and left behind a legacy of activism from which UTEP students and administrators could learn. Corky was the author of "Yo Soy Joaquin," an epic poem that ranks as one of the two most important and influential works on social justice, along with the late El Paso native Abelardo Delgado's poem "Stupid America." These poems should be required reading by UTEP students and faculty who are waking up to the fact that in George Bush's America free speech and academic freedom are under constant attack. Corky's struggle to preserve dignity among Colorado's Chicano community went on for decades in a state that made news throughout 2005 with attempts to fire Native American activist writer and professor Ward Churchill from the faculty at the University of Colorado. His crime? He exercised free speech by writing about September 11 and questioning who the bad guys were. In these times, when individual liberties are being threatened by forces outside and within our country, universities and higher education are often the first to be targeted.

I wonder how many UTEP students of the campus organizations that were being pressured not to conduct political activities on campus know about Corky's life in Denver. In the 1960s, he formed the Crusade for Justice, an organization that united Chicanos against Denver's notorious police brutality and discrimination. In 1970, he established Escuela Tlatelolco, an alternative school for Chicano students that operates to this day. Like farmworker advocate Cesar Chavez, Corky fought in the trenches, marched, and was arrested more than once. In Denver, after a series of local bombings of Escuela Tlatelolco and numerous internal struggles with other activists, the Crusade for Justice declined. The peak of Corky's political career and of the Chicano movement came when delegates from seventeen states met in El Paso for La Raza Unida's party convention of 1972. Leadership battles went on to destroy La Raza, but Corky continued his work in Denver for several more years. By studying what Corky accomplished in a difficult era, UTEP students would be able to negotiate with the university administration from a stronger position, and current issues over free speech might get a fair review. They would learn that you must remain united and use your academic liberty to fight repressive institutional policies that deny students their basic rights as Americans.

Many El Pasoans have forgotten the infamous, though brief, takeover of the UTEP administration building by Movimiento Estudiantil Chicano de Aztlán (MEChA) students in the early 1970s. Back then, I was an undergraduate at UTEP and have never forgotten the image of El Paso police officers handcuffing Chicano students and throwing them into their patrol cars. Those were different times, but to many of us these days are similar. Recent disciplinary action taken by UTEP against several student organizations that were exercising free speech brings back memories of the 1960s and 1970s, when many people didn't know who their friends or enemies were. Questionable decisions by UTEP took place in a region already under pressure from external forces trying to change the quality of life along the border. That my alma mater has joined in the current atmosphere of repression is pathetic and sad. Corky's death is a timely reminder that the concept of Chicanismo, whether it is spiritual, political, or, to some people, dated, is also a life-long commitment to living your life as a free American. In my public role as a university professor, I know that the best example of this freedom begins academically.

El Paso Times, April 8, 2004
PAINTBALLS FIRED INTO JUÁREZ COMMUNITY FROM UNITED STATES

In Anapra, one of the poorest neighborhoods in Juárez, Mexico, across the border from El Paso, residents claim that they are being shot at with paintballs from the United States. On the night of Monday, April 5, the attackers hit two children and three pregnant women. One child was hit in the face, near his eye. The shootings take place at night and Anapra residents say their attackers use laser scopes and night vision gear. They dress in black so as not be easily spotted. *El Diario* reports that they use a tan-colored truck to get into position on a nearby hill. Anapra residents say that the Border Patrol has seen the paintball shooters and has done nothing to stop them. One Anapra resident told *El Diario* that neighbors "will respond" if the harassment does not stop soon.

The paintball explodes on the stray dog in yellow blood, its howls mistaken for the observant coyote in the hills. The paintball flattens against the pregnant woman in blue streaks, the shade of blue impacting how her baby will be born, live, and die. The paintball kisses the adobe walls and spills letters in an alphabet more villagers understand than the black-and-white graffiti of their long-lost gang. The paintball flies in the heat before opening in a geometric shape that changes the face of the child into an image any border justice organization would fight to place on their Web site. The paintball stings the brown back of the shirtless boy with a green star that will form a scar he can never wash off.

The paintball buzzes through the swarm of flies circling the outdoor latrines, its impact against the stalls sending the insects into an orange frenzy. The paintball electrifies the Mexican flag in the plaza with a purple haze that gathers a crowd around the flagpole in the morning.

The paintball miraculously bounces off the baby in the arms of the woman before disintegrating in a pink cloud that gives the clay jars on the well a Wal-Mart competitive design. The paintball zooms into the eye of the innocent old man, the last thing he sees turning red as if red is the only color he remembers from those days in San Luis Potosí when his mother took him to the wall of roses and showed him where his father died. The paintball blends with the olive green Border Patrol van, whose driver mistakes the impact for a bullet and is shocked that the illegals crossing the river are finally armed. The paintball destroys the statue of La Virgen de Guadalupe, its power cracking the figure's right arm as the film of unknown color wraps the statue in a light many worshippers have been praying for. The paintball decorates the door of La Bruja, the town witch emerging into the night with a crooked stick tied in multicolored ribbons that send the shooters scrambling into their van.

The paintball illuminates the border in a storm of bees, the shooters running out of balls as dawn arrives to give birth to the sparkling, broken windshield on their van, the last two boys they targeted holding the warm pistol between them, their three bullets escaping into the air without giving a clue as to what color could describe them best. The empty paintball cases add color to the desert, the rainbow dirt washed by the next sandstorm into the Rio Grande, whose radioactive waters offer more colors than the latest version of the game.

nobody's son: notes from an american life

Luis Alberto Urrea

Nobody's Son

> "You're in big trouble when you got to apologize for being yourself."
> —Cajun folk saying

I

My mom said, "I'm so sick of your God-damned Mexican bullshit!" I was in bed with my wife at the time. It was 7:30 in the morning. My wife was white. So was my mother.

Apparently, the issue of my identity was troubling Mom. She was a good Republican. She tended to work up a good cuss when she was beyond her limit of endurance. I must have come to represent a one-man wave of illegal aliens to her as she sipped her coffee and looked out at a tender New England dawn.

I had finally gotten away from the border. I was teaching writing, at Harvard no less. She saw this development as being due to the force of her own will. That's the GOP for you, I'd say in our frequent and spirited political squabbles—taking credit for someone else's achievements while demonizing their ethnicity. (Did you know that *squabble* is a Scandinavian word? So what, you ask? Just keep it in mind, that's all.)

I was still being called Mexican, Chicano, Hispanic, Latino, Mexican American, Other. These Ivy-League types were taking my name seriously. It drove my mother to distraction.

She barged through the door shouting anti-Mexican rhetoric. Whither goest Mom goest the nation.

We had a miniature Proposition 187 anti-immigration rally right there in my bedroom.

"You are *not* a Mexican!" she cried. "Why can't you be called *Louis* instead of *Luis*?"

Go, Mom.

"Louis *Woodward* or Louis *Dashiell*. One of *my* names. I'm warning you—someday, they're going to come for you, and you'll be sorry."

They.

I've been on the lookout for those scoundrels all my life. So has much of my family. (When I mention my family, I mean Mexicans. The Americans were held at bay by my mother for reasons I only later understood. It turns out she was ashamed of the Mexicans. "They spit on the floor," she insisted, though I never saw my *abuelita* hawk up a big one and splash it in the corner. If your mama's saying it, it must be true.) Many of my relatives were afraid of the border patrol. Others were afraid of the Mexican government. Still others were afraid of Republican white people and Democratic black people. Cops. And perhaps my white relatives back East were afraid of all these things too. But mostly, I got to thinking, they must have been scared of me. I was one of them, but I was also one of *them*.

They.

"They," Wendell Berry writes, "will want you to kneel and weep / and say you should have been like them."

It's a poem called "Do Not Be Ashamed." I read it whenever I'm called upon to give a commencement speech at college graduations. It's not a political poem. It's not a liberal or conservative poem. It's a human poem.

Most students seem to understand what Berry's talking about.

He goes on to say:

And once you say you are ashamed,
reading the page they hold out to you,
then such light as you have made
in your history will leave you.
They will no longer need to pursue you.
You will pursue them, begging forgiveness.

They.

You can almost see thought bubbles above the students' heads as they listen. *Honkies*, some are thinking. *Liberals* and *minorities*, and *commies*. And certainly *666* and *the Antichrist* bubble about up in the air: *Hispanics, Yankees, blacks, queers. Democrats. Women. Men.*

My mother thought: *Mexicans.*

My father, a Mexican, thought: *gringos*.

I, for one, think *They* are the ones with the words. You know, the Words. The ones they called my dad and me—like *wetback. Spic. Beaner. Greaser. Pepper-belly. Yellow-belly. Taco-bender. Enchilada-breath.*

That was my wife's phrase. She thought it was cute. She's gone now. So is my mom.

"Dad?" I said. "What's a greaser?"

He used to tell me I was no *God-damned gringo*. I was, however, white. *Speak Spanish, pendejo!* was a common cry when I spoke some unacceptable English phrase. Utterly forbidden English in our house included many taboos, among them: *my old man* (he was sure this was disrespectful and implied he wasn't a virile young thing); *big daddy* (he was certain this meant big penis); *you're kidding* (another disrespect, suggesting he didn't tell the truth at all times—he didn't); *easy rider* (he thought this meant a man married to a whore); *chicano* (from chicanery).

His only word for *them* was *gringo*. He didn't see it as all that bad. He said it came from the Mexican-American War. The pop hit the American soldiers sang in those days was "Green Grow the Lilacs." Green grows/ gringos. It seemed altogether benign compared to yellow bellies.

I had been called "greaser" by the son of a retired Navy petty officer in my new, all-white neighborhood. We had fled from the ethnic cleansing taking place in Shelltown, California, to which we had hurried from Tijuana. I couldn't quite fathom the name. Surely I wasn't greasy? But I *felt* greasy. And the vivid image of grease, of some noxious *Mexican* grease, collided in my mind with the word "wetback." And suddenly I was certain that my back was wet with grease. A grease I couldn't see. I had an image in my mind of the back of my shirt soaked through with cooking oil and sticking to me, glistening sickeningly in the sun. Everybody could see the grease drooling down my spine. Except me.

My father was whiter than my mother. If he had become an American citizen, he would have voted for Nixon. Twice. Most Mexican immigrants—both "legal" and "illegal"—would vote Republican if given a chance, except the Republicans scare them, so they're forced to support the Clintons and Carters of this nation. It has been estimated that by 2050, Latinos will be the majority population of the world. Not only will America be "brown," but it will also be the home of the new Democrats. The Institutional Revolutionary Catholic Democratic Party ticket led by Edward James Olmos will sweep the elections. The paradigm will shift, as they say: the bogeyman will become the *chupacabras*. Bullfights at the county fair. Baja California will be the fifty-first state. The Buchanan Brigade Aryan Militia will mount an offensive in the Malibu Hills, holding nineteen gardeners and twelve nannies hostage. NASA will land the first lowrider on the moon. Just watch.

"Greaser," my father replied.

I believe he had prepared himself for this. On our first day in the neighborhood, he'd been chased out of our driveway by an irate white man. You don't spend two decades living as a Mexican guest of Southern California without becoming fully aware of the genocidal urge that percolates in the human heart.

Dad transformed before my eyes into a college lecturer.

"During the Americans' westward expansion," he intoned, "the settlers traveled in covered wagons. When they reached the West—Arizona, Texas, California—they often needed repair work done on their wagons after such a long hard trip. A large part of this work consisted of *greasing* the axles, which had dried out. The only ones who had the skill to fix the wagons were Mexicans. Mexicans greased the axles. You see? *Greasers.* So when they call you that, hold your head up. It's a badge of honor. We helped build America."

He's gone now, too.

The last time I was interviewed by the Mexican press, I was in Mexico City, the self-appointed home of all true Mexicans. I was startled to find out that I was not a true Mexican. I was any number of things: I was an American, I was "just" a Chicano, I was a *norteño* (which, in Mexico City, is like saying you're one of the Mongol horde). I was lauded for speaking Spanish "just like" a Mexican, or chided for having what amounted to a cowboy accent. That I was born in Tijuana didn't matter a bit: Tijuana, I was informed, is no-man's-land. Mexicans don't come from Tijuana. Tijuanans come from Tijuana.

That I was an American citizen was apparently a *faux pas*. That I wrote in English was an insult. That I was blue-eyed, however, allowed me to pass for Mexican high society.

I will say this for Mexico City, though: people in La Capital have perfect manners. For all its travails and crises, Mexico City is the most civil city I've ever visited. Imagine a city where a cabbie returns your tip to you because you've paid him too much for his services. Imagine this same city reporting a stunning 700 assaults every day.

In the great museum, you can see a famous Aztec mask. One half of it is a smiling face. The other half is a skull.

I was told by the editor of the newspaper to be out of town by the time the interview appeared. Someone somewhere decided that what I had to say was somehow dangerous. I thought this was a joke. Then an editor took me to the foyer where several of the paper's reporters had been executed. *All I'm saying*, I protested, *is that poor people should be treated with respect*. She lit a cigarette and said, *Be out of town*.

Things that seemed perfectly clear to me turned confusing and opaque.

In the interview, I offered the often-quoted comment from *By the Lake of Sleeping Children* that I, as a son of the border, had a barbed-wire fence neatly bisecting my heart. The border, in other words, ran through me. The journalist said, "Aha!" and scribbled with real vigor.

When the article came out, however, the comment had been transformed. I'm still not sure what it means. It said: "If you were to cut Urrea's heart open, you would find a border patrol truck idling between his ribs."

I was going to write, "Meanwhile, back home . . ." But where is home? Home isn't just a place, I have learned. It is also a language. My words not only shape and define my home. Words—not only for writers—*are* home. Still, where exactly is that?

Jimmy Santiago Baca reminds us that "Hispanics" are immigrants in our own land. By the time Salem was founded on Massachusetts Bay, any number of Urreas had been prowling up and down the Pacific coast of our continent for several decades. Of course, the Indian mothers of these families had been here from the start. But manifest destiny took care of us all—while we greased the wheels.

Them wagons is still rollin'.

I saw a hand-lettered sign on television. It was held up by a woman in stretch pants and curlers, and it said: America For Americans. A nearby man held up a sign exhorting the universe to speak English or go home.

The official language of the United States.

Well, sure. We speak English and, apparently, Ebonics. I want to call Chicano slang Aztonics while we're at it. *Orale*, Homes—we down, *¿qué* *no?* Simón, *vato*—let's trip out the *rucas* of the school board, *ese! Ese torcido rifa, locos!*

It's all English. Except for the alligator, which is a Spanish word. Lariat, too, is a Spanish word.

In fact, here's a brief list, in no particular order. It might help you score points in a trivia parlor game someday. All words borrowed from Spanish:

Chaps

Savvy

Palaver

Hoosegow

Palomino

Coyote

Pinto

Marijuana

Vamoose

Stampede

Buckaroo

Adobe

Saguaro

Rodeo

Ranch

Rancher

Patio

Key (as in Florida Keys)

Florida

Sarsaparilla

Navajo

Nevada

Machete

Texas

Alfalfa

Bonanza

Bronco

Calaboose

Canyon

Colorado

Fandango

Foofaraw

Guacamole

Hackamore

Beef jerky

Lasso

Abalone

Vanilla

Chocolate

Cigar

For example. Perfectly acceptable English. Nary an Aztonic word in sight.

You don't believe me about beef jerky, do you? I find it a little hard to believe, my own self. What's more American than a hunk of jerky? Cowboys, rednecks, crackers, wrestlers, mountain men gnaw away on planks of jerked beef!

Winfred Blevins, in the marvelous *Dictionary of the American West*, notes: "The word is an Americanized version of the Spanish term for jerked meat, *charqui*."

I don't know what we're going to do. Forget about purifying the American landscape, sending all those ethnic types packing back to their homelands. Those illegal humans. (A straw-hat fool in a pickup truck once told my Sioux brother Duane to go back to where he came from. "Where to?" Duane called. "South Dakota?")

The humanoids are pretty bad, but how will we ever get rid of all those pesky foreign *words* debilitating the United States?

Those Turkish words (like *coffee*). Those French words (like *maroon*). Those Greek words (like *cedar*). Those Italian words (like *marinate*). Those African words (like *marimba*).

English! It's made up of all these untidy *words*, man. Have you noticed?

Native American (*skunk*), German (*waltz*), Danish (*twerp*), Latin (*adolescent*), Scottish (*feckless*), Dutch (*waft*), Carribean (*zombie*), Nahuatl (*ocelot*), Norse (*walrus*), Eskimo (*kayak*), Tatar (*horde*) words! It's a glorious *wreck* (a good old Viking word, that).

Glorious, I say, in all of its shambling mutable beauty. People daily speak a quilt work of words, and continents and nations and tribes and even enemies dance all over your mouth when you speak. The tongue seems to know no race, no affiliation, no breed, no caste, no order, no genus, no lineage. The most dedicated Klansman spews the language of his adversaries while reviling them.

It's all part of the American palaver and squawk.

Seersucker: Persian

Sandalwood: Sanskrit

Grab a dictionary. It's easy. You at home—play along.

The $64,000 question for tonight: What the hell are we speaking? What language (culture, color, race, ethnicity) is this anyway? Who are we?

Abbot: Aramaic

Yo-yo: Philippino.

Muslin: Iraqi.

Yogurt: Turkish.

I love words so much. Thank God so many people lent us theirs or we'd be forced to point and grunt. When I start to feel the pressure of the border on me, when I meet someone who won't shake my hand because she has suddenly discovered I'm half-Mexican (as happened with a land-lady in Boulder), I comfort myself with these words. I know how much color and beauty we Others really add to the American mix.

My advice to anyone who wants to close the border and get them Messkins out is this: *don't dare start counting how many of your words are Latin, Baby.*

America—there's a Mexican in the woodpile.

II

Poor Old Ma.

That's what she called herself. She'd sign letters, "Your Poor Old Ma." She was anything but rustic. It amused her *New Yorker* wit to be seen as Ma Kettle among the California hicks and savages. If she'd had her way, she would have worn white gloves every day, and I would have been called Lewis, and I would have called her "Mother Dear."

Her name was Phyllis. (A Greek word, don't you know. It means "the green branch.") She married my dad, Alberto (an Old English name—Aethelberht meaning "noble, brilliant"), in San Francisco's city hall. It was sometime in the late forties or early fifties. My mother had, she often said, "never even *seen* a Mexican." (A Nahuatl word, the ancient name of the Aztec tribe, Mexica.) My father was not only blond and blue-eyed, but he was in uniform and a devil on the dance floor. Even though it was a Mexican uniform, my mother was a fool for that military cut, having served long and dangerous years in Europe during the war. Her heroes remained soldiers, men in her eyes brave and noble and almost unbearably touching. She had seen enough men die and suffer to make of each uniform a small haunting. (Haunt: Old French.)

Alberto was on the presidential staff of Mexico. He had a lot of gold buttons, a couple of medals, and captain's stripes. So did she.

He lived in the presidential palace in Mexico City. He drove a black Cadillac with the number two on the plates. (Número uno, of course, was the president's black Cadillac—despots have always liked a long black car.) Dad spent his free hours zooming over the mountains to Cuernavaca on a huge military Harley. He had access to the president's train, and he regularly flew in the president's DC-3. He had an aunt in San Francisco, and he flew there on ocassion to buy jazz and swing 78s.

He tried to look like Erroll Flynn; she looked (to him) like Merle Oberon.

The fact of them was as unlikely then as the fact of myself seems to me now.

It is a part of our job as writers to betray the dead. Still, there are certain details best left untold. I don't know if you believe in ghosts (Old English) or not. But lately, I feel wraiths (Scottish) hovering over my shoulder as I write. I will give you as much of the story (Greek) as I can. I want to tell you about them. Phyl and Al, though, want to keep some of it to themselves. (Them and they: Old Norse.)

I often wonder if the fact of my mother's life didn't trouble my father in mysterious ways. After all, she'd been to war, and he hadn't. My mother had done something much more macho than my dad ever managed to do. Though his story was by no means bland, as we'll see.

But first I'll tell you about the green branch that was my mother.

She came from Staten Island when Staten Island still had villages and bucolic woods. She was from the village of Richmond. Her family was partially Virginian—Woodwards—who boasted of a plantation in the recent past. Slaves.

When she wasn't lost in the Staten Island woods, visiting families with such awesomely alien names (to me) as "the Van Oppens" (she still had Leonard Van Oppen's faded poems in her trunk—they seemed like letters from F. Scott Fitzgerald), she was in Mattituck, Long Island. There, she was part of a tribe of "terrible" (always said fondly) boy cousins who called her "Gator." They used to hang off the sides of side-tracked boxcars as the morning express shot through, bare inches from their backs.

My mother's mother, the monumentally difficult Louise Woodward, sold antiques in Manhattan. One of her clients was John Steinbeck, who insisted that nobody there recognize him or say his last name. One of her uncles drank beer often with Einstein, but he only knew him as "Al." Eccentrics surrounded my mother. Grannie Effie dressed up in Indian garb and communed with plants, for example. And Auntie Jeanne was "the first woman up the Amazon." I assume they meant the first *white* woman up the Amazon. Auntie Jeanne was also known for hiding her important documents between her voluminous breasts. And, finally, there was "Auntie Piddle-Maker," an old Victorian who stood in the corner of the garden during picnics and smiled as a small puddle ran out from under the edge of her long dress.

In spite of a rich cast of characters, and my mother's endless hilarity over them, I can't imagine it was a happy childhood. Mom boasted constantly of being alone all through her childhood. "I didn't need anyone, dear boy," she'd say. "I didn't need this constant stimulation you seem to need. I made my own stimulation!" Once, my mother confessed darkly, she'd had to jump out of a second-story window to escape a Hungarian stepfather. She fell into a snowbank, then walked in the dark across the woods to someone's house. She was maddeningly unclear about what had happened, either before or after her leap. But it sounded plenty stimulating.

Once, she giggled, she'd saved up her money and bought a ticket on a Ford tri-motor airplane. She flew to West Virginia to see some relatives. She was twelve. Her mother didn't notice she was gone for two days.

After an untidy divorce from her first husband, my mother joined the Red Cross and sailed across the Atlantic on a troop transport to take part in World War II. She drove around battlefields making coffee and doughnuts. She was sitting in a bathtub in London when a buzz bomb went overhead, and the engine cut out, and it fell. She held the hands of flamethrower victims in a MASH tent. She hid in a farmhouse all night as German tanks rumbled past, not one hundred yards from the back wall. She entered Buchenwald with George Patton's troops and took ghastly photographs I was forbidden to see.

And then Mom was hurt.

She and two Red Cross pals were driving a Jeep near the front. I don't know where they were, though I suspect they were in Germany. The women had been serving coffee all day and were in a hurry to get back to base camp. I never knew who was driving.

They were in blackout conditions, so the headlights of the Jeep were taped down to small slits. The light was dim at best, less than the light thrown by parking lights today. It was getting late, and they were in the mountains. The road was familiar to them, so the driver was taking the turns pretty fast.

I imagine them at the head of a ghostly train of dust, their hair flying, the laughter a bit too loud, almost daring the snipers to get them. Laughing in the face of the ever-hungry death that surrounded them. One of the women was named Jill, and I can imagine my mother calling her "Jilly" and "dear girl." The night was getting chill. The trees, ragged negative spaces around them in the dark, smelled heady and beautiful after a day full of the smells of smoke, mud, blood, terror.

What they didn't know was that a mortar round had taken out the middle of the lane on a turn. The driver hit the crater full speed. The Jeep became airborne, and all three women were catapulted over the edge of the cliff.

She never knew how long they were down there.

She used to tell me she'd awakened to the sound of screaming. She was on her hands and knees in mud. She was crawling in the blackness, trying to find the screamer. The mud was actually a pond made of her own blood. And then she realized she herself was screaming.

I realize now, when I'm trying to tell you, that I don't know where the Jeep went—if it exploded, or tumbled, or stayed on the road, or even if it came down the slope on top of them. And I don't know what happened to the "girls." It never occurred to me to ask. Though later, in other stories, there was a "dear Jill" who vanished over the edge of a cliff and was never found.

My mother's leg was nearly severed. It was cut loose and bleeding wildly. The scar disfigured her leg for the rest of her life. You never saw my mom in shorts. She was never able to drive after the wreck. She grew unreasonably fearful of cars, especially in the mountains. And there was no way, for some reason, she would allow you to drive her over a bridge. You could only get Phyl over such barriers as the Hudson River or the San Francisco Bay with a good shot of Baileys Irish Cream.

When their marriage became a long chess game of hate, my father would turn our Sunday drives into small torture sessions. He'd make our '49 Ford take Cuyamaca Mountain's curves a hair too fast, and my Poor Old Ma would frantically stomp her foot on the phantom brake, and my father would laugh at her. "Please, Papa," she'd mutter.

"Jesus Christ, Feliciana," he'd reply, blowing smoke through his nostrils. "We're only going forty-five!"

Feliciana was what he made of Phyllis, a name utterly alien to a Mexican. Most of the relatives called her "La Pillips." My dad's name for her roughly meant "happy woman." One of those tawdry little ironies writers pay a nickel for.

Sometime late in that catastrophic night, Mom became aware of flashlights zigzagging down the cliff toward her. She tried to stifle her cries, for she couldn't know what fate was descending. She was certain the Nazis had found her and would finish her when a light hit her full in the eyes and a good old New York G.I. yelled, "Jesus, it's goyls!" (*Goyls,* my mother always said, remembering this midnight saint and giggling. It never failed to make her laugh—the real, tinkling laugh, the happiness bell she so seldom rang. For the rest of her life, this forgotten soldier's accent turned her into a delighted six-year-old.)

The soldiers dressed her wounds. Again, imagination has failed me until this moment, when I write it. What was the scene? How many men from that patrol bent over her, cut her clothes away? My mother, with her actress looks, ripped and bleeding and naked in the tender hands of these armed men. What did she feel? Did her modesty protest? Was she embarrassed? Did my mother cry?

And the soldiers, out on killing business, suddenly transformed to sweaty angels. What a scene it must have been. I can hear them trying to calm her as they constructed some sort of stretcher and hoisted her to their shoulders. Their rough and dirtied hands holding her steady as they struggled up the slope with her. And the long and mysterious journey in their care. Did they find a truck? Did they carry her all the way?

My mother, bouncing through the night, bleeding her life away into the filthy undershirts of unnamed, faceless warriors.

Six weeks in a hospital tent. The field surgeons stitched her back together. Whenever I watch MASH, I see my mother.

Once, as she lay in her bed, the surgeons came for her. Two men had been using a flamethrower, and it had exploded, cooking them alive. They were in an adjacent tent, and there was nothing anyone could do. The surgeons thought the only one who could bring such burned men comfort as they died was a woman.

She was carried into the tent. She said the men were horribly blackened, stickmen, with their arms raised as if in praise. And when the others set her down beside the reeking cots, she broke down crying. The burned man nearest her broke open charred lips and whispered words of comfort to her. She took his wooden hand and held it, and he told her, "It's all right, lady. It's not so bad." She was guilty for years about crying. But I think it was a gift. I think the suffering appreciate the chance to comfort others.

Those soldiers had done terrible things with their flamethrowers. And their weapons had turned on them and brought a fearsome retribution on them. "Nobody wins," my mother told me about war. "Nobody wins a war." But those two men died lying side by side with her, holding her hand, perhaps smelling her perfume, drinking her woman's voice in shaky gulps, and using their last smoky breaths to try to ease her suffering.

Perhaps they were her only true loves. Perhaps they were her own personal angels. There seems to be a terrible grace in this story. When she finally died, perhaps she was searching for their faces—hoping to find them new and young again, gleaming and unsullied, fresh as a field of snow.

These scenes weren't the only ones that haunted her. There was the night the Russian troops entered a village where she was bivouacked, and the G.I.'s had to hide the Red Cross women because the Russians were raping any women they found. There was the period when she was stationed at a B-17 base and watched as the big wounded planes came in and exploded. There was the time she was ferried across the channel on a B-17; I have the picture. She sits with her eyes clamped shut, praying for mercy. She said the airmen laughed at her all the way across.

There was the time she partied near the front with an artillery unit, and, tipsy on champagne, she pulled the lanyards on the big guns and sent heavy shells into the German lines. In my idiotic childhood innocence I cried, "You *killed* people?"

She just looked away.

"I don't know," she said. "I suppose I might have . . ."

Then she would stare out our window at the sad yellow ghetto lawn.

And there was Buchenwald.

She wouldn't talk about it. Not much anyway. She did say that she was ashamed to be taking pictures, and her shame finally forced her to stop. She said that tractors moved logjams of naked bodies around, and she didn't know what they were at first, since nobody could understand a tall hill of corpses at first glance. You just weren't prepared for such a sight.

Like many soldiers, she kept a clutch of atrocity pictures. She didn't know what to do with them. She couldn't bear to throw them away. That would be like killing those innocent people again. But she couldn't bear to look at them either. And she didn't want me to see them.

She had a footlocker in which she kept her World War II stuff. It was stenciled with her first married name: McLaughlin. In it were captured German items, pictures, dispatches, an army jacket with 7th Army patches on it. A picture of Hitler. A picture of Churchill and Eisenhower getting into a car. Scores of B-17 portraits. And the forbidden envelope of holocaust photos.

I remember opening the trunk and finding them when she was at work. The dead skeletons are some of my first memories.

＊ ＊ ＊

About the Editor

Rigoberto González is the author of eight books, most recently *The Mariposa Club*, a young adult novel. He also edited *Alurista: Poems, New and Selected*. The recipient of Guggenheim and NEA fellowships, the American Book Award, The Poetry Center Book Award, and of various international artist residencies, he writes a twice-a-month Latino book column for *The El Paso Times* of Texas. He is a contributing editor for *Poets and Writers Magazine*, on the Board of Directors of the National Book Critics Circle, and on the Advisory Circle of Con Tinta, a collective of Chicano/Latino activist writers. He lives in New York City and is Associate Professor of English at Rutgers–Newark, the State University of New Jersey.

The editor wishes to acknowledge his assistant, *diego báez,* who is the author of *Illinois Wesleyan University Off the Record* and whose poetry has appeared in the *Santa Clara Review*. He is currently pursuing an MFA in creative writing at Rutgers–Newark, the State University of New Jersey, and teaches English at Essex Community College.

* * *

About the Contributors

Marjorie Agosín is a human rights activist and recipient of the Gabriela Mistral Medal of Honor for lifetime achievement in the arts. Author of several works that have been translated into several languages, she is currently the Luella LaMer Slaner Professor of Latin American Studies at Wellesley College.

*Francisco X. Alarcón i*s the author of numerous books of poetry and award-winning children's books, including *Laughing Tomatoes and Other Spring Poems/Jitomates risueños y otros poemas de primavera*, which received the 1997 Pura Belpré Honor Award and the National Parenting Publications Gold Medal. Alarcón's other recognitions include the American Book Award, the PEN/Oakland Josephine Miles Award, and the 1984 Chicano Literary Prize. He currently directs the Spanish for Native Speakers Program at the University of California, Davis.

Kathleen Alcalá is the author of a collection of essays, *The Desert Remembers My Name: On Family and Writing*; a short story collection, *Mrs. Vargas and the Dead Naturalist*; and three critically acclaimed novels. The recipient of the Western States Book Award, the Governor's Writers Award, a Pacific Northwest Bookseller's Award, a Washington State Book Award, an Artist Trust/Washington State Arts Commission Award, a Latino International Book Award, and a *ForeWord Magazine* Award, she teaches writing in the Low Residency MFA Program on Whidbey Island.

Fred Arroyo is the author of *The Region of Lost Names*. His stories, poems, interviews, and reviews have appeared in a variety of literary journals, and three of his essays are forthcoming in *North Dakota Quarterly*. He is an Assistant Professor of English at Drake University.

Rane Arroyo is the author of five collections of poetry, including *The Buried Sea: New and Selected Poems* (University of Arizona Press, 2008). Arroyo received the John Ciardi Poetry Prize, the Carl Sandburg Poetry Prize, and an Ohio Arts Council Excellence Award in Poetry. He is currently the co-vice president of the Board of Directors for the Association of Writers and Writing Programs, and he teaches creative writing and literature at the University of Toledo.

Kathleen de Azevedo, the author of *Samba Dreamers*, has had work appear in a number of publications, including the anthologies *New Stories from the Southwest, Latinos in Lotusland: An Anthology of Contemporary Southern California Literature*, and *Best American Poetry 1992*. She received a grant from Stanford University's Center of Latin American Studies to research Literatura de Cordel. She teaches English at Skyline College in San Bruno, California.

Richard Blanco's first book of poetry, *City of a Hundred Fires*, won the Agnes Starrett Poetry Prize from the University of Pittsburgh Press. His second book, *Directions to the Beach of the Dead*, won the PEN/Beyond Margins Book Award. He has received the John Ciardi Fellowship from the Bread Loaf Writers Conference, a Florida Artist Fellowship, and a Residency Fellowship from the Virginia Center for the Creative Arts.

Albino Carrillo is the author of *In the City of Smoking Mirrors*. He has published poetry in numerous literary journals and anthologies, including *Library Bound: A Saratoga Anthology* and *The Wind Shifts: New Latino Poetry* (University of Arizona Press, 2007). He currently teaches at the University of Dayton.

Lisa D. Chávez is the author of two books of poetry, *Destruction Bay* and *In an Angry Season*, and has been anthologized in *Floricanto Sí! A Collection of Latina Poetry, The Floating Borderlands: 25 Years of U.S. Hispanic Literature*, and *American Poetry: The Next Generation*. She is currently Associate Professor of English and creative writing at the University of New Mexico.

Juan Delgado is the author of three books of poetry, *A Rush of Hands, El Campo: Poems and Paintings* (with the artist Simón Silva), and *Green*

Web. He is currently Professor of English at California State University, San Bernardino.

David Domínguez is the author of *Work Done Right*, which includes poems previously featured in *Marcoli Sausage*, an edition published as part of Gary Soto's Chicano Chapbook Series. His work has been anthologized in *How Much Earth: The Fresno Poets, The Wind Shifts: New Latino Poetry, Highway 99: A Literary Journey through California's Great Central Valley,* and *The Bear Flag Republic.* He currently teaches at Reedley College in California.

Stella Pope Duarte, author of the novel *If I Die in Juárez,* has also published a story collection, *Fragile Night,* and the critically acclaimed novel *Let Their Spirits Dance,* for which she received a creative writing fellowship from the Arizona Commission on the Arts. She won the 2003 Excellence in Latino Arts & Culture Award, presented by Valle del Sol, the Arizona Highways Fiction Award, the Outstanding Alumni of the Year Award by the American Association of Community Colleges, the Barbara Deming Memorial Fund Award, and first place in the 34th Annual Chicano/Literary Prize from the University of California at Irvine.

Blas Falconer is the author of *A Question of Gravity and Light* and a chapbook, *The Perfect Hour.* He won the New Delta Review Eyster Prize for Poetry in 2000, and his work has appeared in various literary journals. He is currently an assistant professor in Languages and Literature at Austin Peay State University, where he also serves as the poetry editor of *Zone 3.*

Gina Franco is the author of *The Keepsake Storm.* Her poems have appeared in various literary journals and is currently working on a manuscript of poems entitled *Mother Lode,* about copper mining in Arizona. Also an accomplished photographer, she is an Assistant Professor of English at Knox College.

Diana García's collection of poetry, *When Living Was a Labor Camp,* received an American Book Award in 2001. Her work has appeared in such anthologies as *Touching the Fire: fifteen Poets of Today's Latino Renaissance* and *Pieces of the Heart: New Chicano Fiction.* She is the Director of the Creative Writing and Social Action Program at California State University at Monterey Bay.

Ray Gonzalez is the author of nine books of poetry including *Consideration of the Guitar: New and Selected Poems*. Other titles include *The Hawk Temple at Tierra Grande*, winner of a Minnesota Book Award, and *The Heat of Arrivals*, winner of a PEN/Josephine Miles Book Award. His poetry has been anthologized in the 1999, 2000, and 2003 editions of *The Best American Poetry*. He is also the author of two story collections and three books of nonfiction, and the editor of twelve anthologies. He has served as poetry editor of *The Bloomsbury Review* for twenty-five years, and in 2003 he received a Lifetime Achievement Award in Literature from the Border Regional Library Association. He is Professor of English at the University of Minnesota in Minneapolis.

Christine Granados is the author of *Brides and Sinners in El Chuco*, a recipient of a notable book mention in the Pima County Public Library's Southwest Books of the Year Awards in 2006. Her stories have been featured in *Hecho en Tejas: An Anthology of Texas-Mexican Literature* and in *Not Quite What I Was Planning: And Other Six-Word Memoirs by Writers Famous and Obscure*. Most recently, she won the 2006 Alfredo Cisneros del Moral Foundation Award.

Maurice Kilwein Guevara is a Professor of English at the University of Wisconsin–Milwaukee, where he teaches in the MA and PhD programs in creative writing as well as in the Latino Studies Program. His three previous collections of poetry include *Postmortem*, winner of the National Contemporary Poetry Series Competition, *Poems of the River Spirit*, and *The Autobiography of So-and-so: Poems in Prose*. He has served on the board of directors of the Association of Writers and Writing Programs and was the first Latino to be elected as its president.

Juan Felipe Herrera has published fourteen collections of poetry, including *Half of the World in Light: New and Selected Poems* (University of Arizona Press, 2008), which won the 2008 National Book Critics Circle award for poetry. He also wrote the children's books *Upside Down Boy*, which was adapted into a musical, and *Laughing Out Loud, I Fly*, winner of a Pura Belpré Honor Award. Other distinctions include the Ezra Jack Keats Award, the Americas Award, the Focal Award, two Latino Hall of Fame Poetry Awards, two National Endowment for the Arts Writers' Fellowship Awards, four California Arts Council grants, the UC Berkeley

Regent's Fellowship, the Breadloaf Fellowship in Poetry, and the Stanford Chicano Fellows Fellowship. His most recent collection, *187 Reasons Mexicanos Can't Cross the Border: Undocuments 1971–2007*, won both the PEN/USA Book Award and the PEN/Oakland Josephine Miles Award. He holds the Tomás Rivera Endowed Chair in Creative Writing at the University of California, Riverside.

Jack Lopez is the author of *Cholos & Surfers: A Latino Family Album*, an essay collection, and *Snapping Lines*, a story collection. His work has been anthologized in *Iguana Dreams: New Latino Fiction, Pieces of the Heart: New Chicano Fiction, Mirrors Beneath the Earth, Currents from the Dancing River*, and *Muy Macho: Latino Men Confront Their Manhood*, among others. He teaches creative writing at Cal State University, Northridge.

Rita María Magdaleno is the author of *Marlene Dietrich, Rita Hayworth, & My Mother*. She received the Award of Excellence from the Arizona Museum Association and teaches at the Writing Works Center of the University of Arizona Extended Campus.

Carl Marcum's poetry book *Cue Lazarus* was a second place co-winner for Best Poetry in 2002 for the Latino Literary Hall of Fame award. He was awarded a fellowship from the National Endowment for the Arts, a Wallace Stegner Fellowship from Stanford University, and the D.H. Lawrence Fellowship from the University of New Mexico's Taos Summer Writers' Conference. He currently teaches creative writing and literature at DePaul University.

Patricia Preciado Martin is the author of three collections of short stories, *El Milagro and Other Stories, Days of Plenty, Days of Want*, and *Amor Eterno: Eleven Lessons in Love*, as well as two books of nonfiction, *Songs My Mother Sang to Me* and *Images and Conversations*. She was named the Arizona Library Association's Author of the Year in 1997, and she has been active in Tucson's Mexican American community for many years.

Demetria Martínez is the author of two books of poetry, *The Devil's Workshop* and *Breathing Between the Lines*, as well as of the novel *Mother Tongue*, winner of a Western States Book Award for Fiction. Her collection of autobiographical essays, *Confessions of a Berlitz-Tape Chicana*, won the 2006 International Latino Book Award. *The Mystery of Valle San Francisco*, a children's book co-authored with Rosalee Montoya-Read, will be released in 2009.

Valerie Martínez is the author of two poetry collections, *World to World* and *Absence, Luminescent*, winner of the Larry Levis Prize, and recipient of a Greenwall Grant from the Academy of American Poets. Her poetry, translations, and essays have appeared in various literary journals and magazines. An excerpt from her new book-length poem *Each and Her* appeared in the *American Poetry Review* and *Mandorla*, as well as in the anthology *JUNTA: Contemporary Avant-Garde Poetry by Latino/a Writers*. She is currently Associate Professor of English and Creative Writing at the College of Santa Fe.

Ana Consuelo Matiella is the author of *The Truth About Alicia and Other Stories*, editor of several books on multicultural education, and producer of fotonovelas on educational topics. Her work has been anthologized in *Walking the Twilight: Women Writers of the Southwest*. She is a columnist for the *Santa Fe New Mexican*.

María Meléndez is the author of *How Long She'll Last in This World* and has been anthologized in *Sisters of the Earth*, *Hunger Enough: Living Spiritually in a Consumer Society*, and *Under the Fifth Sun: Latino Literature from California*. She has edited two anthologies, *Nest of Freedom* and *Moon Won't Leave Me Alone*. She currently lives in Logan, Utah, where she teaches creative writing and American literature at Utah State University.

Pat Mora is the author of six collections of poetry, including *Adobe Odes*; two nonfiction titles, *Nepantla: Essays from the Land in the Middle* and the acclaimed memoir *House of Houses*; as well as of many award-winning children's books. She received the Luis Leal Award for Distinction in Chicano/Latino Letters (2008); the University of Southern Mississippi Medallion for Outstanding Contributions to Children's Literature, Hattiesburg (2008); the Roberta Long Medal for Distinguished Contributions to Celebrating the Cultural Diversity of Children, University of Alabama at Birmingham (2007); and the National Hispanic Cultural Center Literary Award (2006), among many others.

Braulio Muñoz is the author of two novels, *The Peruvian Notebooks* and *Alejandro and the Fishermen of Tancay*. Currently Centennial Professor of Sociology at Swarthmore College, he has also authored a number of critical texts, most recently, *A Storyteller: Vargas Llosa between Civilization and Barbarism*.

Dixie Salazar is the author of three books of poetry, including *Blood Mysteries*, and of the novel *Limbo*. She has taught extensively in the California prison system and the Fresno County jail. Currently, she teaches writing and literature at California State University and shows oil paintings and collage work at the Silva/Salazar studios in Fresno.

Luis Omar Salinas (1937–2008) is considered one of the founding fathers of Chicano letters. He authored seven collections of poetry before his death. He was considered a key figure of the "Fresno School" of poets, though he was born in Robeson, Texas. He was highly respected for his ardent activism and his belief in the transformative power of poetry.

Virgil Suárez is one of the nation's most prolific poets and anthologists. His milestone volume, *90 Miles: Selected & New Poems*, was published in 2005. He has been awarded the Florida State Individual Artist Grant, a G. MacCarthur Poetry Prize, and a National Endowment for the Arts grant. He is an Associate Professor of Creative Writing at Florida State University, Tallahassee.

Margo Tamez is the author of two poetry collections, *Naked Wanting* and *Raven Eye*. She has been awarded a Poetry Fellowship from the Arizona Commission on the Arts, a First Place Literary Award from Frontera Literary Review, the Environmental Leadership Fellowship Award, and an International Exchange Award from the Tucson Pima Arts Council. She is the co-founder of the Lipan Apache Women (El Caláboz) Defense, a land-based Indigenous People's Organization, recognized by the United Nations Permanent Forum on Indigenous Issues.

Sergio Troncoso is the author of *The Last Tortilla and Other Stories*, which won the Premio Aztlán and the Southwest Book Award, and *The Nature of Truth: A Novel*. His stories have been anthologized in *The Norton Anthology of Latino Literature*, *Latino Boom: An Anthology of*

U.S. Latino Literature, Hecho en Tejas: An Anthology of Texas-Mexican Literature, and *New World: Young Latino Writers.* He currently lives and writes in New York City.

Luis Alberto Urrea is the author of eleven books, including *The Devil's Highway,* which won the 2004 Lannan Literary Award and which was a finalist for both the Pulitzer Prize and the Pacific Rim Kiriyama Prize. His first book, *Across the Wire,* was named a *New York Times* Notable Book and won the Christopher Award. He won an American Book Award for his memoir *Nobody's Son: Notes from an American Life* and in 2000 he was voted into the Latino Literature Hall of Fame following the publication of *Vatos.* His book of short stories, *Six Kinds of Sky,* was named small-press Book of the Year by the editors of *ForeWord Magazine.* He has also won a Western States Book Award in poetry for *The Fever of Being.* He is Professor of English at the University of Illinois–Chicago.

Luis Humberto Valadez received his degrees from Columbia College in Chicago and from the Jack Kerouac School of Disembodied Poetics at Naropa University. He is the recipient of the Lily Endowment and of awards from the Hispanic Scholarship Fund. Also a musician and a performer, he is currently Program and Education Coordinator for Chicago HOPES and lives in Chicago Heights. *What i'm on* is his first poetry collection.

Marcos McPeek Villatoro is the author of two collections of poetry, *They Say That I Am Two* and *on Tuesday, when the homeless disappeared,* as well as of three Romilia Chacón crime novels. The debut title in that series, *Home Killings,* was listed by the Los Angeles Times Book Review as a Best Book of 2001, and was awarded a Silver Medal from *Foreword Magazine* and First Prize in the Latino Literary Hall of Fame. He holds the Fletcher Jones Endowed Chair in Writing at Mount St. Mary's College and is a regular commentator for NPR.

* * *

Bibliography

The following is the complete list of Camino del Sol books.

1994
Night Train to Tuxtla, Juan Felipe Herrera

1996
El Milagro and Other Stories, Patricia Preciado Martin

1997
Breathing Between the Lines: Poems, Demetria Martínez

1998
Nobody's Son: Notes from an American Life, Luis Alberto Urrea

1999
Border-Crosser with a Lamborghini Dream, Juan Felipe Herrera
Days of Plenty, Days of Want, Patricia Preciado Martin
The Last Tortilla and Other Stories, Sergio Troncoso
Memory Fever, Ray Gonzalez
In Search of Snow, Luis Alberto Urrea
Wandering Time: Western Notebooks, Luis Alberto Urrea

2000
Amor Eterno: Eleven Lessons in Love, Patricia Preciado Martin
Thunderweavers / Tejedoras de rayos, Juan Felipe Herrera
Turtle Pictures, Ray Gonzalez
When Living Was a Labor Camp, Diana García

2001
In an Angry Season, Lisa D. Chávez
Cue Lazarus, Carl Marcum
The Ghost of John Wayne and Other Stories, Ray Gonzalez

Giraffe on Fire, Juan Felipe Herrera
Palm Crows, Virgil Suárez
Snapping Lines, Jack Lopez

2002
The Devil's Workshop: Poems, Demetria Martínez
*From the Other Side of Night / Del otro lado de la noche: New and Selected
    Poems*, Francisco X. Alarcón
Home Movies of Narcissus, Rane Arroyo
Notebooks of a Chile Verde Smuggler, Juan Felipe Herrera
The Truth about Alicia and Other Stories, Ana Consuelo Matiella
The Underground Heart: A Return to a Hidden Landscape, Ray Gonzalez

2003
Blood Mysteries, Dixie Salazar
Marlene Dietrich, Rita Hayworth, & My Mother, Rita Maria Magdaleno
Naked Wanting, Margo Tamez
A Rush of Hands, Juan Delgado
Work Done Right, David Dominguez

2004
In the City of Smoking Mirrors, Albino Carrillo
The Keepsake Storm, Gina Franco
on Tuesday, when the homeless disappeared, Marcos McPeek Villatoro
World to World, Valerie Martínez

2005
Directions to the Beach of the Dead, Richard Blanco
Elegy for Desire, Luis Omar Salinas
How to Name a Hurricane, Rane Arroyo
The Religion of Hands: Prose Poems and Flash Fictions, Ray Gonzalez

2006
Adobe Odes, Pat Mora
Brides and Sinners in El Chuco: Stories, by Christine Granados
How Long She'll Last in This World, María Meléndez
The Peruvian Notebooks, Braulio Muñoz
Samba Dreamers, Kathleen de Azevedo

2007
Agua Santa / Holy Water, Pat Mora
The Desert Remembers My Name: On Family and Writing, Kathleen Alcalá
A Question of Gravity and Light, Blas Falconer
The Wind Shifts: New Latino Poetry, edited by Francisco Aragón

2008

The Buried Sea: New and Selected Poems, Rane Arroyo
Alejandro and the Fishermen of Tancay, Braulio Muñoz
If I Die in Juárez, Stella Pope Duarte
Half of the World in Light: New and Selected Poems, Juan Felipe Herrera
House of Houses, Pat Mora
The Last Supper of Chicano Heroes: Selected Works of José Antonio Burciaga,
    edited by Mimi R. Gladstein and Daniel Chacón
The Region of Lost Names, Fred Arroyo
Renaming the Earth: Personal Essays, Ray Gonzalez

2009

Of Earth and Sea: A Chilean Memoir, Marjorie Agosín
Faith Run, Ray Gonzalez
Havana and Other Missing Fathers, Mia Leonin
Odalisque in Pieces, Carmen Giménez Smith
POEMA, Maurice Kilwein Guevara
what i'm on, Luis Humberto Valadez

Index of Authors